REVOLUTION AND UNION:

THE AMERICAN DILEMMA
1763-1877

Richard Allan Gerber

CENGAGE
Learning

**Revolution and Union:
The American Dilemma
1763-1877**

Richard Allan Gerber

Executive Editors:
Michele Baird

Maureen Staudt

Michael Stranz

Project Development Manager:
Linda deStefano

Senior Marketing Coordinators:
Sara Mercurio

Lindsay Shapiro

Senior Production / Manufacturing Manager:
Donna M. Brown

PreMedia Services Supervisor:
Rebecca A. Walker

Rights & Permissions Specialist:
Kalina Hintz

Cover Image:
Getty Images*

* Unless otherwise noted, all cover images used by Custom Solutions, a part of Cengage Learning, have been supplied courtesy of Getty Images with the exception of the Earthview cover image, which has been supplied by the National Aeronautics and Space Administration (NASA).

For product information and technology assistance, contact us at
Cengage Learning Customer & Sales Support, 1-800-354-9706

For permission to use material from this text or product,
submit all requests online at **cengage.com/permissions**
Further permissions questions can be emailed to
permissionrequest@cengage.com

ISBN-13: 978-1-4266-4195-4

ISBN-10: 1-4266-4195-8

Cengage Learning
5191 Natorp Boulevard
Mason, Ohio 45040
USA

Cengage Learning is a leading provider of customized learning solutions with office locations around the globe, including Singapore, the United Kingdom, Australia, Mexico, Brazil, and Japan. Locate your local office at:
international.cengage.com/region

Cengage Learning products are represented in Canada by Nelson Education, Ltd.

For your lifelong learning solutions, visit **custom.cengage.com**

Visit our corporate website at **cengage.com**

Printed in the United States of America

REVOLUTION AND UNION:
THE AMERICAN DILEMMA 1763 - 1877

TABLE OF CONTENTS

REVOLUTION AND UNION:
THE AMERICAN DILEMMA 1763 - 1877

TABLE OF CONTENTS

REVOLUTION AND UNION:
THE AMERICAN DILEMMA 1763 - 1877

INTRODUCTION

<u>Revolution and Union: The Dilemma of America 1763-1877</u> examines two episodes in American history. **Part I**, titled "**Revolution,**" examines the enactment and the institutionalization of the idea of republican government in America. "**Revolution**" contends that the definition of republicanism evolved between 1776 and 1800 and required an entire generation to reach completion.

"**Revolution**" asserts that the seeds of republicanism began in 1763 with colonial resistance against efforts by the British government to address the problems of imperial administration. Republicanism was forged in the tumultuous events leading to the American struggle for independence and the emergence of republican governments of the United States in the Articles of Confederation and those of the states. The construction of the Constitution of 1787 and its consequent ratification play prominent roles in Part I as the definition (or redefinition) of republicanism unfolded. "**Revolution**" ends with the Bill of Rights of 1791 and the impact of the election of Thomas Jefferson in 1800. Those events may be considered as the full expression of republicanism. They completed the American Revolution.

Perhaps the most important political assumption of any definition of republican government is the idea of government by consent. People enjoy the undeniable right to decide who rules them and how they are ruled. American revolutionaries in 1776, in 1787, in 1791 and in 1800 shared that basic concept, however variously they may have understood and applied it. They rejected arbitrary governance that did not possess their approval. The American nation was born in self-determination. That is the meaning of the American Revolution in each of its sequential phases.

Part II, "**Union**" considers the efforts of the United States government to prevent the shattering and disintegration of America, to preserve the United States as a sovereign nation. "**Union**" contends that the concept of nationhood included both the territorial integrity of America's borders and the implantation of America's free institutions throughout the United States between 1848 and 1877. The definition of Union evolved between 1848 and 1865 to include emancipation and took until the completion of Reconstruction to guarantee freedom to those formerly enslaved.

"**Union**" emphasizes the struggle of the North to prevent the intrusion of slavery into the territories of the United States and the victory of the South in achieving constitutional protection for slavery in those regions between 1848 and the election of Abraham Lincoln in 1860. [It is most reasonable to recognize the dynamics of escalation and polarization of that decade as comparable to the period 1763-1776.] **Part II** also demonstrates the redefinition of the idea of Union to include the abolition of slavery by implementation of the Emancipation Proclamation and the 13th Amendment. **"Union"** examines Reconstruction as a series of sustained actions by the American government between 1866 and 1875 to protect the freed people against their white neighbors as the alternative to permanent military occupation of the South. The Civil Rights Acts of 1866 and 1875 spanned a decade that witnessed enactment of the crucial 14th and 15th Amendments to the Constitution. **Part II** concludes with the winding down of Reconstruction and the ultimate victory of white supremacy in the South.

The most significant underlying value of the Union was that each nation state is entitled to maintain its territorial and institutional integrity as a nation. Open rebellion by internal factions that reject the forums for redress of their grievances can scarcely be justified by labeling that revolt as "self-determination." Fragmentation destroys the fabric of society. It frequently leads to perpetual violence and certainly to anarchy. National integrity, conversely, exemplifies the patriotic loyalty that members of the society feel for their homeland. In America's case saving the Union in 1861 meant preserving the constitutional system, that very republic their fathers had struggled to achieve in the American Revolution.

The dilemma of America, however, is that self-determination and national integrity contradict one another. How can a nation founded on the consent of the governed deny that very idea to others who wish self-determination? How could the Union reject the actions of the Confederate States of America to enact a revolution similar to that of 1776? In that respect did the United States stand in the position of the British Empire in suppressing a population attempting to enact self-determination? Was Jefferson Davis another Thomas Jefferson?

On the other hand, what gives any angry group with a road-side bomb and a sense of frustration against the national regime the right to destroy a legitimate government? Does not the logic of that brand of revolt end in anarchy? If it was legitimate for the Confederacy to destroy the Union, is it not equally legitimate for State of Connecticut or even the Town of Glastonbury? Or the Whiskey rebels of 1794? Were not Southern rebels traitors to their country? Was not Jefferson Davis another Benedict Arnold? If it is legitimate for a nation to defend its integrity from external invaders, why cannot it also defend itself against internal enemies?

Please note that **Revolution and Union** is an interpretive book. It represents the ideas and attitudes of the author. What is presented in these pages is highly selective. There is no attempt to be comprehensive. While this is a work of years of research, the scholarly apparatus is omitted in order to facilitate reading. Neither does this volume substitute for a textbook or any reference work. The challenge to readers is to think with some intellectual consistency about this huge dilemma in American history and to form their own opinions.

Dr. Richard Allan Gerber received his doctorate in History from the University of Michigan in 1967. He has taught American history for more than forty years, first at Herbert H. Lehman College and at the Graduate Center of the City University of New York, and since 1992 at Southern Connecticut State University. He has received recognition for his excellence in teaching.

His most recent scholarly works include The System: The American Constitution in Historical Perspective (2007); Not Your (Founding) Fathers' Constitution (2007); and "The Civil Rights Act of 1875: A Reexamination," with Dr. Alan Friedlander (2007). He has won recognition for his scholarship from the Organization of American Historians. In addition to his career as an historian, Dr. Gerber also served for two decades in senior level academic administration positions.

Dr. Gerber lives in Glastonbury, Connecticut with his wife, Carolyn, a retired school social worker who traded the little bad boys she formerly counseled for the one little old bad boy she has left. They also have two cats, Hamilton and Jefferson, of course.

PART ONE

REVOLUTION

CHAPTER ONE: HISTORICAL KNOWING

Welcome to the examination of the study of history! Chapter One: Historical Knowing, discusses the most fundamental ideas and concepts that historians use in their examination of the past.

What is History? The Study of Change through Time

The first question for any historian is, of course, what is history? We recognize that history is about time. About the study of time. About the study of change through time. But what does that idea actually mean?

For most students, history is what the historian says it is. This is because we were taught to memorize and to regurgitate information only, probably to pass some test. In that environment the historian is the expert, unquestioned and infallible. We were not given any apparatus for critical thought. For example: This moon is made of green cheese. If the historian tells you that the moon is green cheese, you write down "The Moon is Green Cheese." Since early American history centers in Philadelphia, it is doubtless Philadelphia brand cream cheese. And then you memorize it – "the moon is green cheese; the moon is green cheese." You don't write down: that idiot professor has the nerve to say that the moon is green cheese! Instead, you surrender or suspend your independent thought. Even though you know better. And even if it is just for the exam! Okay. The moon is not made of green cheese! So now do you write that down?

Or take the example of **Abraham Lincoln's** murder by John Wilkes Booth. Once as a young history professor Richard Gerber exploded into his lecture class waving a letter that he declared he had just discovered in the library's collection of rare documents. This "document," he announced, was written by **Senator Benjamin Wade** of Ohio, the Republican leader. Students were appropriately skeptical. Then he read the letter:

When Lincoln was shot, the document explained, he did not really die. Rather, his injuries caused him to live in a vegetative state, with some occasional brain function. But the Republicans put out the word that Lincoln had in fact died. They could hardly permit the nation to think they

1

had an demented president or one in a vegetative state. At this point a few students began to write down what they were hearing.

Next, the document continued, the Republican leaders spirited Lincoln away on that famous funeral train that finally arrived in Springfield, Illinois, Lincoln's home town. They put the President's coffin into the ground. More students began to take notes. But Lincoln remained alive. As he grew older, the letter went on, Lincoln began to write some pretty weird children's poetry. Gerber actually began to read some pretty weird children's poetry that he told the class Lincoln had written. By now well more than half the class was furiously taking notes.

Finally, Professor Gerber exclaimed: "One day his gingerbread house fell down." The students groaned. "You were kidding us all the time, weren't you," they said out loud, understanding that they had been bafflegabbed. And off course they had been bamboozled.

There is a point to this story, however. If you can be shaken or fooled into abandoning, or even disbelieving, what you know to be true – such as that **John Wilkes Booth** murdered **Abraham Lincoln** – then how do you know the historian is telling the truth if he talks about something you know nothing about, such as Ulysses Grant's foreign policy? Or some unemployment statistics from the 1930's? Or Alexander Hamilton's ideas? Anything about which you are not in total command? Answer: you take the historian's word for it! History is what the historian says it is!

What happens is that students digest history as a mass of concrete, unchanging and unchallengable factual information. To compound the problem, if the historian gives you reasons for why things happened the way they did, then those reasons are themselves added to the list of facts to be memorized for exams. And promptly forgotten.

What is bad about this is that not only does it waste everybody's time, but also that you are being manipulated and you do not recognize it! You have lost the capacity to think critically. And, of course, that is not what history is. So please be skeptical about every book you read, every lecture you hear, and certainly every internet site you log onto. Even every primary document that seems authentic. Do not succumb to the adage that "history is what the historian says it is." That guideline applies even to this current historian, the author of this book and to the lectures for your history courses.

Of course there is one sense in which history is indeed what the historian says it is! There is, after all, no history without the historian.

HISTORICAL KNOWING

There is just a huge mass of undigestible and formless material out there in the unknown. It takes the trained historian to craft a narrative or an analysis from this quarry of data and information. It is the role of the historian to create the statue from the unformed block of marble – to form or make history from this staggering array of factual data – to make some accurate form from this essentially formless material out there. It is up to every student to substitute his or her own critical thinking for previous rote learning.

This we begin to do right now by introducing **seven** fundamental concepts by which we begin to answer the question: What is History?

Concept One: Thesis

A thesis is an interpretive generalization which sets forth the assertion or argument that an author (or a document) intends to prove. A thesis is some combination of data and reasoning that supposes a conclusion. Typically, a thesis is composed of information and the reasons for the meaning of that information. Sometimes a thesis statement is overt and sometimes you have to dig it out from the document. The idea of **thesis** is the most fundamental concept in historical methodology.

An illustration. Consider the Declaration of Independence of July 4, 1776. This significant document contains a thesis statement: *America declared its independence from Great Britain in 1776, because British laws were tyrannical.* That thesis statement may be historically accurate or it may not be at all accurate. At this stage it is simply an assertion which must now be proved. The validity of the thesis – this one and every one – depends on the quality of the evidence offered to prove it. If that idea seems a difficult one to comprehend right away, do not worry. There are plenty of professional historians running around loose who do not know a thesis from a turkey.

Concept Two – Evidence

Evidence, obviously, is the proof which validates or fails to validate a thesis. The use of evidence is the single most critical analytical weapon the historian has in her or his arsenal. So here comes the million dollar question: how do we know that the evidence offered proves or fails to prove the thesis? The most complex question for historians is how do we know when the evidence offered proves what it says it proves? How do we know when the evidence proves or fails to prove the thesis?

HISTORICAL KNOWING

Let us come back to our thesis statement and examine the evidence. Is the **Declaration of Independence** – all by itself – conclusive and definitive evidence for proving the thesis that America declared Its independence from Great Britain in 1776, because British laws were tyrannical? The document indicates that the leaders of the American Revolution gave this thesis as the reason. However, did the leadership of the American revolution represent the thinking of all American revolutionaries? Even if they did, was the Declaration the accurate truth? Were British laws tyrannical? And if so, was that issue the cause of the American independence?

Or could this official statement simply be good propaganda, hiding a more fundamental motive, such as a desire to advance certain economic interests or to take political power? The honest historian would have to conclude that just by using the Declaration alone the thesis has not been proven. The thesis may still be true, of course! But not without lots more evidence than that presented solely in the Declaration.

Here is the bottom line! If there is any doubt, then the evidence is not conclusive. This is not about just reasonable doubt; this is not a courtroom. But any doubt whatsoever. If there is any doubt, then the evidence is not conclusive. And since we are pledged to accuracy, we must either find additional evidence, or hold the thesis to be true in part only, or scrap it altogether. What methodology do we employ for determining the validity of evidence.

Step 1: Project Thesis From Known Facts

A thesis is an educated guess! Your best shot at what you think is true. We theorize. We think. Sometimes we just have a hunch. We "feel" or we intuit that something is true. We draw that guess, or hunch, or hypothesis – or thesis – from what we already know. From the facts we have. We draw the interpretative generalization or assertion and project it into a thesis. We have a sort of historical intuition about it. We articulate that guess! That is our thesis. That is Step 1.

Step 2: Compare Thesis With All The Facts

Next we compare that thesis to evidence. We do research and find all the facts, not just those that support our thesis. We compare our assertion with all of the researched facts. We measure our thesis against all of those facts. If they square, if they match, the thesis is valid.

But if the facts conflict with the thesis, or if you ignore those facts that do not match the thesis, or if you do not have enough facts, then there is only one conclusion to be drawn: the thesis is wrong! If our theory does not match the facts, the theory is wrong! Wrong!

It does not matter how beautiful the thesis is. It does not matter how logical the thesis is. It does not matter how much the thesis fits our preconceived ideas of what ought to be true. It does not matter how smart you are. Or if you got your reputation peddling this thesis. The thesis is wong! The thesis is wrong! Wrong!

The good historian – like the good scientist – will accept the results of an honest comparison of thesis and facts – and scrap the thesis if need be. You might feel sorry it isn't what you thought. You might wish it otherwise. It might screw up your perfectly good ideology or logic or thinking or even all the investment you made in time and effort and reputation in developing the thesis. But it is still wrong! You might still hang on to it, because it fits so nicely with what you think about your politics today.

But it is still wrong. You may not manipulate the facts to prove that your thesis is accurate. You may not select only those facts which prove your thesis and include them in your presentation and ignore others. Or omit others. Those actions are forms of dishonesty, which do not change the facts, and still do not validate your thesis. It is still wrong!

What is required is a brutal – even clinical – honesty. This brand of candor requires courage. It reflects a commitment to the historical process which goes beyond anyone's pet thesis. Or the amount of time until your paper is due! Even though it is sometimes difficult to accept, the process comes first. The process is more important than the outcome. Accuracy must be honored!

Concept Three: Bias - Detecting an Author's/Speaker's Point of View

Once we raise the question of "whose opinion is this?" we must confront directly the concept of **bias**. Bias is not a four-letter word. Okay it is a four-letter word but not a dirty word. Bias is not intended to make you suspicious of the speaker or author or document. But it is intended to make you aware of where the author or speaker is coming from. The point of view tells much about the validity of evidence.

Literally, a bias is a slant. We cut on a bias. Everyone has a bias or a slant. Let us just say that everyone has some point of view, whether it is stated or conscious, or is unarticulated or subliminal. This point of view, this bias, is complex and complicated. It is composed of a person's background and experiences and location and gender and race and perhaps a hundred other variables, ranging from the time of day or the person's place in a power structure.

To illustrate consider an American Revolutionary, **Samuel Adams** of Boston. The beer! Actually Adams was a brewer. If you call this man a freedom fighter, you get one image of him. If you call him a terrorist you should get quite a difference impression. And, of course, one man's freedom fighter is another man's terrorist. His actions were exactly the same, whatever terms we use to describe him. But when you choose the terms that describe Adams that language reveals your bias, not Adams's.

Similarly, there is clearly a difference in bias if you call **George Washington** a liberator, the father of his country, rather than calling him a traitor, as the British did. The point is that an historian can isolate and detect and test a person's bias through examining the speaker's words. Even the most objective sounding statement reveals and reflects the speaker's or author's bias. There is a skill in uncovering a bias, which we will practice this term. You will never never never again read a book or a document with the innocence of today. Ah, sweet innocence. No more virginal readers.

Concept Four: Fact *Versus* Interpretation

Now we move to Concept 4: the difference between **Fact** and **Interpretation**. We all use terms like fact and interpretation and we tend to take them for granted. Historians ought to be more precise about these two concepts. So what is the difference between a fact and an interpretation?

Facts are, if you will, objective. That is, they exist independently of what we think about them. For example, a statistic is a fact. In 1710, to qualify as a Knight in England, one had to own land worth £600 per year in rental value. That is a fact. A date is a fact. Example: **Thomas Jefferson** wrote the Declaration of Independence in 1776. A fact. This next is a little more complex. An idea is also a fact. Example: Thomas Jefferson thought that human nature could be improved. This is not to say that human nature can actually be improved, but only that Jefferson thought so. It is a fact that he thought so. We have his frequent statements to that effect.

Facts do not need to be proven. If we have enough evidence, of course, they can be. But facts exist whether we can prove them or not! Jefferson wrote the Declaration whether we can prove it or not. We can prove it, however. We have his statements about it. You can just hear him, in his

HISTORICAL KNOWING

Virginia drawl, saying: "I wrote it, y'all." We have other people's statements about it also. Moreover, we have the handwriting analysis of the draft.

If we didn't know the author, it would still be Jefferson, whether we could prove it or not? And if we did not know the year in which it was written, it still would be 1776 So some facts we know. Most facts – maybe 90 percent – we do not yet know. Some facts we can prove. Some we cannot prove – even some of those we know to be facts.

Interpretations, by contrast, are what we think about the facts. They are, if you will, subjective or relative to us. A simple example: suppose someone said "1776 was a good year for independence." That's an interpretation. Another example: "July 4 is too hot a day for observing Independence Day." That's an interpretation. Example: "Gerber does not admire Thomas Jefferson." That is his interpretation. In his opinion the man is over-rated and he does not Like Thomas Jefferson. Can that also be a fact?

Interpretations are eminently debatable. No problem here, of course! Interpretations are debatable. Try this example: **Abraham Lincoln** issued the **Emancipation Proclamation** [fact], because he wanted to win the Civil War faster [interpretation]. Or another example: Lincoln issued the Emancipation Proclamation [fact], because he believed in racial equality [interpretation]. Or another example: Lincoln issued the Emancipation Proclamation [fact], because he thought his wife Mary was angry with him for cluttering up the White House with his papers. [Interpretation].

In these forms the differences between fact and interpretation appear simple. But I do warn you to be careful. In complex form the differences are very tenuous and obscure and muddy. This happens often when everybody accepts the reason – or the interpretation as a fact itself. Interpretations are frequently accepted as fact when there are no other interpretations open or available. Here's an example:

Henry VIII divorced [got his marriage annulled] his first wife, **Katherine of Aragon** [fact], because she did not give him a male heir to the throne [interpretation]. Despite the obvious conclusion that this is accurate – and these days there is little argument among scholars that this is indeed the reason – this is still an interpretation. None of us is inside the mind of Henry VIII.

We do accept the reason, the interpretation, as a fact, because even in the absence of hard evidence, it appears beyond challenge. There are lots of instances like this one. Please take warning to be cautious. So encyclopedias are books of facts. Books of essays are interpretations. That last statement is a fact. The statement that the last statement is a fact is also a fact.

Do not get the wrong idea about this. One interpretation is not necessarily as good as the next. Perhaps in the sight of God they are all equal. Sometimes even absolute conflicting proof will not cause an interpreter to change her or his mind. But the validity of an interpretation depends as always on the use of evidence. Always the evidence. In this respect it is like "CSI – Crime Scence Investigation." Always accuracy!

Concept Five: Historical Cosmology:
Common Mental Equipment or Time Frame of Reference

Closely related to the problem of interpretation is the concept of Historical Cosmology. What is Historical Cosmology? The term Historical Cosmology, or just simply **Cosmology**, refers to a time-bound set of Ideas, truths, assumptions, notions, biases, views, experiences and concepts that all add up to a common mental equipment shared by all the people of a society or a region who are alive at any given moment.

Common mental equipment is sometimes referred to as a milieu, or a vantage point, or the mind of an age, or some other term. But common mental equipment is what is at stake. Sometimes we can refer to this as a **time frame of reference.** Here's an example:

If you are an early Church Father, such as **St. Jerome**, you are writing about the fall of the Roman Empire in the 6th century. Your thesis might be that the Roman Empire fell because it failed to accept Christianity. It was too heathen, lacked morals, and was internally weakened to the point that it was divided. In that divided condition it easily fell prey to the barbarians.

Alternatively, you are **Edward Gibbon**, writing a most significant book, called The Decline and Fall of the Roman Empire in a very secular century, the 18th. Your thesis might be that the Roman Empire fell

because there was a serious divisive force in the land --namely Christianity. The empire became half heathen and half Christian. And this conflict caused internal dissension which weakened and divided the empire. In that divided condition it easily fell prey to the barbarians.
Between St. Jerome and Edward Gibbon there is no dispute about the facts. There was a Roman Empire. There was internal division and

dissension over the acceptance of Christianity. That dissension caused the Empire to become weak and divided. The divided Empire easily fell to the barbarian hordes.

But we have two absolutely opposing viewpoints here. One says the Roman Empire fell because it did not sufficiently accept Christianity. The other says it fell because it accepted Chrisianity too much! Who is right? And why? Perhaps neither is right, and there is some other cause or causes to consider. But the point is that one difference between St. Jerome and Edward Gibbon is related to the cosmology of their own centuries.

Every generation has its own values, concepts and beliefs – its own way of looking at the world. That perspective determines and colors a generation's way of looking at the world. All of the people of a culture, or even among cultures, perhaps unknowingly, share in this body of thought, values and assumptions. It is their time frame of reference. It is their Historical Cosmology!

That time frame of reference – cosmology – evolves as the world changes. People think differently in one moment in time than they do in another. Their world outlook changes. That is what history is! In a very real sense, History is the Evolution of Cosmology.

Here's another example: What ideas or words come spontaneously and instantly to mind if the historian asks you to define "progress?" For most of us the word "progress" has something to do with space, technology, science, future, or moving forward. However, what would happen if we asked that question, "What is progress," to people in the Italian Renaissance of the 13th century? 700-plus years ago. Now the dictionary definition of progress might be the same. They would say, just as we do, that progress is the striving for perfection – or something like that.

However, they would just as spontaneously say that "progress" was not the future, but rather the recovery of a perfection that had already occurred in the past, in the classical world of Greece and Rome. We would achieve progress, not through science and technology, but rather through great works of art and music and literature

One difference between the 21st century and the 13th is the difference between the two cosmologies. The mental equipment with which we view the world is shared, despite the fact that we come from different
parts of the country, different social classes, different races, genders, and every other difference. These variations do not seem to matter. We share the same cosmology, Of course if this is true about "progress," then that

is only one idea, one notion, one concept, one of thousands and thousands of such beliefs, ideas, and assumptions floating around in the mental environment. We are time-bound. We can no more think with the same mental equipment as the people of the 13th century than they could about us.

This means that history is relative to the period in which it is being interpreted. Let us note that the idea of the relativity of history to the time of its interpretation -- the idea of cosmology - led our old buddy Thomas Jefferson to exclaim that "every generation should write its own history." It made no sense to him to view the past through someone else's point of view or time frame of reference. Generation X would regard one thing as important about an event, while to Generation Y what was important to Generation X would just be irrelevant.

The French philosopher, **Voltaire** (Francois Marie Arouet 1694 - 1778), perhaps expressed this idea best when he said: "History is a pack of tricks we play on the dead." He meant that we incorporate our values, our ideas, our assumptions, our time frame of reference - our cosmology - into our reading of the past. In order to make the past meaningful to us we project our values and ideas onto the people and events of the past. In doing so we distort and alter the way the people who lived that past understood their own moment. We play tricks on them by inventing meanings they never intended.

Alas, we cannot help it. We cannot escape our cosmology. We are time bound. What the successful historian must do is to begin to reconstruct the time frame of reference, the mental equipment, the cosmology of the period we are studying, and attempt to see the past through the eyes of the people who lived it. Not an easy task, to be sure.

In order to do that, we have to know ourselves - our own time frame - well enough to distinguish ourselves from the historical moment we are studying. To think like them, we must know who we are first, then make the appropriate distinctions. This means no ivory towers for historians. Rather, historians must always be active in their own moment, actively aware of our own world.

Now suppose we turn Voltaire around for a minute. Instead of saying "History is a pack of tricks we play on the dead, suppose we said: "History is a pack of tricks the dead play on us." What does that mean?

Try the following example: you read in the newspaper, "Dog Bites Man." Does that get your attention? Probably not, but why not? Perhaps it is because this is such a common occurrence that is essentially not news. It is the usual stuff. How about this, though! You read in the paper: "Man Bites Dog!" Does that get your attention? These days we invent dinosaurs made out of DNA; some of those dinosaurs are among your teachers and White House staff. So even "man bites dog" might not be such a big deal after all. Anyhow, "Man Bites Dog" should get your attention because it is news. It is the record of the abnormal. Not the record of everyday occurrences.

But what about history? History also records the abnormal, the unusual – the news. That's its job. That's what it does. So how do we discover that part of the past which is the norm? How people lived and what they thought and did every day? You are not going to email your sister in Cincinnati and tell her that you got up in the morning and brushed your teeth with recycled sewage and put plastic in your coffee. Neither are people in St. Jerome's time, or Edward Gibbon's or anyone's. And they don't even know your sister in Cincinnati.

We can only reconstruct that part of the past through factual creativity, through immersion in other cultures and through attempting with caution and sensitivity to put ourselves into another cosmology.

Concept Six – Historical Sources

We have already touched on the view that evidence is the proof which we use to demonstrate the validity of a thesis. Here it is important to appreciate that historical evidence is constructed of some combination of data and reasoning. It is not just facts alone. It is not just analysis alone. Evidence is the combination of data and reasoning logically advanced to persuade a reader or listener that a particular general statement or thesis has merit and validity.

The addition of combining reasoning with information is critical to the idea of evidence. That is because facts alone usually do not persuade. Facts are the bricks with which you build the building. But what shape is the building? Reasoning gives shape or design to the structure of the historical building – or thesis – we are attempting to prove. We earlier raised the question of how we know when evidence (data plus reasoning) proves what it says it proves. To assist in this quest – or perhaps to muddy things further, this is the place to introduce the concept of primary sources. All right, then: what is a **primary source**?

Is it the closest eye witness to an historical event? Is it the most proximate? It is hard to dispute the view that being on the scene makes the eye witness a primary source. But is it because of the proximity? Does the condition of **proximation** make the eye witness primary?

Alternately, is primary defined as the first source to report? Is that what primary means? As a third possibility, does a primary source mean the most reliable source? The source that is most accurate or valid? Does the condition of reliability – the best source – make that source primary?

As always an example: What if you are a soldier in a foxhole in World War II? Are you a primary source for that war? There is a famous cartoon by war correspondent **Bill Mauldin**, depicting two GI's, whom he called Willie and Joe. Willie says to Joe: "Yestiday you saved my life and I swore I'd pay you back. Here's my last pair of dry socks." Are Willie and Joe primary sources for World War II? They have only a foxhole's view of the war, after all. So does this portion or degree of proximation promote them to primary? [And while we're at it, is Mauldin's cartoon a primary source?]

What of **General Douglas MacArthur**, the chief American commander in the Pacific theater of World War II. What if you are a general in Washington D.C. in World War II? Or you are in China? Are you a primary source? If the answer is affirmative, it should dispose of the idea of proximity as a criterion for the definition of primary sources. The general in D.C. is not proximate. But he is likely to be more reliable than the GIs on the ground.

So we have now disposed of both definitions of primary sources as proximate or most reliable. For MacArthur is a more reliable source than Willie and Joe – and he is not proximate. And Willie and Joe are surely proximate, but they are not the most reliable.

Let's try another example. What if you write a book on the ancient Greeks? Is this a primary source for ancient Greece? It is quite possible that you know more about ancient Greece than the ancient Greeks knew, because you have 1500 years of scholarship under your belt. You have the big picture. You also have the advantage of historical perspective. Moreover, you have all those proximate sources. Is your book a primary source? The book is more reliable, not proximate, nor first.

By now it should be clear that the condition of proximation, because that is essentially spatial in nature is not the way historians define a primary source. Similarly, the condition of reliability, because that is essentially related to validity, also falls short of the definition of a primary source. So what do historians mean by "primary?"

HISTORICAL KNOWING

Let us suggest that primary means contemporary – anyone who was alive at the moment an event occurred is primary, regardless of any association with the event or not. It does not matter if the source is an eye witness. It does not matter if the source is the first source. Nor does it matter if the source is the best source or not.

Why? This relates to what we have been discussing in the past few paragraphs. Primary is related precisely to cosmology – to the time frame of reference. It is because the people of that time share the same mental equipment, the same time frame of reference. They share the same historical cosmology. History is about time, not space. It is about time, not reliability.

Please do not confuse primary with valid, except that the cosmology of a particular moment is more important to know as an historian than almost anything else. We are all primary sources for the election of 2008. Willie and Joe, Bill Mauldin, and Douglas MacArthur are all primary sources for World War II, because they were alive at the time. They share the same cosmological moment. Reliability is another matter.

That said and understood, what is a secondary source? A secondary source is someone who was not yet living at the time of an event. That source may be an excellent source or a complete dud. Like your book on ancient Greece. But this is about time. Sources born after an event do not share the same cosmology – and hence they are not primary, no matter how valid or reliable they are.

To summarize: a source is any record – whether verbal, visual or numerical – of a specific event, person, thing or idea. Any source who participated in an event and any source who knew the event first-hand is a primary source. Anyone alive at the time an event occurs is a primary source. Otherwise the source is secondary. To be primary the source has to be contemporary. Otherwise it is secondary. regardless of its validity. Validity is a wholly different species.

Concept Seven: Cause and Effect

What is a "cause?" What is an "effect?" Of course, what is critical is the relationship between causes and effects. Let us accept the idea that causes cause effects and all effects are themselves causes of the next effects – and so on and so on. Sequence is the key to cause and effect. Events simply cannot preceed the events that preceed them!!

A man has a loaded pistol pointed at his head. His wife enters and breaks out laughing. "Why are you laughing," he says. "You are next." That cannot happen, can it? Sequence is essential.

If all causes cause some effects, and all effects are the causes of the next effects, what are the implications of that thought? Does it mean that everything is caused? It might seem so. But if that is true then is history – are all events – determined? If all events are caused, then is "chance" just a set of causes we don't know yet?

Even more important, if everything is caused, what if we could find the key to that causation? Could we predict the future, too? Is history a science of causation? There are many who thought so. Here is a very brief selection. Their keys to prediction continue to fascinate us. Each is nonetheless unfulfilling to most of us

Begin with the 19th century political philosopher **Karl Marx**. As you may know, Marx believed that economic motivation, buried in human nature, could predict history. We want to make clear that this is not about any political systems that others concocted out of Marx's ideas. Rather, we are suggesting that Marx believed that each person was driven by his or her own personal economic interests. From economic causation he projected how socioeconomic classes would behave and hence what would happen eventually over time. Marx comprehended that economic motivation was the key to the unfolding of historical events.

For **Charles Darwin**, the English naturalist, the key to historical development was his concept of evolution through natural selection. Darwin made no distinctions between the laws of evolution which governed the natural world and the laws which governed humankind. Darwin's followers applied his idea of evolution to human society. They essentially invented laws of history. To understand evolution was to perceive how history would ultimately unfold.

Consider also the Austrian psychiatrist **Sigmund Freud**. For Freud it was the operation of the human psyche – and the sexual drive, even under control – which determined human behavior. Again a systematic all-encompassing explanation for the development of human interaction and, by logical reasoning, to historical change. Another single-factor explanation which, should it be ever completely understood, would reveal how events are caused.

HISTORICAL KNOWING

For theologian **John Calvin**, the 16th century Protestant Reformer, the key to history was to understand history as God's plan known in action. While one could never exactly predict historical events specifically, they were nonetheless predetermined. One's devout faith would serve to allow events to unfold.

In all of these systems – and Gerber's guess is that you could suggest others – there was one law or principle which determined historical events. And perhaps humans will continue to explain the past and predict the future by inventing ideas which are tributes to human creativity and intellect. So far, we haven't done it. It remains to be determined – a bad pun – whether history is a science of causation.

What Is the Use or Value of History?

To conclude this topic we must consider the use of history. What good is history, anyhow? Who cares? Why study the past? Perhaps the best answer was offered by Benjamin Franklin. Franklin was often asked the justification for learning and knowing and studying anything. Particularly history. What good was all that knowledge anyhow? He always answered: "What good is a newborn baby?"

What follows are Gerber's own personal reasons for studying history. You are obviously most welcome to decide whether any of them makes sense. These are interpretations. They are not facts. They represent this author's opinion. There are, actually, three reasons:

First, history helps liquidate ignorance. Every one of us as humans is obligated to learn as much as we can about our heritage and human experience. This thirst for inquiry exists in every human being, until society corrupts the drive for pure learning in favor of funding and other less noble motives.

Second, history permits meaning in a life built on memory. History is our collective memory. Just as we don't think any of us would get very far if we started each day with no personal memory, we do not believe society can become more civilized or progress without the collective

wisdom that history provides. Thus, history provides roots and guidelines in our own chaotic time. History offers standards for ethical behavior and unethical behavior, which give us some roots to live by in our own fragmented and chaotic world.

HISTORICAL KNOWING

Third, history, as the record of the experience of other human beings, has humanistic objectives. Tolerance and appreciation of the values and cultures of others flow diretly from historical inquiry. All the moral choices in the world, all the choices between right and wrong, between sticking to principle and selling out – all of the expressions of human nature have been articulated many thousands of times before. Human nature hasn't changed much, if at all. We have only been out of the trees for a few million years. Humans still have the same basic needs, drives and qualities which compose humanity as a species.

If we can strip away the foreground of circumstances, if we can distinguish the human dilemma from the conditions in which individuals make choices, we can ourselves learn – vicariously, without having to suffer each and every experience personally in order to learn. Thus we can ourselves make better choices for ourselves. That is, qualitatively preferable choices, because we have studied the consequences of choosing one choice or another as others made them before us. In other words, by studying the past we can improve how we live our own lives.

Thus the study of history is a major force for tolerance, for the teaching of love and community and individual self-fulfillment. It is as strong a force for humanity as there is. If we can learn to be sensitive to others in the past, and avoid seeing them as stereotypes, and appreciate other cultures as complicated, mortal and significant, then we can profit by their examples to us in our relations with others in our own times.

It was the American philosopher **George Santayana** who taught us: that "Those who forget the past are bound to repeat It" For many, that is an overdone and hackneyed phrase – but it still rings true. Or as Gerber's children always tell him: those who forget the pasta are bound to reheat It!

CHAPTER TWO: THE AMERICAN REVOLUTION -- PHASE ONE

It is quite possible to define the period leading directly to the American Revolution as a struggle between Colonial Autonomy and (British) Imperial Reform. That is the thesis of this chapter.

Colonial Autonomy Versus Imperial Reform

What does that phrase mean, Colonial Autonomy versus Imperial Reform? There is a pattern of action which you should notice in the years after 1763. The issues stemming from the acquisition of the enormous empire taken from France in the Treaty of Paris of 1763 began a process of active measures enacted by a reform-minded English ministry. Imperial reform, in turn, led to colonial protest, as colonists, long used to being essentially left alone, resented intrusions on what they considered to be their discretion, indeed their right, to make decisions.

Colonial protest, again in its turn, led to British responses to protest, and then to colonial reactions to those responses, and more British reactions to those responses - and reactions to the responses to the reactions - and so on, leading ultimately to the American Revolution and then to the Declaration of Independence of 1776.

Escalation and Polarization

It is important to notice a second pattern in this struggle. We might label this a pattern of **escalation** and **polarization**. Escalation refers to the growth of the intensity or anger as the conflict evolved from issue to issue. The heat level goes up as people become increasingly outraged at the other's ideas and behavior.

Polarization refers to the increasing inability to communicate or compromise or even hear one another that develops from one issue to the next issue. The adversaries talk past one another. They turn a deaf ear to the ideas of the other. Negotiating room disappears. This process of escalation and polarization means that both sides dug their heels in so that what had been disagreements about problems to solve become abstract principles which must be defended to the death.

THE AMERICAN REVOLUTION – PHASE ONE

Once we understand the pending conflict between the British government and the Colonies as an issue of imperial reform versus colonial autonomy we can take up the set of issues which we can categorize as the first phase of protest. The first phase of protest runs from 1763 – 1769.

Western Problems

An abbreviated list of five western problems might be noted.

(1) Conflicting land claims. Conflicts among colonies as to boundaries and land claims top the list. (2) Land Use. What use should be made of western lands now suddenly in British hands? (3) Defense. Issues of defense and protection against Indian attack and perhaps the next French attempt to regain its lost territory were also significant and complex. (4) Indian relations. Relations with the various tribes still must be settled – somehow. (5) Government for Canada. And of course a new government for 60,000 French Canadians must be determined and implemented.

Perhaps the key point to notice is that each of these issues required a decision from the central government in London, because they were beyond the capacity of any of the thirteen colonies to address. British problem-solvers, reformers of the empire, were needed to resolve any and all of them.

Royal Proclamation of 1763

The first attempt to tackle this array of western issues was King George III's Royal Proclamation of 1763. In some ways the Proclamation of 1763 was a statesmanlike measure. It contained several provisions:

(1) The Proclamation prohibited colonial settlement beyond the watershed of the Appalachian Mountains. This is the famous **Proclamation Line**, about which some American colonists complained so bitterly. If there had been no stoppage of settlement – if colonists had poured into the new West with no regulations – all the problems related to land would be resolved by the realities of people carving homes and settlements out of the wilderness. It would then be too late to make any other decisions. The line was designed to be temporary; to sit in place until the other policies could be determined.

Unfortunately for British relations with the colonies, the ministry of Lord Grenville was ousted in England, replaced over British issues which had nothing at all to do with the colonies. Future ministries simply overlooked the Proclamation Line or did not realize how important it was. What had begun as a temporary measure froze and became permanent. It was permanently put on the back burner.

(2) New governments were set up for the new territories acquired from France. These included Quebec, East and West Florida, and the Granada territories of the West Indies. The government of **Quebec** was set up to Anglicize French Canada – that is, to make Englishmen out of French Canadians. For Quebec an English Common Law system of government was installed in place of French Civil Law. Worship in the Catholic Church was prohibited, replaced with an established Anglican Church. English, not French, became the official language of Canada. A representative system of governance was substituted for the French Governor General.

(3) There would be no future grants of land to any private land companies until the conflicting land claims were settled. No purchases could be made by private citizens from the Indians. Indian claims were to be handled entirely by the Royal Administration. This meant that the entire western area was reserved for Indians. Only troops and fur traders were allowed west of the Line.

(4) The fur trade was opened to anyone. That put a stop to the private monopolies that the colonies had been granting to fur lobbyists. Posts were to be set up to issue trapping licenses throughout the west. A small fee would get you a trapper's permit. The money from licenses would be used to buy land from the Indians.

(5) Finally, all colonial laws which ran contrary to any provision of the Proclamation were declared abolished. This meant that London, not Boston, New York or Philadelphia had taken control of this complex set of issues.

Implementing the Proclamation

What settlements were made under the Proclamation of 1763? How did it work out? For one thing, four major treaties were signed with Indian tribes, to establish reserved areas for the Indians and to buy land from them. This portion of the Proclamation seemed to work out well. At least there was peace in the west. The United States inherited this problem. Americans solved it in the end by a policy first of Indian removal, then of reservations, then by some attempts at extermination of native Americans, and ultimately by assimilation.

Regarding protection and defense: The British commander in America, **Lord Jeffrey Amherst**, had recommended to the ministry that 6000 British regulars would be enough troops for defense purposes. The ministry, however, preferred 10,000 redcoats. There were, to be sure, large numbers of French-and-Indian War veterans who needed jobs. They got them. Partly the larger number, and the higher cost, was based on the thought that the colonists would pay part of the expense, since they were the ones being protected, were they not? American colonists were very suspicious of these troops, and as it turned out, many of them were used to keep order in eastern cities in the years ahead.

Regarding the Proclamation Line itself, as indicated earlier, changing ministries proved fatal, because there was a lack of continuity in the policy. The colonial population, especially in New England, was ready to spill over into the West. Land-hungry settlers were tired of growing rocks. They could not understand why, with so much open land out there, they could not just settle it. Colonists, moreover, had little respect for the Indian treaties. Some violated the Proclamation and went into the West. British troops went in after them and brought them back.

The attempt to Anglicize French Canada had been designed to calm the fears of Protestant New England about a Catholic colony on its borders. Well, New England calmed down, but the French Canadians did not. The policy was a dismal failure. It took ten years, but the British government eventually recognized that the policy was not working and changed it in 1774. Relations between the French Canadians and the surrounding English Canadians is still a live issue in Quebec today, *n'est ce pas?*

The decision was made, but never implemented, to favor the claims of the land companies, rather than the eastern settlers who wanted free western land. The U.S. inherited this problem and did not solve it until 1862 with the Homestead Act of that year.

In short, the Proclamation antagonized many colonists: those with western land claims, settlers who wanted to go west, land speculators, and, of course, the French. Indians were not happy, either, because there were so many treaty violations. Let us say that British policy regarding this set of western issues was certainly well meant, but it was not particularly successful.

THE AMERICAN REVOLUTION – PHASE ONE

With American independence, the United States inherited the entire set of western problems. Most significant was the major issue of the relationship of the colonies to the mother country, which the British were never able to solve. The U.S. government would instantly face these western issues – and a treacherous new problem over whether slavery was legal in the territories.

Financing the Empire and the First Phase of Protest

The second set of problems facing the ministry involved complex issues of finance. How would the government manage budgetary problems of taxation and revenue? How would London finance its newly acquired empire?

Revenue Reform #1: Revenue Act of 1764 (Sugar Act)

In the face of the need for new revenue, Parliament established the **Revenue Act of 1764** – also called the **Sugar Act** – you might know it by either name. It was designed to raise money and also to tighten the administration of the trade laws – to enforce the law. The Sugar Act, or Revenue Act may be noted as Revenue Reform #1.

Under the Sugar Act the tariff duties on foreign molasses, from which rum was made, was shifted from a **protective tariff** to a **revenue tariff**. The protective tariff of 6 pence per gallon had been designed to keep out foreign made rum from the colonies – colonists would have to buy rum from English merchants only, if at all! The protective tariff rate had encouraged an almost customary practice of cheating, bribery and smuggling. It could not be enforced. Rum, significantly, was a very popular drink in America. Some say it still is. Moreover, rum was used in trade for African slaves.

In the Sugar Act the Ministry reduced the tariff to 3 pence per gallon and established mechanisms for strict enforcement. This reduction, coupled with enforcement, was intended to raise money and stop illegal trade outside the empire at the same time. Clearly a reform measure.

Vice-Admiralty Courts were set up to try violators. In these Courts there were no local juries. Colonial courts would not convict anybody for doing what everybody did routinely. Would any jury today convict you for going 65 mph in a 55 mph zone?

THE AMERICAN REVOLUTION – PHASE ONE

Violators of the trade laws were moved to Halifax Courthouse, in Nova Scotia, Canada, for trial. This move emancipated the courts from colonial control – you certainly get decisions closer to justice! In that sense it was a reform measure.

The reaction to the Revenue Act in America was way out of proportion to its economic influence. It aroused merchants in Boston, New York and Philadelphia, whose lucrative illegal trade would now be curtailed. They did not mind the 3 pence duty. The Act could have said 30 pence or 1 pence. As long as it wasn't enforced, who cared what it said? It was the reality of enforcement, the change in the practice of local autonomy, that was most disturbing! But surely, Parliament had a right to enforce its own laws.

Colonists did not see the Act as reform legislation. They saw it only as it affected them. It hit New England hardest – particularly rum runners and those who sold rum to Indians. And they occasionally reacted violently against the Customs Officers. Customs Officer **John Malcolm**, for example, was tarred and feathered, a terrible, painful punishment for anyone.

It is interesting that many southern planters favored the Act. There was a provision in it for a subsidy on naval products – particularly indigo and hemp – rope, not marijuana, which would bring economic advantages for southern planters. Indigo plantations obviously thrived on the backs of slave labor.

Colonial Protest Over the Revenue Act

Colonists did protest the Revenue Act. **James Otis** of Massachusetts, for example, argued against the law before the Governor's Council in Massachusetts. Of more significance was the pamphlet that Otis wrote, titled "The Rights of the Colonies Asserted and Proved." Otis was a sort of fiery agitator, an 18th century rabble rouser with ideas! Otis claimed that the power of Parliament was not absolute, but rather a declaration of what he called the Old Law, which came from God. Any act of Parliament which violated the Old Law, such as the Sugar Act, was invalid. Parliament, Otis emphasized, could not tax the colonies without consent of Colonial Assemblies. Taxation without consent became a core principle underlying assertions of colonial autonomy.

Where there had previously been a distinction in some minds between a tariff (an external regulation and hence legal) and a tax (an internal tax and hence illegal), Otis eliminated the distinction. There was no difference. A tax was a tax was a tax. Otis also condemned trials without juries as un-English, as violations of the rights of Englishmen.

The legal protest over the Sugar Act was, in Gerber's opinion, a smokescreen. Clearly Parliament had authority to regulate the empire's trade. It was enforcement that mattered, because enforcement ran counter to the patterns of autonomy which had been built up over a hundred years of benign neglect. In any case the Sugar Act was a legitimate exercise of Parliamentary authority. It was implemented in the colonies, raising some £40,000 yearly.

Despite the controversy over the Sugar Act, Lord Grenville was not discouraged from continuing his efforts to solve the empire's financial problem. He quite naturally believed that the colonies should bear a part of their own expense. But he had no desire to bully them or abuse them with arbitrary levies of money. Grenville first consulted with the agents of the colonies who lived in London, including **Benjamin Franklin**, to try to find an acceptable substitute for the proposal that eventually became the Stamp Act. The agents had nothing much to offer.

Franklin did tell Grenville that the proposed Stamp Tax would create bad feeling in America. Grenville, however, looking at the whole puzzle of the empire, had to do something. If the colonies would not tax themselves, and since reform of the empire required money, then Parliament would have to tax the colonies – especially if the Colonial Agents could offer no other alternatives. Moreover, if Grenville's ministry would not act, it would be replaced in London with one that would!

Revenue Reform #2 – Stamp Act of 1765

Accordingly, Parliament passed the **Stamp Act** in 1765. Under the Act, stamps [excise taxes such as cigarette, gasoline, or liquor stamps today] would be purchased from the British agent in each colony. Stamps were to be affixed to newspapers, legal documents, wills, court proceedings, business transactions, licenses – essentially anything bought or sold in the colonies. The Act was expected to bring in some £60,000 per year. That amount would go far to reduce the British debt and the burden on English taxpayers.

The Act would be easy to administer, because the stamps cost next to nothing to print, and only one Stamp Agent per colony was needed to distribute them. As far as taxes go, it was almost pure profit, with very little overhead. Violations of the Act were to be tried in Vice Admiralty Courts. The Colonial Assemblies were requested to appoint the Agents, a move to try to win some colonial support for the measure.

Colonial Protest Over the Stamp Act

The reaction to the Act in the thirteen colonies was spontaneous and surprising. People went ballistic! Riots broke out in the port cities. Mobs demanded that the stamps not be permitted to land and that the Agents resign. Actually, by the time the Act was to take effect, every single Stamp Agent had resigned, had been run out of town, or was on the verge of quitting.

Some opponents to the Act used the occasion as an excuse to badger their political enemies within the colonies. Mobs attacked conservatives who, while they, too, disliked the law, believed in obeying laws until they were changed. People who disliked violence sometimes became the targets of mob violence. In New York a mob wrecked the home and property of the **Delancy** family, wealthy merchants who obviously would have to pay more taxes under the Act than the people who attacked them. In Massachusetts a mob destroyed the house of then Chief Justice and later Governor **Thomas Hutchinson**. Hutchinson became a sort of scapegoat for the general discontent people felt for folks higher up the socio-economic ladder.

In addition to riots there was a well-organized intercolonial response. Indeed, in the Stamp Act crisis there was probably more unity in the colonies than at any time before the War for Independence. While the actual economic burden was not heavy, the Act worked against the self-interest of the vocal middle class: business people, lawyers, and journalists in particular. While they used the language of the right to tax themselves, what was really at stake was a precedent against their class self-interest. It should be clear that the issue of reform *versus* autonomy was escalating rapidly.

Actually, the mobs were led by prominent merchants and organized into associations calling themselves the **Sons of Liberty**. The Sons began as a secret organization, with local cells eventually making contact throughout the colonies. They had their own passwords, their own secret handshakes, and so on. The merchants took over these organizations and used them for their own purposes. This was quite an unusual alliance between middle and working classes. The alliance was one reason the opposition to the Act was successful. It became the role of the Sons to arouse the populace to the cause of the merchants.

In addition to rioting and violence, a drive to get the Stamp Act repealed began as soon as it was passed. In Virginia, **Patrick Henry**, an inflammable opportunist if there ever was one, led the way. You have to love people with two first names! Henry introduced in the Virginia House of Burgesses several resolutions phrased in constitutional rhetoric.

The most significant of Henry's resolutions asserted what became a slogan: "Taxation Without Representation Is Tyranny." Taxation without representation is tyranny? Maybe it is!! But in Henry's mouth the phrase was, in Gerber's opinion, utter nonsense. Consider the scenario under which the colonies received representation based on population. They might receive one-fourth of the votes in Parliament. Now what happens? Parliament votes on the Stamp Act. The colonists would be outvoted by an overwhelming majority. But no one could argue that the colonies weren't represented!

What Henry really meant was that we colonists do not want any taxes. Period! The colonists wanted neither taxes nor the representatives that would eliminate their argument against taxation. If taxation without representation is tyranny, then presumably taxation with representation isn't tyranny. Does anyone believe for one instant that Henry failed to understand that scenario?

We must note here that there is a major escalation from James Otis's idea of "no taxation without consent" to Patrick Henry's "no taxation without representation." Consent could be granted by the colonial legislatures. Representation would be much harder to achieve. Nonetheless, Henry's slogan inflamed the colonies.

In response the Massachusetts Sons of Liberty called for a **Stamp Act Congress**, composed of representatives of all the colonies, to meet in New York City in October 1765. When that Congress met, it took several actions. First, it sent a petition to Parliament and the Crown, requesting repeal of the Act. Then Congress declared the Stamp Act unconstitutional, because the colonies were not represented in Parliament. They vowed that the stamps would never be used.

THE AMERICAN REVOLUTION – PHASE ONE

Next, the Congress invoked economic pressure to get the Act repealed. It was agreed that merchants would stop importing British goods. That is, an **embargo** would be placed on British products. To enforce the embargo the Sons of Liberty published in the newspapers the names of merchants who continued to import British goods. Customers were urged to boycott those merchants. This measure was actually unnecessary, because the merchants were wholly unified in opposition to the Act, whatever it cost them. Instead, American-made goods were to be used, so as to become independent of the British economy altogether. American colonists would cut out luxuries and make what they needed.

The embargo was extremely effective. English merchants who relied heavily on colonial trade felt the pinch of lost profits. The estimated losses in revenue in a few short months amounted to something like £345,000, a drastic cut in trade. Nearly six years of collected Stamp Act tax revenue was lost to merchants in a very short time. English merchants instantly put the heat on Parliament to repeal the Act. Members of Parliament who wanted to stay in office listened to their constituents.

Benjamin Franklin, who had earlier acquiesced in the Stamp Act, now testified in the **Privy Council** that the Act ought to be repealed. His performance was so good that he actually saved his reputation in the colonies. It is perhaps ironic that quick repeal of the Act probably slowed down the drive for separation from England. Repeal lengthened the time toward independence by restoring peace.

In any case The Stamp Act was repealed in 1766 by the new ministry, headed by the **Duke of Rockingham**. Rockingham's ministry had replaced Grenville's over an issue that had nothing to do with the colonies. Many in England were disappointed that so fruitful a measure was sacrificed on the alter of economic pressure. Cartoons portrayed the ministers burying the Stamp Act. The Stamp Act had never really gone into effect in the colonies.

Parliament also passed the so-called **Declaratory Act** of 1766! The Declaratory Act stated, in effect, that Parliament had a right to legislate on any subject whatever regarding the colonies. It was a claim of Parliamentary supremacy, pure and simple. To be sure it was rather petty, saying that "OK, you won this time, but we're really right." No colonists protested the Declaratory Act. They were too busy building bonfires and burning the stamps in celebration of repeal.

THE AMERICAN REVOLUTION – PHASE ONE

Can it be that the "taxation without representation" argument was a propaganda ploy? You are welcome to decide for yourselves! Repeal of the Stamp Act was, however temporary, a victory for colonial autonomy. But the new ministry faced the identical problem of raising revenue that had plagued Grenville. Reform was still required.

Colonial affairs were put in the charge of an arrogant aristocrat named **Charles Townshend**, known in some circles as "Champagne Charley." Townshend had little sympathy for the self-interested provincials in the colonies. His major objective was to reduce the taxes of English homeowners and landowners. To that end he even took private lessons in economics. It is quite probable that Townshend studied the ideas of *laissez-faire* free market competition soon to be made popular by the father of classical economics, **Adam Smith**, author of the 1776 best seller, The Wealth of Nations.

Some people even today think Smith's classical economic views are some sort of biblical text which the American government ought to follow. And some people still think the earth is flat! And that evolution is not science. And that the New York Giants will win another Superbowl in our lifetime. At any rate, Townshend was pledged to make up for lower English taxes by raising them somewhere else.

Accordingly, he persuaded Parliament to pass the Acts that bear his name, the **Townshend Acts** of 1767. These laws placed customs duties on English paint, lead, paper, glass and tea. Please be clear: these were duties on English goods for the first time, rather than foreign goods. They were to raise some £40,000 per year. The money was earmarked for the colonies, to be used to pay for the cost of defense and to pay customs officers. This last provision is significant, because it was a reform measure to free colonial officials from financial dependence on the colonists, and hence end the pressure toward dishonesty and corruption.

Specifically, the law provided for an **American Board of Customs Commissioners** (with headquarters in Boston) to supervise the collection of the customs duties. The Commissioners were made directly responsible to the English Board of Trade. They were paid directly by the Crown, not by fees or commissions paid by colonists. The law thus created the **Civil List** [today we might say civil service] for customs and judicial officers in the colonies, a much needed reform. The Crown would now pay salaries to its administrative personnel. This would allow them do their work professionally and honestly, so they could fairly administer the the trade laws.

THE AMERICAN REVOLUTION – PHASE ONE

Americans called the Civil List tyranny, which it clearly was not. The British government had every authority to pay its own officers. The Civil List was, however, another clear departure from the practice of local autonomy. Its implementation would further escalate the issue of reform versus autonomy.

The Townshend Acts also contained a provision for the use of General Warrants or what were then called **Writs of Assistance.** Writs of Assistance permitted British officers to search and seize ships and goods – more or less on suspicion – in order to find smuggled property. Those writs were, indeed, gross violations of privacy. Americans said so. It is also true that they were in use in Britain. At least no double standard was in effect.

American distaste for General Warrants was an influence on the Fourth Amendment to to the U.S. Constitution. Note how specific warrants have to be! "The right of the people to be secure in their persons, houses, papers and effects, against *unreasonable searches and seizures*, shall not be violated, and no warrants shall issue but upon probable cause, supported by oath or affirmation, and particularly describing the *place to be searched, and the persons or things to be seized.*" Thus says the Fourth Amendment. Were the Writs of Assistance influential in creating that provision?

Coming on the heels of the Stamp Act, before memories had cooled down, it was most natural that colonists would object to the Townshend Acts. Again there were riots, but this time the merchants controlled the mobs, so that they did not get out of hand. Again, for the second time, non-importation – embargo – was declared and implemented. This was Embargo #2. As with the Stamp Act embargo two years earlier, there were lists of English products to be excluded. Again, domestic manufacturers were encouraged, in order to take up the slack.

Moreover, the theory behind colonial protest also escalated. Recall that James Otis had claimed that Parliament could not tax the colonies without their consent. Then Patrick Henry had claimed taxation without representation was tyranny! Now, under the leadership of **Samuel Adams** of Boston – the Beer – Massachusetts began to organize colonial resistance. Adams, who actually was a brewer, drew up in 1768 a document called the **Massachusetts Circular Letter**.

The Circular Letter did not refer to its shape – but rather to its circulation to the other colonies. The Letter had the approval of the General Court, the Massachusetts Assembly. Adams escalated the rhetoric. He drew on Otis and Henry, but he added that because Americans could not be represented in Parliament in any practical manner, then American colonial legislatures were co-equal to Parliament. The letter asked a united colonial protest to win repeal of the Townshend Acts.

Co-equal to Parliament? Such an idea, if accepted, would drastically change the constitution of Britain by creating legislative bodies with the same powers as Parliament. It might be the same as saying that each state legislature in America today possesses the same powers as Congress does. Adams's Circular Letter surely escalated the ideological rift between London and the colonies to substantial proportions.

We must also note that some Americans were really convincing themselves that this phony constitutional argument was legitimate. For example, "**Letters of a Pennsylvania Farmer**", written by **John Dickinson** of Pennsylvania. These letters were actually fourteen editorials written between November 1767 and the end of 1768. Dickinson invoked the now-familiar slogan that taxes without representatives were illegal. He cited many other constitutional arguments against British intervention into colonial affairs.

It is important to remember that Dickinson was no incendiary like Patrick Henry, nor a cynical politician like Sam Adams. He was certainly no more a farmer than you are. He was a Gentleman Farmer; the only thing he raised was his hat! Dickinson was, in fact, one of the only members of the Continental Congress who refused to sign the Declaration of Independence. Dickinson would become the principal author of the Articles of Confederation.

At any rate, the Royal Governor of Massachusetts, **Francis Bernard**, saw the Circular letter as sedition. Sedition may be defined as criminal language (spoken or written) directed at government, subject to severe punishment, even death. Bernard suspended the Massachusetts Legislature and sent them home. The Governor then decided to enforce the Townshend laws. As soon as the regulations were offically in effect, the Customs Officers decided to make an example of wealthy Boston merchant **John Hancock** [the Insurance Company], the man who signed the Declaration of Independence with a signature so large that, said Hancock, George III wouldn't have to put on his glasses to read the name.

Hancock liked to import Madeira wine from the Canary Islands, which was illegal, but before the Townshend Acts Civil List, his actions had been "overlooked." Customs officers seized Hancock's ship, the Liberty, and confiscated the wine.
Hancock proceeded to call out the Boston Sons of Liberty and they attacked the Customs House. The Customs officers fled and called for

help in the form of British troops. This action established Hancock as the leader of the Radicals. We can define "Radical" in this context as that group of colonists most advanced in protest. That is all the term means, at least ideologically, although we can associate radicalism with a willingness to advocate violence as protest!

It also made Hancock the puppet of Sam Adams. Some historians, including Gerber, think that it was Adams who tipped off the British about Hancock's Madeira, knowing that their enforcement action would bring a very influential merchant over to the Radical side once and for all. There is no evidence for that opinion. Just a hunch.

Violence compelled the Governor to call for troops. Redcoats arrived in Boston in October 1768 on the pretext of restoring order, although order had long since been restored. This move in turn caused the people of Boston even more strongly to resist the Act. Because the legislature of Massachusetts had been suspended, 96 representatives of that legislature met unofficially and privately in their own Provincial Convention, the **Massachusetts Provincial Convention**.

This provincial convention was an illegal and unconstitutional legislative body. It was the first to meet in the colonies without official sanction. Nevertheless, it acted as an unofficial "legislature," which ordered non-importation, another embargo, in an effort to repeat the success of the Stamp Act repeal.

In Virginia the response to the Townshend Acts was also strong. The **House of Burgesses**, Virgnia's colonial assembly, passed something called the **Virginia Resolves**. The Virginia Resolves were written by **George Mason**, someone you absolutely must know as the future author of the **Virginia Bill of Rights**, the model for the United States Bill of Rights, and George Washington, a wealthy planter and slaveholder.

Using the argument in the Circular Letter, The Virginia Resolves claimed that only the House of Burgesses could tax in Virginia. The Burgesses had the sole right to levy taxes within the colony's borders. They called on the Crown to repeal the Townshend Acts. In response, the Royal Governor of Virginia, named **Norborne Berkeley, Baron de Botetourt**, dissolved the Burgesses and sent the members home.

THE AMERICAN REVOLUTION – PHASE ONE

That caused the Virginia protesters to call another illegal provincial congress, much like that of Massachusetts. This one met in **Raleigh's Tavern** in Williamsburg, in the building that still stands in that city. The Virginia Resolves also called for a policy of non-importation. Virginia's embargo included a suspension of the African slave trade.

It should be pointed out here how the escalation of the issue of reform *versus* autonomy had grown, and in particular how it divided the colonists. The British government certainly had contributed to the growth of protest and the emergence of desires for separation, not only by the passage of tax reform, but also because they flatly ignored the petitions sent to them by one colonial body or other.

Ignoring petitions may seem a small thing. But ignoring petitions angered the large number of moderates in the colonies who wanted autonomy just as much as any Radical but who disliked mob violence and other illegal protest. These people could not help but feel that if legal, moderate channels of protest were given no attention, perhaps the only method left was confrontation and violence. In short moderates were being forced to choose between radicalism and violence on one hand and accepting British policy on the other. Ignoring petitions served to radicalize moderates, to convert moderates into Radicals.

At the same time many conservative colonial Americans decided that violence was wrong. Government must be obeyed until laws could be changed internally by legal processes. These numerous folks would become Tories or Loyalists. Make no mistake! There were every bit as many of them as people who became active revolutionaries.

We can now identify three positions in the colonies regarding British reform. Radicals were determined to change British policy even by violence. Moderates wished to protest policies through the legal channels. Conservatives were willing to support British reforms, because they believed violence was wrong. Each incident or event caused more people to take a stand, some on one side, some on the other.

There is one thing more to notice: the embargo following the Townshend Acts did not hurt British merchants as had the Embargo which followed the Stamp Act. Out of sheer necessity, British merchants had found new markets for their goods in Europe and in the Mediterranean. England prospered, despite a massive reduction in trade with the colonies.

It is estimated that American trade was reduced by half the usual volume. New York, for example, reduced the value of its trade with Britain from £490,000 to £75,000 in one year. The British made it up elsewhere. The embargo, in short, hurt only American commerce. The embargo was not a factor in the repeal of the Townshend Acts.

It is clear that **King George III** was seriously concerned about the deteriorating relationship between the empire and his American colonies. Rather than perceiving this king as some benign monarch, we might instead appreciate the recent scholarship that demonstrates that George III was quite militant, even hawkish, when it came to the colonies. He would brook no disobedience to London's decisions. He would quell violence.

After experimenting with numbers of ministers, he finally hit on the man he thought could facilitate British policy. Namely **Lord North**. North is frequently seen in American history high school textbooks as a villain, a tyrant whose actions led directly to the American Revolution. Historians now know, however, that North was little more than George III's mouthpiece. The King made policy. North got it implemented because he had significant influence in Parliament. In any case that tyrant's first act was to get the Townshend Acts repealed. Some tyrant!

North did it not out of colonial pressure, but rather because he believed in a freer trade policy -- without tariffs – than did Townshend. Note that Parliament did leave the tax on English tea, as a symbol (like the Declaratory Act) of Parliament's right to tax.

Period of Relative Calm Between 1769 – 1773

From the repeal of the Townshend Acts in 1769 to 1773 and the Boston Tea affair, Lord North succeeded in bringing a period of relative peace and restoration of "normal" relations between the Mother Country and the colonies. During those nearly five years years the colonial air remained relatively calm. There were incidents, brawls and tragic events that revealed that the problems had been patched over but not really solved. Yet there was nothing truly disruptive. There was a period of relative peace starting in 1769. It was as though the colonies and the Mother Country had kissed and made up. Indeed, it was all that Radical leaders like Sam Adams could do to keep any anti-British sentiment alive. How's that for a commentary on British tyranny? How's that for a statement of the drive for the rights of Englishmen, which colonists had claimed they wanted.

Three incidents during the period of calm are worthy of mention, because they suggest how little, rather than how much, anti-British spirit existed in the colonies.

THE AMERICAN REVOLUTION – PHASE ONE

Boston Massacre: 1770

1st: the so-called **Boston Massacre** of 1770. You may know that British troops had been chasing some little boys who had been throwing snowballs at the troops. Some say that the snowballs had rocks in them. They hurt. At least one soldier suffered a bloody head wound. A mob gathered, and began hurling clubs, ice and whatever else they could find at the Redcoats, who finally formed up in the snow with bayonets fixed.

No one knows who fired the first shot. It is thought that a club knocked down a soldier whose musket discharged. That shot caused troops to fire into the crowd, although no order to fire had been given. Five citizens of Boston were killed. Traditional portrayals, such as those by engraver and silversmith **Paul Revere**, picture the king's troops as menacing, while the colonists are made innocent victims. This reflects a pro-colonial bias.

Revere, incidentally, at first included the death of one African American citizen of Boston named **Crispus Attucks**. Then he whited out Attucks in the engraving that most Americans see. Certainly African-Americans consider Attucks a patriot – and so should we all – if indeed any of these men should be considered that way. You will have to ask yourself why Revere omitted Attucks in the commonly viewed portrayal.

The Boston Massacre was a tragic incident, to be sure, but historical accuracy suggests that the troops were under serious threat, and were essentially defending themselves. In any event the Radical press in Boston made the streets run red with blood. That is a huge overstatement, in Gerber's opinion. But it made good propaganda for the Radicals. Sam Adams now had martyrs at last which he could use to revive his faltering Radical organization. Indeed, the "massacre" was a violent confrontation, a tragic confrontation, certrainly, but hardly the one-sided slaughter of innocent civilians. Can the Boston Massacre be compared to the Kent State shootings of 1970, two hundred years later, in which four students were killed? Can the British Redcoasts be considered analogous to the Ohio National Guard?

At the trial of the troop's officer, one Captain Thomas Preston, no less a citizen than prominent lawyer **John Adams** (Sam's cousin) got Preston acquitted on a legitimate plea of self-defense. Actually, nine soldiers were tried, seven were acquitted outright, and two were found guilty, branded on the thumb and released – an ancient ritual called **Benefit of Clergy** – which in this case amounted to a suspended sentence.

One result of the incident, however, was that Governor Thomas Hutchinson, whose house had been attacked by a mob during the Stamp Act riots in 1765, ordered the withdrawal of British troops from Boston. Hutchinson's action also contributed to the general aroma of peacefulness.

Golden Hill Riot – NYC 1770

The 2nd event, also in 1770, is known as the Golden Hill Riot. In New York City, from January 13-16 of 1770, there were tremendous riots around the stump of the Liberty Pole, the symbol of the Sons of Liberty. The Sons printed up pamphlets attacking the people of New York City and the Sons of Liberty themselves. Then they signed British soldiers' names to them. The riots started when the troops tried to rip up the pamphlets that they had never written. The riots lasted for three days. The troops were surrounded by some 3000 New Yorkers who disarmed the Redcoats and forced them into their barracks. Once again this was a trumped up incident. Once concluded, a relaxation of tensions resumed in New York.

Burning of the Gaspée

The third Incident was the burning of the British revenue cutter, the Gaspée, off Newport, Rhode Island. Some 150 Radicals including wealthy merchants who just happened to be some of the biggest smugglers on the east coast sailed out to the Gaspée, removed the captain and crew, and then burned the ship. Some say they were led by one **John Brown**, for whom Brown University is named, but we can't say for sure!! Some of the mob were picked up and sent to Canada for trial, because, as noted, American juries would not convict them. While Americans claimed that the trials undermined the jury process, Englishmen were growing increasingly alarmed over the lawlessness in the colonies. At any rate, this incident, too, ended with the return of peace and normal relations.

Evaluating the First Phase of Protest

In evaluating the period from 1763 to 1769, from the Proclamation of 1763 to the repeal of the Townshend Acts, we can identify what we can truly call, with historical hindsight, of course, the first phase of protest. British reforms of the Empire produced enough antagonism in America to create intercolonial protests out of isolated incidents. It is clear that the enforcement of the law was more a threat to traditional patterns of autonomous behavior than the laws themselves. The Civil List was more important than any issues of principle, and certainly more important than taxes. With the repeal of those laws, however, the life of agitation wore down and lost enthusiasm.

During the period from 1769 to 1773 the trade laws were better enforced than ever in colonial history. Of some £257,000 collected in customs duties, only about £83,000 went to Britain. The rest, some £174,000 was used in the colonies to pay crown officers and soldiers. Smuggling just about stopped. Prosperity returned. We have no CNN polls, of course, but as late as 1773, despite the actions of the Radicals, probably no more than 1% of American colonials would have favored independence from Britain. 99% would likely have felt independence unnecessary and even inconceivable. That picture would change.

CHAPTER THREE: SECTIONALISM IN PRE-REVOLUTIONARY AMERICA: WHO SHALL RULE AT HOME?

Sectionalism in Colonial America

We arrive next at a topic rarely taught in secondary schools and only infrequently in college level surveys of American history. Yet it is absolutely critical to understanding the American Revolution. This is the matter of colonial sectionalism – the issue of "**who shall rule at home.**" Who will take power in each colony?

It would be a serious historical error to view the struggle between the colonies and the Mother Country strictly and solely as a question of home rule or independence. What colonists thought about British policy was certainly crucial in deciding whether or not to strike for independence or remain loyal to the Crown. But it was not the only issue. If it had been, then we must logically expect colonial unity and solidarity in the period from 1763 to 1776, and real unity in 1776. Such unity did not exist even for five minutes.

We must be clear about the distinction between these two ideas that sound roughly alike. The issue of British-Colonial relations, ultimately the choice between American independence or loyalty to the Crown, we may characterize as the issue of Home Rule. The issue of which power group or interest or faction inside each colony would prevail if independence succeeded or failed we characterize as Who Shall Rule at Home. Home Rule is the external issue. Who Rules at Home is the internal issue. Both mattered.

The reality is that in 1776 probably only 1/3 of the colonists were actively for independence. These were the **Radicals or Whigs or Patriots**. Another 1/3 were for the Crown, against independence. They were the **Loyalists or Tories or Conservatives**. The final 1/3 might have been either or neither but kept silent. Were they too busy slopping their hogs to notice? Being passive or neutral, they were a force for the *status quo*.

SECTIONALISM IN PRE-REVOLUTIONARY AMERICA

There were, however, in each colony, local conflicts or differences, based on political or economic or religious or regional or social issues or some combination of these. This was nothing new; it certainly exists today. How we feel about our President's budget depends in part on how it affects each of us in our own city and state just as much as it does on our understanding of the national economy.

Each person's decision about independence or loyalism depended in large part upon the question of what historian **Carl Becker** first called: "Who shall rule at home?" In deciding whether to support independence or not to support independence each person had to determine whether he or she would be better off in their local community and their region if the Crown remained in control or if the Radicals took control. In other words, home rule or not home rule was also a question of local or internal, even personal, interests.

Make no mistake about this! The issue of who shall rule at home also means that the American Revolution and the War for Independence was also a Civil War among colonists. Not just between Redcoats and colonists but colonists against colonists as well.

In determining what issues most separated colonists from each other, we must consider an array of issues which we can term **Sectionalism**. Most colonies were divided; they had been divided historically between the eastern or Tidewater region of the colony and the western or frontier or Piedmont areas of the colony into the frontier. These East versus West sectional issues are critical to understanding the American Revolution.

More specifically, in most colonies the western frontier areas held a set of grievances against the eastern establishment. These grievances were the basis of sectional arguments. We can review them briefly in general terms.

Frontier Grievance #1: Representation

(1) Representation. Western frontiersmen always claimed that they were under-represented in the colonial legislature and therefore they did not have a genuine voice in policy and government of the colony. [We should strike while the irony is hot!] Representatives were customarily elected by county, with each county having the same number of representatives in the colonial legislature. Eastern counties, the Tidewater counties, were small in size and numerous in population. The size of counties got larger

as you went west but had fewer people. Therefore, in practice there were many more eastern counties and eastern representatives. Westerners were always outvoted. After 1763, colonial legislatures were deluged with petitions to reform the representation system.

Frontier Grievance #2: Law and Order

(2) The West lacked institutions of law and order. There weren't enough local courts, judges, sheriffs, or Justices of the Peace in the west. These were not Royal Officers, but rather colonial officers. Westerners complained that there was inadequate law enforcement.

Yet Westerners wanted law and order. It is simply inaccurate that people went west to get away from law. That's a myth. They went west for opportunity. We see this in the establishment of vigilante law; people had to do something to escape a state of anarchy. As for Easterners, they simply didn't wish to pay good tax money for frontier officers.

Frontier Grievance #3: Indian Danger

(3) The West faced danger from Indians – a defense grievance. A dispersed population could not cluster in towns to defend themselves. They needed forts, troops, and presents for the Indians. The East didn't kick in much to help. It wasn't their scalps! Easterners took a pretty relaxed view of the Indian danger.

Frontier Grievance #4: Internal Improvements

(4) Internal improvements. Westerners complained bitterly about the lack of communication with the East. It got worse the further west you went. There were no roads to speak of and what roads existed were impassable most of the year. It was hard for westerners to ship farm products or pelts to the eastern part of colonies and get goods in return.

In many cases it was customary to ship goods by wagon west to the Mississippi River, travel down the Mississippi to New Orleans on a flatboat, and unload the goods at the New Orleans docks. Then reload the goods to an ocean-going vessel and travel by ship around Florida and up the coast to Boston or New York. That method was faster and cheaper than to ship directly east, over the mountains, to reach eastern cities by land. Without commerce it was hard to maintain contact. This issue would produce a widespread demand for roads and canals.

Frontier Grievance #5: Land Issues

(5) Land issues. There were a series of land-related issues. One was fear of the Crown's Land Officers who collected **quitrents** and who could evict settlers if they were not paid. Quitrents were small annual payments to the Crown for your land, even though you owned it – a feudal relic carried into the new world. Westerners might have feared more the land speculators who swindled them out of their land. But there was considerable sentiment against the King's men.

Another land issue was the problem of agricultural debt. Western farmers were largely poor and marginal folk who needed loans or credit from eastern lenders. If they got any help at all, which was infrequent, the farmers must mortgage their land. One bad year of weather, or Indian raids, or severe competition and there would be a quick **foreclosure**. The farmers would lose their land. Credit was largely an absent commodity in the west.

As a remedy for quick foreclosures, westerners asked for **Stay Laws** and paper money. Stay Laws extended the time that a debt could be paid. Stay laws, in effect, were the equivalent to refinancing loans over a longer period. Paper money was also desirable because it tended to be inflationary. Of course it was easier to pay back debts in paper than in specie money (that is, gold or silver). Westerners did not normally have specie money. Frequently barter was used. Whiskey often became a medium of exchange.

Frontier Grievance #6: Religion

(6) Religious Grievances. Particularly in the Southern and Middle colonies, and especially after the **Great Awakening**, westerners were frequently taxed to support the established churches, usually the **Anglican Church**. But Westerners were frequently non-Anglicans. There were **Scotch-Irish Presbyterians** and numerous German sects. They resented the tax. They wanted tolerance for their own religions. Even in western Anglican areas there were not enough clergy to go around; this, too, became a western grievance. This was not a serious issue in northern colonies, especially in New England, where **Congregational** churches flourished.

SECTIONALISM IN PRE-REVOLUTIONARY AMERICA

Taking this array of frontier issues as a package suggests that there were a lot of kissed- off westerners. As a generality we may argue that if easterners went in favor of independence, westerners were very likely to support the Crown, because for them local issues were more significant than relations with London. If easterners remained Tories, westerners fought for independence.

The issues of sectionalism illustrate what political scientists call **negative reference group theory**. You take positions and actions, not just because you are for something, but because you are opposed to someone or something – your negative reference group. People often vote against those they most dislike, even if they are not enthusiastic for their own candidates.

One way to test this negative reference group theory is to take each colony, one by one   and examine this prospect.

Sectionalism Colony By Colony

South Carolina. This southern colony was   dominated   by   planter-merchants,   who were as aristocratic in attitude and behavior as any class in the colonies. The seat of the colony was located at **Charleston**, a thriving city in the 1770s of some 14,000 people, the largest in the South.

Charleston had begun as a frontier fort and became a fortified city. For a century until the French and Indian War, Charleston had been under threat from Cherokees, Creeks, French, and Spanish. That necessity had required a rigid, military, centralized form of government. The threat disappeared in 1763, but the form of government remained. Planter-merchants lived in Charleston in the winter social season, making the society a tight little circle of the rich, the well-born and the few.

They also governed the colony. There were high property qualifications to hold office and to vote, including land and slaves. In religion, the east was some 80% Anglican and about 20% **French Huguenots** who became Anglicans.

Planters raised cotton, tobacco, hemp and **indigo**, using slave labor, for a lucrative trade with England. The Acts of Trade did not hurt South Carolina planters. Indigo planters got bounties (subsidies) and didn't have to ship first to England. They were the sort of folks who profited from the Bush administration income tax revisions.

SECTIONALISM IN PRE-REVOLUTIONARY AMERICA

Out in the western part of South Carolina lived the poor farmers, who moved there from Virginia and Pennsylvania. Most were Scotch-Irish. They founded a little cattle town called "**96**," which still exists today as Old District 96. This was the ancestral home of the family of **John C. Calhoun.** They disliked the Charleston hotshots so much that they drove their cattle north to Philadelphia, not east to Charleston. Many farmers were in serious debt to eastern creditors. In religion they were primarily **Presbyterian,** and, after the Great Awakening, **Baptists.**

Westerners in South Carolina had all the grievances against the east that you could have. For example, there wasn't a single law court in the west until 1770. Indeed, they eventually rioted, trying to coerce the planters into reforms. This movement, called The **Regulator Movement**, was summarily repressed.

With the American Revolution, independent, wealthy eastern aristocrats generally opposed the King and became Whigs. You better believe that the farmers of the west became Tories nearly to a man, supporting the Crown's army with men and equipment.

North Carolina had perhaps the sharpest sectionalism of any colony. It contained all the problems of South Carolina and some of its own. The colony's earliest settlers had been runaways from Virginia and South Carolina. It had a somewhat democratic local life, except for a small clique of tobacco planter-aristocrats.

These folks were close to the Royal Governor in Raleigh who ruled in their interests. The west was a royal pain (pun intended) to these slaveholding snobs. One special problem for North Carolina occurred when settlers from Virginia and South Carolina came into North Carolina, causing incessant arguments over the land ownership. That argument enlarged into a full-scale conflict between the Governor and western settlers. To make it worse, we might mention that western North Carolinians came from every sect – **Scotch-Irish, Moravians, Dunkers,** and **Pennsylvania Dutch,** just to name a few.

The pot of grievances boiled over in 1769, 1770, and 1771. When the Charleston government raised taxes for the established Anglican Church, westerners formed a Regulator Movement of vigilantes in 1770. This armed cavalry planned to go east to compel the government to recognize all their grievances.

SECTIONALISM IN PRE-REVOLUTIONARY AMERICA

The Governor called out the local militia. In May of 1771, the **Battle of Allemance Courthouse** was fought between the militia and the Regulators. The Regulators were badly beaten and many were killed. The Governor then went into the back country and captured the leaders of the movement. He put the area under military rule. The revolt was suppressed.

This fight marked the opening battle of the issue of Who Shall Rule At Home. In deciding about independence, just as in South Carolina, the North Carolina slave holding tobacco aristocrats decided as a class to support American independence. Westerners, who hated the tidewater aristocrats much worse than they disliked George III, produced some of the strongest support for the Tory cause.

Both Carolinas offer a classic case of negative reference group behavior at work. Both western areas supported British **General John Burgoyne**, raided Whig plantations, and fought hard for the Crown.

Virginia. To examine a map of Virginia is to notice that it is marked by a proliferation of rivers that crisscross the colony. Virginia had no port city akin to New York or Charleston or Boston. There was no need for a market concentrated in a single place, because ocean-going ships could sail up those rivers to the private docks of plantation owners. That means that tobacco planters became quite independent. They learned marketing, management, accounting, finance, banking, international business, and labor relations – all the other services cities usually provided for a fee by city experts.

Many planters had run up huge debts to English merchants. In the 18th century, eastern tobacco lands had begun to deteriorate; proper fertilizers had not yet been invented. Virginians needed loans to bail out their declining businesses and to maintain their life styles. If you think that getting out from under those debts was a factor in deciding to favor the American Revolution, then you are absolutely right!

Nevertheless, Virginia was different from the Carolinas, even though the colony was run by slave-holding aristocrats. It is intriguing to note how many slave-holding families were also fervent revolutionaries and advocates of individual rights and liberties. For example, **Thomas Jefferson**, author of the Declaration of Independence is prominent. Note also **George Mason**, author of the Virginia Bill of Rights and **James Madison**, Father of the Constitution and author of the United States Bill of Rights.

SECTIONALISM IN PRE-REVOLUTIONARY AMERICA

Of course we must not omit **George Washington**, **Patrick Henry** and numerous others. What made these slaveholders such advocates of liberty? Guilt? Hypocrisy? Environment? DNA? Cosmology? You are most welcome to decide.

Anyhow, with eastern tobacco lands in decline, many planters simply moved west to find new rich soils. The Byrd family of Westover, for example, who continue to control what is now West Virginia, is an example. There is a (Robert) Byrd in the United States Senate even in 2008!

The point is that because wealthy planters lived in both the east and the west there was no neat line between the tidewater and the frontier. Because of their wealth and status westerners could demand and receive a decent system of courts, law enforcement and usually sufficient representation in the Burgesses. The rivers were their roads. Western planters ran their local communities and learned to govern wisely.

It is also of note that farmers in the west, who came mostly from Pennsylvania and Maryland, settled on small farms or raised cattle, not tobacco. That means that they got good land, but were not, unlike the Carolinas, under the economic thumb of the planters. Farmers in western Virginia disliked slavery. As you may know in 1861 when Virginia joined the Confederacy, the western part of the State broke away and became West Virginia.

As to religion, true Anglicanism in Virginia was laxly enforced, although there was a tax collected to support the Church. Jefferson, Mason and Madison, incidentally, considered the tax a serious grievance. Lots of Baptists lived out there in the west. In 1755 the Burgesses passed a Toleration Act recognizing free worship. In the 1770's dissenting (non-Anglican) clergy were licensed to preach and administer sacraments. In the Revolution, it was the aristocrats who led the movement to dis-establish the Church or at least to support other religions with the tax.

In summary, the grievances which tore apart the Carolinas were largely absent or mitigated in Virginia. In the American Revolution, once the planter-aristocrats in both east and west, obviously including Washington, Jefferson, Mason, Madison, Henry and other natural leaders of the colony decided for Independence, they brought the entire colony with them against the Crown.

SECTIONALISM IN PRE-REVOLUTIONARY AMERICA

Maryland. Recall that Maryland was a Propriety Colony, founded by **Lord Baltimore**, whereas the others in the South were Royal Colonies with Royal Governors. **Cecilius Calvert**, the original Lord Baltimore, built Maryland into a tobacco economy. While Maryland continued quite prosperous for the moment, the fact is that much like Virginia, Maryland was fading fast as its soil became depleted.

The city of Baltimore, the urban center of the colony, was not in the plantation area. It grew from wealth from the Susquehanna River of Pennsylvania. Indeed, Baltimore was a commercial challenge to Philadelphia; it was certainly more like the City of Brotherly Love than it was like Charleston. The city was also the jumping off point for settlers headed west.

As with the Carolinas, Maryland was deeply divided between the tobacco planters of Annapolis and the poor farmers of the West. In Maryland the westerners disliked everyone: the Calvert family and the tobacco planters. After 1763, they disliked the Crown as well. They complained that the government was too expensive. They claimed that taxes went back to England to support the Calverts and their friends, rather than being used in the colony. They also complained about under-representation. We should note that the planters in this colony were in huge debt to England, as in Virginia.

In the American Revolution, the planters as Radicals utilized anti-Proprietor grievances to bring the west into the Whig side against both the Loyalist Proprietor and against the King. They convinced people that the decision of most planters to favor separation was in their best interest. With some exceptions the entire colony joined the movement for independence.

Georgia. This colony does not properly belong in our discussion of sectionalism. Frankly, the colony was not particularly significant in the Revolution. On some maps it isn't even shown. Georgia was the youngest of the thirteen colonies. It is not known if dog-fighting was in vogue in the colony.

A fascinating place, it was founded by **General James Oglethorpe**, an idealist who saw the colony as a place to rehabilitate all sorts of personal hard cases. Oglethorpe was frequently seen in London with groups of his "downtrodden" as he called them. A kind and benevolent character, this James Oglethorpe! He befriended the Indians as well. However, the colony was a pure paternalism. Georgia had no legislature; every decision, even the most local ones, was made by the Directors in London. Paternalism as a practicing political system, did not work in Georgia. Recognizing that reality, London eventually appointed a royal governor with powers conventional to those officials. Bottom line: Georgia was only beginning to develop during the revolutionary years.

Pennsylvania. Moving north to the middle colonies, we ask: what kind of sectionalism existed in Pennsylvania, New York and New Jersey? First, the proprietary colony of Pennsylvania, the "Keystone" as it likes to label itself! From 1680 to 1770 Pennsylvania enjoyed spectacular growth. **Philadelphia** was the largest city in the colonies, with a population of around 40,000 in 1770. Despite the burgeoning of towns and commerce on the seaboard and inland – **Lancaster** and **York** each had some 5000 people in 1770 – the economy was primarily agricultural. Pennsylvania was essentially a land of small farms. And one heavy duty seaport!

The population was also the most diverse or cosmopolitan. About one-third were English. Another one-third were Scotch-Irish. The remaining one-third was of German sects. **Quakers** merchants had governed the colony until 1756, when they lost control. Quakers, as pacifists, refused to support the French and Indian War and they were unseated. After 1763 no group was powerful enough to control the colony, although the Quakers were the strongest – and that was without oatmeal!

Religious animosity was one key to Pennsylvania's problems. Anglicans, a strong force around Philadelphia, were feared, possibly because there were always rumors about the appointment of an Anglican Bishop in the colony. The German sects detested one another and especially hated Presbyterians, who were Scotch-Irish. Pennsylvania was a maelstrom of religious antipathy, which opened the door for the Quakers, because they seemed the safest to everyone.

Western grievances were also particularly strong. The three eastern counties around Philadelphia (Bucks, Chester, and Philadelphia counties) each had eight seats in the unicameral (single house) legislature of Pennsylvania. A total of 24 seats out of a 36-seat Assembly! That circumstance prevented the west from gaining seats, despite a growing population. Further, Quaker merchants effectively ignored the cries for protection against Indians. Pacifists would not supply soldiers or arms to keep the west pacified. That pacifism explains a tradition of friendship with the Indians ever since **William Penn**, the original proprietor and a Quaker, founded the colony.

SECTIONALISM IN PRE-REVOLUTIONARY AMERICA

Land was also a major issue. The Penns were a family of benign proprietors, who gave much of their own land in western Pennsylvania to settlers. Politically, an alliance formed between westerners and the Penns – **Thomas Penn** now the head of the Penn family -- against the Quakers and their Philadelphia allies, led by the most formidable figure in Pennsylvania politics – Benjamin Franklin.

Among his many achievements, intellectual, scientific, and diplomatic, Franklin was a major speculator in western land and he was a most effective political force. The Penns, nonetheless had control of western lands. In a power grab, Quaker landowners and Anglican land speculators united to oppose them. Franklin disliked Thomas Penn; he continually lobbied the government in London to supplant the proprietors with a royal governor. In any case the west had another reason to detest the east.

Internal communication was also an issue. The Proprietors had failed to provide for east-west roads. Many Susquehanna valley farmers shipped south to Baltimore instead of east to Philadelphia. Taken together, we might say that Pennsylvania contained every sectional issue there was.

In 1763 and 1764 Pennsylvania almost had a civil war. Despite repeated protests, the government refused arms for the west against Indian attacks. A group calling themselves the **Paxton Boys** went out and slaughtered a group of Christian Indians who they thought were spies for **Pontiac**. Actually they were! Recall that 1763 was the year of Pontiac's rebellion – a rebellion eventually put down by Redcoats. The Paxtons started to march on Philadelphia. The city armed itself for attack.

At this point Franklin intervened. He promised military aid for the west. He delivered it, too. It bothered the Paxtons that Philadelphia Quakers were arming for civil war, but would not provide arms against Pontiac. [You will find the current town of Paxtonia located off Route 81 not far from Wilkes-Barre, Pennsylvania.]

In the decision for Revolution the Quakers and most Anglican merchants in Philadelphia remained Tories, loyal to the Crown. Franklin split with them; he was certainly an exception among Philadelphians. The Pennsylvania legislature similarly refused to be manipulated into promoting independence, unlike Virginia and Massachusetts, where the legislatures became organs for Whig policies. As one might anticipate, western Pennsylvanians became Radicals almost to the last man and woman.

SECTIONALISM IN PRE-REVOLUTIONARY AMERICA

What is significant is that even though western Pennsylvania was a land of small farmers exactly like the farmers in western North and South Carolina, and with the same grievances against the East, in Pennsylvania the West was for independence, while in the Carolinas the West was strongly Tory.

The Franklin faction in Philadelphia was for independence. Once war began, Quakers were run out of the government under threat of tar and feathers. The Radical leaders of the colony paid the Penns £300,000 for their lands. They were much better treated than the Calverts of Maryland, who lost everything. If Pennsylvania is not an instance of negative reference group behavior at work, there isn't any!!

New York. New York is always and forever confusing. This Royal Colony was divided into two geographical regions: **New York City**, the metropolitan-urban center and the upriver region, the Hudson River Valley, an agricultural area with the center at **Albany.**

The upriver area was dominated by planters who were genuine land barons. These included **Robert Livingston**. And **George Clinton**. And **Philip Schuyler**. They and others were land barons, landed aristocrats who hired more tenant-farmers than in any other colony. These tenants had few rights. They were almost peasants in the European sense. They hated the land barons.

New York City was controlled by affluent merchants, of whom the family of **James Delancey** was perhaps the most dominant. Everyone knows where Delancey Street is in the City! You may remember that mobs had attacked Delancey's property during the Stamp Act riots of 1765. In a certain sense the working classes of the City were as subordinate to the merchants as the tenant farmers were to the land barons. The middle class in the City held an uneasy balance of power between the aristocratic merchants and the working class poor. In New York there were high property qualifications to hold office and even a substantial £40 per year freehold just to vote.

To make a long and complex story short: when the decision for independence arrived, the upriver land-barons, led by the Livingstons, the Schuylers and the Clintons became Whigs, favoring separation from England. The Delanceys and most of the City merchant class remained staunchly loyal to the Crown. The City's middle classes reacted against their natural enemies – the merchants – and threw their support to the upriver aristocrats, creating a large and powerful Whig coalition. The City masses joined them as Radicals.

SECTIONALISM IN PRE-REVOLUTIONARY AMERICA

You can guess what's next. The oppressed tenants of the upriver area allied themselves with the New York City merchants, in order to oust the land-barons. We have the rural lower classes backing the Crown – as in the Carolinas – while the New York City working classes, became Whigs. Sectionalism was surely a vital force in New York.

New Jersey. A word about New Jersey is sufficient. If you tell people you are from New Jersey, they are likely to say: Oh yeah! Which Exit! New Jersey was a colony of small farms. It, too, had a sectional split, but this one was North/South – not East/West. Southern New Jersey, then as now, fell within the orbit of Philadelphia in economic, social and religious policy. Southern New Jersey usually followed where Philadelphia led. The north, likewise, then as now, was dominated by the influence of New York City. You got a problem with that?

As to the Revolution: northern New Jersey, following this pattern, allied with the Whigs for independence, just as the City had. Southern New Jersey joined with the Tories, as did most of Philadelphia. This includes the Royal Governor of New Jersey, **William Franklin**, the son (actually the illegitimate son) of Benjamin Franklin. Old Ben never spoke to his Tory offspring again.

Delaware. Much like Georgia, Delaware was not particularly significant either way in the revolution. When the tide was out, Delaware was the three lower counties of Pennsylvania and when the tide was in (high tide) Delaware was the two lower counties of Pennsylvania. No nasty letters from Delaware patriots, please.

New England. One general characteristic that made the lower New England colonies – Massachusetts, Rhode Island and Connecticut different from all the others is that the area was filled up with people. Massachusetts, Rhode Island and Connecticut were well settled. In Rhode Island that only took fourteen minutes. People were land hungry.

A shortage of land and a growing population created pressure to spill over somewhere. They could not go very far west, because of Indians and after 1763 because of the Proclamation Line. They could not go into New York, because the upriver land barons would not permit it. *Ergo*, they frequently migrated to the Royal colony of New Hampshire, or to Maine, which at that time belonged to Massachusetts. Or to the area called the

SECTIONALISM IN PRE-REVOLUTIONARY AMERICA

New Hampshire Grants, which would become Vermont. This migratory activity drained off the kind of anger that western farmers might have felt for their eastern neighbors – the ire that plagued other colonies. Discontented farmers could go north.

We might say that the open land provided a kind of **"safety valve"** to reduce the population/land pressure. The land/man ratio problem! The "Safety Valve" notion of open land is one that would influence American territorial expansion until the 20th century. It is significant that both **Vermont** and **Maine** would be firmly Radical in politics.

New Hampshire. This Royal colony was dominated by a merchant aristocracy located in Portsmouth. Who do you think started all those outlet stores? Western and northern New Hampshire, however, had been settled by farmers from Rhode Island and Connecticut, who very much disliked the city merchants. Sectional rivalries existed in New Hampshire as elsewhere in the colonies. With the American Revolution those merchants generally became Tories. That made the decision for independence easy for westerners in New Hampshire. They made it!

Massachusetts, Connecticut, and Rhode Island were almost wholly unified in favor of independence. They were three Whig colonies with very few loyalists. Unification on this point meant that New England, particularly Massachusetts, along with Virginia, would lead the protest against Great Britain and take leadership in the Revolution itself.

Massachusetts. A sense of unification was most natural in the Bay Colony of Massachusetts. Farmers, town dwellers and the primary city of Boston all had a community of interest. Massachusetts possessed a residual sense of community, a legacy from Puritan days, but still very powerful. There were also good communications between cities, towns and farm areas as well. Local participation in government, such as the Town Meeting, permitted folks a sense of inclusion in government. Everyone who wished to act (more or less) had forums for participation which prevented isolation and hence discontent. Rowdy town meetings in Boston were frequent, but people participated.

While westerners had grievances against the east, they were not divisive as in New Hampshire. The Massachusetts General Court, to add a point, had itself developed ways to control or neutralize the power of the Royal Governor. The grievances in the Bay State – perhaps most conspicuously represented by the rebellion of **Daniel Shays** in western Massachusetts broke out in 1786, long after America had become an independent nation under the Articles of Confederation.

Moreover, the three colonies were prosperous. People of all stations were more literate than in other colonies. They were generally better educated as well. Recent scholarship has demonstrated a clear relationship between the literacy rate and local participation in government. This is a strong argument which implies the connection between literacy and support for independence in New England.

We can also say that the populace in these three colonies trusted their leaders, both clerical and secular. Perhaps this may be historically traceable to the Congregationalist form of church organization and to traditions of local participation. The leaders of Boston who often met in Faneuil Hall (today a market with more outlet stores) did not antagonize the west. Moreover, western Massachusetts had good representation in the **General Court**, as the Massachusetts legislature was called.

Connecticut and Rhode Island. Remember, too, that Rhode Island and Connecticut were settled as Charter Colonies. The citizens of the colony elected their own Governors. There was, consequently, no government clique appointed by the Crown, no set of officeholders beholden to the King to oppose the home grown leadership. Therefore: New England in the American Revolution produced three generally unified colonies for independence. Massachusetts, Connecticut, and Rhode Island all big on starting a new nation!

Conclusion.

So where does all this discussion leave us? Understand that there is no simple formula for determining who will be a Whig and who a Tory once the American Revolution broke out into warfare. Local internal conflicts certainly played a significant role in people's decisions.

Were Whigs all enlightened, benevolent merchants and planters, rebelling on principles, for the rights of Englishmen? That would be an inaccurate generalization. Alternatively, were the Whigs all working class democrats, farmers and craftsmen, revolting against the established aristocracy? Another inaccurate generalization! So what generalization can we make for determining who's who?

Whigs came from all geographical sections, all social classes, all religions and all economic levels. And so did Tories!

SECTIONALISM IN PRE-REVOLUTIONARY AMERICA

If you want to know who's who, look hard at the intra-conflicts, the internal issues within each colony. Much of the question of home rule (independence) was shaped and even determined by one's interest in the question of "Who Shall Rule At Home." If that is an accurate generalization, then the War for Independence was also a civil war among Americans.

CHAPTER FOUR: THE AMERICAN REVOLUTION - PHASE TWO

The Second Phase of colonial protest began with the passage of the **Tea Act** in 1773 and concluded with the Declaration of Independence of July 4, 1776. Lord North's fateful decision to give the **East India Company** a monopoly of the tea trade in the British Empire destroyed the period of calm which had existed in the colonies for the previous five years. The Tea Act threw the proverbial fat in the proverbial fire!

The Tea Act and Its Consequences

The Tea Act revived the Radical organization. After passage of the Tea Act the political factions in the colonies divided permanently. With the Tea Act people chose up sides. The forces of moderation and adjustment and compromise never had a chance. The Tea Act of 1773 was, it may be argued, the single critical turning point in the momentum toward the American Revolution. After the Tea Act there was no turning back!

Looking backward with hindsight, it might look as though England consciously and even deliberately intended to antagonize the colonies by a "tyrannical" action, namely the Tea Act. That is what we were all taught on our momma's knee. But there is a need to understand the dilemma of the ministry.

Lord North's ministry was trying to bail out the East India Company, to prevent it from sliding into bankruptcy. This giant enterprise was a major source of revenue for the Crown. Moreover, the company was perhaps the equivalent of today's Microsoft in terms of its impact on the economy. The company had been mismanaged for years; by 1773 it was facing economic collapse.

If it failed, there would be a serious economic depression in England. No ministry could afford to permit the East India Company to fail, any more than the U.S. government could afford to let Chrysler fail. Or Lockheed. Or Wal-Mart. Or Microsoft. Serious economic and political consequences would result from the demise of the East India Company.

THE AMERICAN REVOLUTION – PHASE TWO

The ministry decided to give the East India Company a monopoly of the tea trade. "Cheerio and pip-pip to that!" The English drank tea. American colonists did, too, when they weren't into rum! Tea was a big seller. It was also easy to ship: tea was small, light, and very profitable. **Lord North** knew that Americans would be unhappy about the Act.

But what choice did North have? If he did not take action, his ministry would likely be voted out of office and the next Prime Minister would take that action anyhow. Accordingly, Parliament passed the **Tea Act in May 1773**. While only the Company would sell tea in America, the price was lowered for Americans, as a salve to ease the anticipated antagonism that was sure greet the news.

It didn't work. Colonial merchants in every colony, whose 1769-1773 prosperity had caused them to relax their pressure for redress of grievances, and who had restored cordial relations with their English counterparts, were now, because of the Tea Act, driven back into the arms of the Radicals. "We told you so," Radicals could declare with some satisfaction. "We knew they'd do something like this. It was just a matter of time." Radicals pictured Lord North jamming the tea down American throats.

Many moderate American merchants now began to think that the principles of economic competition and economic independence were at stake. They had long outgrown the British "company store" sort of economic system. The Company's price permitted it to bypass the colonial wholesale merchants and sell for less. Merchants feared what businesses might be taken over next.

We all know the hysterical reaction that followed the announcement of the Tea monopoly. The Sons of Liberty fomented riots. They intimidated Crown officers. The action was hardly a regional phenomenon. In Charleston, South Carolina, the Sons of Liberty forced the East India Company to store the tea in locked warehouses; it was not sold. In Philadelphia the Sons refused to permit the tea ships to land. In Annapolis, Maryland, the Sons burned the tea ship, the "**Peggy Stuart**."

And in Boston, Massachusetts, in December 1773 a group of influential "Mohawk Indians," organized by Samuel Adams, marched two-by-two down to the waterfront, boarded three tea ships, the "**Beaver**," the "**Eleanor**" and the "**Dartmouth**," and dumped 45 tons of tea – 342 chests – into Boston harbor. This was the famous, or infamous, **Boston Tea Party**.

THE AMERICAN REVOLUTION – PHASE TWO

George III was shocked and alarmed. The King had not been overtly involved up to this point, preferring to direct the actions of North's ministry from behind the scenes. Indeed, many unknowing colonists regarded him as a sort of peacemaker between Parliament and the Colonists. However, the actions of the Boston "Indians" caused him to think that his personal authority as the protector of persons and property had been personally affronted. It is surely a myth that George III remained above the political battle. As previously noted he was quite hawkish when it came to the rebellious provincials in the colonies.

For the King, the Boston Tea Party was different than previous protests. For this was an illegal destruction of private property. Even the Stamp Act riots were directed against a government agency. But the East India Company was a private enterprise. Why would that difference matter?

This issue was about mob violence, riots and looting. Is it all right for a mob to destroy houses, stores, cars or banks? Or burn people out and loot what's left? Is not the first function of any government to maintain social order? What should the punishment be for rioting, for destroying private property or for looting? Is rioting for a "good cause" any sort of justification?

Please do not misunderstand this point!! That is exactly what the Boston Tea Party is about. Isn't it ironic that people who claimed that the government denied them their right to profits – by taxation laws – now destroyed someone else's private property? What does that reveal, if anything about their principles?

The Tea Party brought to a head the whole issue of home rule. It made people take a stand. Folks had to decide if law, order, and non-violence were more important than the power to act independently and make their own decisions? Were you for order or for liberty? Or to enlarge the issue, were the colonies going to continue to manage their own local affairs (the concept of local autonomy) or were the needs of the empire going to supersede local control (the concept of imperial reform)?

Was the Tea Party just an angry protest? Or did the Radicals of Boston deliberately provoke the London government into harsh measures, knowing that London's stern laws would create support for the Radical cause? Gerber thinks so. And they got just exactly what they wanted.

Most New England merchants threw in with the Radicals, violence and all. Unlike the first phase of protest, however, they no longer led the movement. Rather, they followed in the wake of the Radicals. British merchants, quite naturally and quite unlike the Stamp Act, chose the opposite course, as did all the colonial Tories. They favored strong measures to protect their property rights against mob action. The anger of British merchants led Parliament to pass a set of measures that can only be labeled blundering. They were designed to punish and cure the colonies all at once. This is the series of what the British called **Coercive Acts** and the Radicals called the **Intolerable Acts** of 1774.

There were four of these. (1) **The Boston Port Bill**. This Act closed the port of Boston to all shipping, in or out, except for shipments of firewood, until Boston paid back the East India Company for its losses. This Act was supposed to bring the economic life of Boston to a slow grinding halt. Actually, it put the town under siege. In Gerber's opinion, The Boston Port Bill was a serious overreaction, because it punished the innocent people of Boston along with the guilty perpetrators of the Tea Party.

(2) **The Administration of Justice Act**. This law provided that any British Officer or Agent who, in the course of doing his duty, such as enforcing Parliamentary laws, was charged with some offense against the colony, would be tried in England, not Massachusetts. This law would have protected someone like Captain Preston in the Boston Massacre. It was certainly seen as a threat to the Massachusetts court system and local justice.

(3) **The Massachusetts Government Act.** This law changed the governance of the colony. The Governor could now appoint his own Council, instead of having it elected by the Massachusetts General Court. The Governor had power to prohibit town meetings from meeting. He, not the towns, could appoint local judges and sheriffs. Those sheriffs, not the towns, in turn, would select jurors. No officer could be removed from office without approval from the Governor and his Council.

The purpose of the Massachusetts Government Act was to reestablish order and prevent subversion of the entire British system by Radical-led mobs. But it was drastic action, to be sure. The law created an extra-powerful governor, financially independent of local pressure. This worked against the habits of representative government in all the royal colonies. As such it was the most serious threat to the notion of local autonomy. The other colonies certainly saw it that way.

(4) **The Quartering Act.** Under this law, British troops, led by General Thomas Gage were sent to New England and stationed in Boston. The town was required to supply barracks. If it did not, then taverns and

private dwellings were to be commandeered by the troops and used for quartering them. This was a peacetime instance of quartering troops on the populace. It created absolute fury and hatred in the colonies for standing armies in peacetime.

Parliament also passed a fifth act, not at all intended to respond to the situation in Massachusetts. The colonists, nevertheless, viewed it as part of the coercive package. This was the **Quebec Act** of 1774.

Recall that the attempt to Anglicize French Canada under the Proclamation of 1763 had failed dismally. Now Parliament tried again. The Quebec Act set up a civil government in which (French) Roman law, not the English Common Law, would be used. It was also a highly centralized government with a Governor-General appointed by the Crown. The Legislature and the Governor's Council would also be appointed by the King, not elected. There would be no jury trials in civil cases, but only judges, as in France. French was restored to official usage and, of course, the Catholic Church was recognized. The Quebec Act essentially reversed the 1763 law and gave the French Canadians what they wanted.

New England certainly perceived the Quebec Act as part of the Coercive Acts. After all, it restored Catholicism and centralized government. To Congregationalists used to local institutions, the Quebec Act lurked as a systematic threat to English institutions and law.

In Gerber's opinion the Quebec Act was a statesmanlike piece of legislation. It was the first recognition by England of the problem of governing peoples and cultures, not just mercantile units. The principle of the Quebec Act promised that loyal, contributing parts of the empire were not required to be English in customs and institutions. If you were loyal, you could be British without being English!

Would there ever have been any American Revolution if London had understood that very principle in 1763 and applied it to the 13 colonies? One thing is sure: if Parliament had not passed the Quebec Act there would have been 14, not 13, colonies striking for independence. The Quebec Act saved Canada for the British Empire.

To the Radicals the Coercive Acts (including the Quebec Act) seemed to threaten the heritage of local civil government. The several laws addressed the representative system, the courts, even the English religions. Some firebrands added that the acts were designed to punish the colonies for agitation and even to deprive them of their rights as Englishmen.

THE AMERICAN REVOLUTION – PHASE TWO

That colonists had deliberately disobeyed the law and that they had destroyed private property as a mob they promptly forgot. All the colonies sent supplies to the besieged city of Boston – by land, of course.

The (First) Continental Congress

The **Virginia Provincial Convention**, meeting, you recall, in Raleigh's Tavern in Williamsburg, proposed a Continental Congress to meet in Philadelphia, in September 1774, to decide what to do about these Coercive Acts. They did not call it the **First Continental Congress**, of course, because they could not know there would be a second.

We call it the First Continental Congress, for blessed with historical hindsight are we! Virginia's proposal divided Conservatives and Radicals down the middle. Conservatives believed they could still control the situation and get the Coercive Acts repealed through the traditional methods that had worked in the past, as British subjects petitioning for redress of grievances.

Radicals believed that the old methods were useless now, and that Parliamentary supremacy would have to be fully overthrown in order for Americans to regain their autonomy. Conservatives felt that they could still get the old system changed from the inside. Radicals did not. It is fair to say that in the summer of 1774, just before the Congress met, Radicals were still in the vast minority. Conservatives agreed to attend the Congress, because they thought they could control it.

Carpenter's Hall still stands on Chestnut Street between 3rd and 4th Streets in Philadelphia's historical district. All the delegates who attended the Continental Congress in that building recognized the need for unity. Any protest would have to have the stamp of approval of the whole body; otherwise it would be useless. Exactly here the Radicals showed their powerful organizational ability. They utilized perfect timing, so as not to frighten the Conservatives with anything drastic before the time came. Radicals from Virginia and Massachusetts met in secret to agree on their stand, but in the sessions they stayed away from each other as though they were strangers. They behaved like a well-oiled political machine.

The Radicals jumped in first with the Suffolk Resolves, a document with the formal title **Declaration and Resolves**. The **Suffolk Resolves** are named for Suffolk County, Massachusetts, (not Long Island). The Suffolk Resolves declared that Parliament had no authority to govern the colonies at all! Whatsoever! Hence the Coercive Acts were unconstitutional and the changes made under them were all illegal.

What the Suffolk Resolves declared bears repeating: Parliament had no authority to govern the colonies. Period! Please understand that this is bigger than taxation or trade regulations. Parliament has zero authority. Instead, the Resolves proposed a separate, elected government for the colonies – an elected Inter-Colonial Assembly – loyal to the Empire, but entirely self-governing. A colonial government independent of Parliament!

This was certainly radical. Radical, too! But it was also a logical step from previous arguments. First there had been "No taxation without colonial consent (Otis)". Then "No taxation without representation (Henry)" Then they had added that since representation was impractical – the Colonial legislatures were thus co-equal to Parliament (Massachusetts Circular Letter). Now, in the Suffolk Resolves they asserted that Parliament had no authority to govern the colonies whatever!

Given the pressure of events, in ten years the situation had moved from 1763, when Parliament had total power to tax, to 1774 when, the Radicals announced in the Suffolk Resolves, Parliament cannot govern the colonies at all. Everyone should comprehend this dynamic as escalation and polarization in its most classic demonstration.

There was a tremendous political battle in the First Continental Congress to pass the Suffolk Resolves that makes our current congressional political strife seem tame, indeed. The Suffolk Resolves passed by one vote!

But the Radicals were not finished. Another part of the Declaration and Resolves enacted a renewal of the economic embargo against British goods. In itself economic boycotts were not new; remember the embargoes after the Stamp Act in 1765 and the Townshend Acts back in '67! So this is embargo #3.

The Continental Association

The enforcement of this embargo was brand new. It was truly revolutionary. In every port city along the east coast local Associations of citizens were to be organized to enforce the embargo. These local associations were responsible to an inter-colonial association called the **Continental Association**. The Continental Association would have the real power to set the policies and direct local associations in enforcing those policies.

THE AMERICAN REVOLUTION – PHASE TWO

Local Associations had power to investigate the economic activities of individuals, and to punish anyone who violated the embargo by continuing to trade with Britain. Someone's goods might be confiscated, tar and feathers might be employed if necessary, but enforcement most routinely occurred by boycotting violators. Boycott notices listed the names of those who continued to import British goods. Merchants complied – or else!

Ergo, the First Continental Congress had passed the Suffolk Resolves, established the embargo, and created the Continental Association. It then dissolved itself and went home, leaving the Association(s) in control. How significant were their actions?

Was the Continental Association the Emergent American Revolution?

Consider what makes a government a government. Whether it is the drama club, the local labor union, or the Congress of the United States, there are two essential elements of any government. (1) the power to make policy, or if you will, the power to make law; whether policy is called rules, or bylaws, or law. (2) the power to compel obedience to the policy, or if you will, to enforce the law they make.

How does the Continental Association fit this definition? Certainly it had the power to set policy. It also had the power to enforce that policy. It had the power to make law, and the power to enforce the law as well. The Continental Association was an illegal body, which would now take over the role of the Parliament. The Continental Association would now govern the colonies, if not officially, legally or constitutionally, then certainly in reality and in practice.

This situation should now be plain. The Continental Association was the essence of revolution. In Gerber's thinking: the birth of the American Revolution occurred at the moment that the Association was established and put into effect. This means that the American Revolution did not occur in 1776 with the Declaration of Independence. It did not occur in April 1775 at Lexington and Concord. It occurred at the end of 1774 or in the early weeks of 1775 with the establishment of the Continental Association.

John Adams understood. The American Revolution was, said Adams, a Massachusetts delegate to the Continental Congress, "in the hearts and minds of his countrymen."

THE AMERICAN REVOLUTION – PHASE TWO

The Revolution was the conscious determination in the heads of the Radicals – to be independent of the legitimate government. To be rid of parliamentary sovereignty. In different wording the Revolution was the conscious awareness among some Americans that they really weren't British any more. By Adams's definition, the revolution had taken place at the end of 1774 or by early 1775.

We must make a clear distinction between that Revolution and the War for Independence. The War was an attempt to make the Revolution stick. If George Washington had been caught and hanged for treason, there still would have been an American Revolution. It just would have failed. The Revolution and the War for Independence were quite different events.

To summarize, by the end of 1774 all of the old colonial legislatures, whether Royal, Proprietary or even Charter colonies, were outmoded. Their word was acceptable to no more than one-third of the people, because they were no longer adequate to meet the tasks of protest. Thus this new revolutionary (illegal) body had been formed – the Continental Association – to fill the void. The Association was backed up by the illegal Provincial governments meeting in Virginia and Massachusetts and before long in every colony (except New York and Pennsylvania). Those vigorous governments now expressed the views of the protesters, even if they did not represent the majority of colonials.

The old regime had not been turned out by force. It had just withered on the vine. The Radicals had committed this revolution in the First Continental Congress. We may interpret these events to say that the American Revolution – that shift in mental equipment – had become a fact by the end of 1774 or early 1775. The War for Independence was a battle to make the Revolution succeed!

What was Lord North's reaction to the actions of the First Continental Congress? That "tyrant" drew up what was called the **Conciliatory Resolve**, early in 1775. North offered to return to the old **Requisition** System of colonial contributions in lieu of parliamentary taxation, for any colony which would support British measures – especially defense – through requisitions. For example, if a colony would voluntarily pay the costs of troops, then Parliament would not levy taxes on its subjects. North did not deny the right to tax. He just said there would be none, if any colony would do its part.

Actually, this idea might well have been an acceptable proposal in 1774, before the capture of the colonial governments by Radicals. As it was, it was too little, too late. It is also difficult to imagine that either North or the King thought the Conciliatory Resolve would fly! As usual, moreover,

THE AMERICAN REVOLUTION – PHASE TWO

British pride had to be protected. Parliament coupled the Conciliatory Resolves with the **New England Restraining Act.** That law simply prohibited the New England colonies from trading with anyone except England and the British West Indies. The intent of the Act was to divide the colonies, in the hope that middle and southern colonies would be happy to pick up the slack of trade outside the empire and would abandon New England. That ploy didn't work, either.

Indeed, these two British actions reached the colonies only after the shooting had started. By that time the Radicals were so entrenched in power that they could simply disregard both the Conciliatory Resolves and the New England Restraining Act.

The War for Independence Begins

Following the conclusion of the Continental Congress, Boston, still under siege, began a period of waiting for the British to make a move. They did not have to wait long. General **Thomas Gage**'s attempt to seize a storehouse of colonial arms began a shooting war. Some now highly - patriotic names and settings entered American vocabularies: **The Battle of Lexington Green** and **Concord Bridge** on April 19, 1775. Then the battle of **Bunker Hill**....actually **Breed's Hill**, in Boston, a most severe defeat for the British. Then came American General **Ethan Allen's** capture of British **Fort Ticonderoga** in upstate New York. **General George Washington,** appointed by the Continental Congress to lead an army of continental soldiers had, together with local militia, compelled the British to evacuate the city of Boston in April 1776. To be sure the War for Independence, a bloody conflict, however sporadic, was on!

And yet, there was an unreal quality about the period between April 19, 1775 and July 4, 1776. Despite the realities of warfare, with men dying on both sides, both camps seemed genuinely to be shocked that the colonies were in insurrection. There was a fiction of law and order in the face of battle. Were the Radicals so far out in front of public opinion that there was not widespread support for revolution? Had all the options but killing been exhausted?

The Second Continental Congress and American Independence

The outbreak of warfare led to the calling of another meeting: The **Second Continental Congress** met on May 10, 1775 in Philadelphia, at what is now **Independence Hall.** The building, located on Chestnut Street between 5th and 6th Streets is a much-visited national shrine. This time the Conservatives stayed home. The Second Continental Congress was wholly a Whig conclave. By the time the Congress met, the Radicals had made many converts; the most important was Benjamin Franklin, the great gentleman-scientist-philosopher from Philadelphia.

Even in this Radical body the unreal world prior to independence was reflected. Congress was engaged in creating an army, building inter-colonial defenses, raising $2 billion in credit to finance a war against the Mother Country. Washington had been appointed General-in-Chief. Yet Congress could not yet take that last "leap in the dark" (as John Adams referred to it) to independence. After all it took 14 months between Lexington and Concord in April 1775 and the Declaration of Independence of July 4, 1776. This was a period of time of some 14 months! Why?

What took so long? The clearest explanation is that the Radicals themselves were split between independence and reconciliation with England on American terms. For most Radicals reconciliation with the Mother Country – albeit on terms that would restore local autonomy outright – was a live option. Wouldn't restoration of the old order, prior to reform, be far less dangerous than creating a wholly new country and having to fight the strongest power on earth just to give birth to an infant nation? Could not Radical objectives for renewal of colonial autonomy be achieved inside the empire? Many thought so.

Thus even the most advanced Radicals tried once more for reconciliation. They wrote something called the **Olive Branch Petition** of 1775. The Olive Branch remains the symbol of peace. It was the last serious formal attempt to maintain ties to England. The petition was written by **John Dickinson** of Pennsylvania, the man who refused to sign the Declaration of Independence, who fought valiantly in the war as a private soldier, and who later wrote the Articles of Confederation. Dickinson was a fascinating man! The second author of the Petition was Thomas Jefferson of Virginia. As a young man Jefferson had a full shock of red hair. [Was he a suicide redhead, dyed by his own hand?]

The Olive Branch stated America's loyalty to the King, while attacking Parliament's violations of what Dickinson and Jefferson called American rights. Then it stated that the current war was not a rebellion, but rather only the legitimate defense against attacks by the British army.

THE AMERICAN REVOLUTION – PHASE TWO

George III ignored the Olive Branch Petition (as he had so many others) as the declaration by an illegal body. He refused to yield. He was determined to "stay the course." Instead, in August 1775, he pronounced the colonies in a state of rebellion. From his angle of vision he was surely correct! This hawkish monarch was determined to suppress open rebellion by force! He was dedicated to maintaining the union of the British Empire.

Yet even with the Crown's disdain of the Olive Branch, even with both sides hardened and killing each other, even then the indecision continued. The curious, tentative quality of this rebellion continued to manifest itself. The Radicals inched toward independence but could not quite proclaim it. Conservatives feared the destruction of America. People chose sides. The popular heart would not quite beat either way. It was, after all, one thing, to claim the right to make your own decisions and to reject Parliamentary authority. It was emotionally quite a wrench to give up your allegiance to your country altogether. Even the most advanced Radicals maintained this nagging loyalty to the Crown, to being British!

Then a bombshell burst. It was a pamphlet, written by a great friend of liberty and a propagandist with a powerful pen. Franklin had introduced him into the Whig camp and at this choice point in time he earned his pay. Of course this was **Thomas Paine**. His pamphlet was titled **"Common Sense."** It appeared in January 1776. Paine praised the virtues of liberty and spelled out the idea of freedom as the uniqueness of America. Paine demanded independence. Then he took a new tack and attacked the King personally as a corrupt aristocrat from a decadent Europe.

"Common Sense" was the first direct assault in all the literature of American protest on the very idea of hereditary monarchy. Paine advocated a republic! He said that word out loud. There were no republics in Europe, except for a few obscure Swiss cantons and the small Dutch Republic. "Common Sense" proclaimed a republican form of government with no king at all! And no hereditary aristocracy! And no established state religion! And no standing army, either! This was truly radical. The notion that government rested on the consent of the governed, that people should actually determine their own rulers, was theory, not reality. The idea of a republic had held little sway since the fall of Rome.

Yet, lifted on Paine's fiery words, it struck exactly the right note at the right time. "Common Sense" created electricity all across America in favor of independence. It uplifted public opinion. People were suddenly galvanized to action. This attack on the King as a tyrant stimulated colonists into accepting the Radical position. Sometimes words capture dreams, sometimes! John Fitzgerald Kennedy's Inaugural Address was one of them. The "I Have a Dream" speech of Martin Luther King Jr., was another. "Common Sense" was one of those rare moments. Suddenly it all seemed clear.

Or at least clearer! In the Congress, **John Adams** had been prodding and provoking and badgering the delegates toward that final fateful decision. Adams rarely receives sufficient acknowledgement for his contribution toward American independence, but if anyone in Congress deserves to be recognized as taking leadership against reconciliation and for a new America, Adams is that person.

Shortly after the widespread favorable reaction to "Common Sense" **Richard Henry Lee** of Virginia – a man with three first names – offered into the Second Continental Congress a Resolution declaring the independence of the colonies from Great Britain. The first unofficial vote on **Lee's Resolution**, historians believe, resulted in a 7 – 5 split in favor of independence. What would have occurred had one vote changed and the outcome had been 6-6? Even a split vote was unacceptable. Unity was needed and everyone understood it so.

The motion was suspended for a time, during which delegates sought counsel from their various state governments. The vote was retaken on July 2, 1776. There was a strenuous debate. The official public vote was declared unanimous. Congress then set up a drafting committee of five members to write an appropriate statement to the world – a **Declaration of Independence.**

The committee was composed of prominent persons from each section of the colonies. They included **Thomas Jefferson** of Virginia, **Benjamin Franklin** of Pennsylvania, **Robert Livingston** of New York, **John Adams** of Massachusetts, and **Roger Sherman** of Connecticut. The famous group picture of them is available everywhere and is ready for framing in your residence hall.

Jefferson actually wrote the draft, as everyone knows. There was a fair amount of editing by the Congress, too. However, nobody asked for extra time, unlike some students, to get their work done. The Declaration was signed at Independence Hall on July 4, 1776. The Declaration was then read publicly – with apparent great relief!!

In some quarters it was read with great pleasure and joy. The statue of George III was toppled, much like that of Saddam Hussein in 2003.

THE AMERICAN REVOLUTION – PHASE TWO

George got melted and made into musket balls to be fired at his own troops.

Conclusion

How can we evaluate this process to Independence? What kind of Revolution was this American Revolution? The following interpretation is a Gerber invention, not fact. You are free to interpret these events any way you like, as long as you deploy your evidence with historical precision. The moon is not green cheese.

In one respect this was a conservative revolution, with even the most advanced Radicals drawn into it by the chain of events. It was not inevitable, bound to happen because of the distance between Great Britain and America. It was certainly no rampaging, guillotining class struggle such as the French Revolution was to be just a few years hence in 1789.

Its purposes were restorative, conservative, and perhaps even backward-yearning. American revolutionaries wished to recapture the simpler, autonomous days of the pre-1763 period. A time they remembered – or thought they remembered – when they made their own decisions. A time before all that imperial reform started. A time when their self-interest operated without restriction from an empire attempting to reform itself and saw the American part of the empire as a needful part, but a part only, of the big picture. In this sense the objective of the Revolution was a restoration of the past.

In another sense, if we take a longer view, the Revolution can be seen not as completed in 1774, or 1776, but continuing until the adoption of the Constitution of 1787 and the Bill of Rights in 1791. In that view independence was the beginning of a process, certainly radical for the 18th century. It was built on republican principles of representative government without monarchy, without established religions, without hereditary classes, and without standing armies. Its heart was a system of individual rights and liberties. The idea of a republic in the 18th century was genuinely forward thinking, progressive and indeed, revolutionary.

One thing is certain. The United States would inherit all of those problems that the British government couldn't solve. Would America do any better?

CHAPTER FIVE: THE AMBIGUOUS REVOLUTION
FROM CONFEDERATION TO CONSTITUTION

America's First Governments – The States

The U.S. had declared its independence from Great Britain. So now what happens? First and foremost, there was a war to be fought and won. Second, there was a government for a brand new nation to establish. Actually, we should observe that there were fourteen new nations to establish: the thirteen states and the United States.

The Second Continental Congress provided guidance for the drawing up of the thirteen new state constitutions and the organization of those governments. That Congress continued to function until a new government for the United States of America was established and ratified. That means that the Second Continental Congress officially stayed in office from 1775 until 1781, when the Articles of Confderation officially replaced it.

Between 1776 and 1780 all the states except Rhode Island and Connecticut adopted new written documents embodying their state governmental structures. Those two states continued to utilize their original charters as their constitutions; those lasted well into the 19th century.

What kind of governments were these first state governments? In large measure, as noted, the American Revolution was a struggle to preserve local autonomy. Many Americans intended to restore the past, the glory days prior to 1763. The new governments of the states and also of the United States reflected the perceptions of what the ideal (if not the reality) of constitutional forms had been back then. In that sense what they established was restorative. It was what local autonomy felt like to them!

What they enacted was, in another sense, quite genuinely revolutionary. We are so used to it that we take it for granted. They established a Republic! The elimination of monarchy may seem obvious to us, but it was astonishing for the 18th century.

FROM CONFEDERATION TO CONSTITUTION

For the American revolutionaries **republicanism** was more than merely the substitution of an elective system for kingship, as remarkable as that was all by itself. It was also the enactment of Enlightenment ideals. People like **John Adams** and **Thomas Jefferson** and **John Dickinson** knew that society required legal agencies of authority. What made their actions so revolutionary was that they demanded fresh agencies, resting on popular consent. Not the Crown. Not the standing army. Not the established religious structure. Not the hierarchy of hereditary classes!!

Instead they wanted the authority of government to rest with the people themselves. Not coercion from above, based on fear. Instead the state would be based on the willingness of persons to obey. Government by the people based on consent freely given. A republic resting deliberately on the principle that those who were governed should determine who governed them!

Leaders such as **John Dickinson**, the primary author of the Articles of Confederation, knew very well the risks of both anarchy or tyranny. That had been the fate of the republics of Greece and Rome, after all. They would have stated, further, that they were not little "d" democrats. Democracy as a system was a 19th century invention – and not perfected yet! Nonetheless, this set of framers believed that a republican form of government, based on an informed public, could work if authority were limited. There had been no successful sizable republics in Europe for centuries. Were they operating on faith?

In order to strike a balance between their belief in republican principles and their suspicion of authority, they created something else innovative in the 18th century, namely written Constitutions. They wrote down just what powers would be exercised by the delegates of the people and just what rights and liberties those governments could not abridge. Written constitutions were logical enough after what they felt the British had done. Of course, each colony, now each state, already had some written document as a charter. There was at least some experience with documents of governance. Written constitutions, moreover, helped to give the fourteen new governments legitimacy in the eyes of the world.

Constitutional arrangements always reveal the realities of who has power. These constitutions certainly did. They were written by people who held power and would determined to keep it if they could. It is useful now to look briefly at the first State Constitutions and then at the Articles of Confederation.

The new state constitutions reflected the drive to restore local autonomy. They indicated the restorative – even nostalgic – nature of the Revolution.

FROM CONFEDERATION TO CONSTITUTION

They were based on popular government, but they were definitely not democratic. State Constitutons drew on colonial and British experience. They were quite similar in their provisions, precisely because they were built on the power of property and the upper classes.

Legislative supremacy, an Enlightenment notion, was the order of the day. No checks and balances here. Governors and judges – the executive and judicial branches of government – held functions that were minimal and structured so as not to intrude on what the people decided through their legislature. Of course the popular will was to be enacted, especially since it served the propertied interests. Except for Pennsylvania, each state had a bicameral (two house) legislature, with popularly elected representatives in the lower house. The upper house, customarily elected by people of property, existed to check the Governor and the undisciplined popular lower house. The legislature would prevail in cases of conflict between it and the other branches.

Except for Massachusetts and New York the Governors exercised quite limited power. In the context of 1776 and 1777 the mind set of Americans would not let them surrender back to a strong executive the power they were bleeding to get out from under. Only in Massachusetts and New York did Governors have the power to veto legislation. By 1790, we might note, most states, much like the United States government itself, had amended their documents to give their Governors considerably more executive power. Judges were made independent of the executive branch. They were either appointed by the legislature, or elected. They could not be removed without good cause. Lifers, generally, as is the case today.

Every state except Vermont enacted a property qualification for voting. It was felt that without a tangible stake in society, one would not care enough about the common good. Government without property was considered anarchy. This means that the people who wrote these constitutions and got them ratified, were the same people who had the most stake in society, and stood to lose the most by having their rights curtailed. Property qualifications, frequently quite high, protected their interests. We witness this concept demonstrated in the provisions against governmental seizure of property without "**due process of law.**"

Perhaps the most unique features of these state constitutions were their Bills of Rights. Eight states even began their constitutions with

Bills of Rights. The most important of these documents was the **Virginia Bill of Rights**. It was written by **George Mason**, himself quite an

68

aristocratic figure, and a slaveowner. Yet Mason wrote this most liberal of documents of individual rights. In the Virginia Bill of Rights we can see what Americans disliked about what they claimed were British abuses. There were to be no general warrants. There were to be no cruel and unusual punishments. Bail must be moderate and a person could obtain a writ to free himself or herself from jail – the **writ of habeas corpus**. No standing armies in peacetime, but the militia (not individual citizens – the National Rifle Association notwithstanding) had the right to keep and bear arms. Further, a person was entitled to a fair trial, with speedy justice by his or her peers. There was to be a free press, and freedom of conscience. A number of these provisions would be hijacked by **James Madison** when he wrote the Bill of Rights that was appended to the U.S. Constitution.

The Articles of Confederation

We must look next at the first government of the United States: the **Articles of Confederation**. It quite amazes this historian that the states were willing to set up any kind of general government whatsoever. Historically, they had developed independently of one another. Despite a common language, law and government, they were as different as scotch and beer. Everyone must understand that people's loyalties were to their individual state.

They were New Yorkers. And Virginians. And Nutmeggers. Not Americans. John Adams sometime stated that "Massachusetts is my country." Today we are Americans first, with state loyalties secondary. These long-standing state loyalties were intensified by trade rivalries, by conflicts over land, and differences in attitude and life styles. Perhaps this situation resembles the various republics of the old Soviet Union, different and antagonistic to one another, yet held together by the central government. Only the power of Parliament had on several occasions prevented open warfare between colonies, now states.

The idea of one single national government of the United States, of a single continental republic was unheard of and totally unimaginable to most all of them! The American Revolution created thirteen quite distinct and independent countries. Only the pressures of war and the hope of recognition as a member of the family of nations compelled any need for a loose alliance. Indeed, once the fighting stopped, the Congress of the Confederation governed but very little.

FROM CONFEDERATION TO CONSTITUTION

We can examine just how the Articles of Confederation reflected the powerful concept of state independence in its very structure. There are six examples noted here. In the first place, Section #2 of the document says "Each state retains its sovereignty, freedom and independence, and every power, jurisdiction, and right which is not by this Confederation expressly delegated to the United States in Congress Assembled." Section #1, by the way, was the name, the United States of America (emphasis on States, not United). To men fighting the centralized tyranny of the British government, the idea of establishing another central government – even one of their own choosing – was flat out impossible. A loose alliance among the several states was all they could agree to. Central government, such as existed, was merely a means to an end. The goal was the independence of each of those states from Britain. State independence was what they were fighting for.

Second, representation to the Confederation Congress was by state: one state, one vote. Proposals to elect delegates for every 30,000 people (which would have helped the big states), were soundly defeated. Moreover, all major laws had to be passed by every state. One negative and the law would not carry. The very idea of a majority vote signaled that some states were less sovereign than others. Any amendments to the Articles, similarly, must pass unanimously.

Third, the executive power in the Articles rested with a series of Congressional committees. At one time there were actually 99 committees, with confusing rules, overlapping jurisdictions and redundant responsibilities. What was wrong with this system was not, as most students were taught, that the executive function lacked power. It was instead the fractured or divided nature of the committee system that proved fatal. Committee members sat on too many committees – we would say today they wore too many hats. Had four or five departments been created, the government might have worked much more efficiently.

Fourth, there was no federal judiciary, just as there was no separate executive branch. The highest courts of the several states were the highest courts. Period. Fifth, Congress did not have power to enact tax laws or laws regulating trade, such as tariffs. This was entirely natural, was it not, for folks whose experience with the taxing and tariff powers of Parliament was so dismal? Without tax or tariff power, Congress was dependent on the states to volunteer money to operate the government and enact its programs. It was much like today's United Way – and that is about all they ever received! Sixth, Congress had no power to enforce

its own laws. It had no power of coercion whatsoever! It had to rely on each of the several states to enforce congressional legislation. If a state chose not to obey a congressional act, or refused to enforce it on its citizens, it just didn't. And there was absolutely nothing Congress could do about it!

The closest analogy we have today is the United Nations. Each member nation of the U.N. is a sovereign nation. If the U.N. passes a resolution and a country decides not to obey it, the U.N. does not have any power to enforce its will. Member nations may decide to enforce U.N. Resolutions in the name of the U.N., as with th deployment of American troops in Korea in 1950. But if member nations do not take that action, the U.N. is powerless.

Was the Articles of Confederation a "Weak" Government?

We all learned somewhere in our distant youth that these governmental elements of the Articles were weaknesses. Gerber thinks, by contrast, that the idea of weakness is a present-minded bias. We are unable to imagine the ideology of decentralized authority. Or state sovereignty! We instinctively and unconsciously compare the central power of the Articles to that of the Constitution. This bias skews our understanding of the nature of the Articles. Limited powers does not mean weaknesses. Here our United Nations analogy proves instructive.

How many of us today would approve power for the United Nations to tax Americans? Or to set American tariff rates? Would we consider it a weakness in the U.N. structure that the U.N. does not have those powers? Of course not. Most of us would object to a foreign power, or even a collective of foreign powers taxing America or telling Americans what we could or couldn't export. America is sovereign.

That is exactly what would have occurred had Congress been granted tax powers or commerce powers or enforcement powers! Each state was a sovereign entity, just as America is today. The writers of the Articles did not forget to include centralized powers. Rather, they regarded centralized powers as tyrannical. Of course the Articles was not weak. It enacted precisely the limited powers that the American states decided it should have. We simply cannot look at this with post-Constitution eyes. Please put yourself into the cosmology of the decade between 1776 and 1787.

To summarize, the Articles of Confederation was based on the principles of state independence, local autonomy, and legislative supremacy. That was what the War for Independence was being fought to achieve. The Articles clearly reflected the localistic objectives of the revolution.

Unities in the Articles of Confederation

Let us also understand that the Articles contained a degree of unity greater than any other league of states in world history. Congress was given powers which must have struck the 18th century as unique. They ranged from the power to make war and peace, to coining and borrowing money; from making treaties to raising an army and navy. These (and some others) are exactly those which make a nation a nation.

Why did advocates of state sovereignty and local autonomy invest Congress with such significant powers? You may rest assured that if the American states could have escaped from the British Empire without war, those powers would never have been granted to Congress. Only the wartime emergency – the need for survival – accounts for any degree of unity among the states. Thus Congress deliberately did not have the power to govern the sovereign states within its own American borders, but it did have all the powers needed to relate on an equal footing with any other nation outside the United States of America. In this respect the powers of Congress were remarkable for people fighting for local autonomy.

One other provision of the Articles should be noted. This is the "full faith and credit" clause. That provision was later inserted into the U.S. Constitution and remains intact today. The full faith and credit of each state was pledged to the acts, records, and judicial proceedings of every other state. "Full faith and credit" meant that if you owned land in Connecticut and moved to New York, you still owned that land and New York would recognize and protect your rights to that ownership just as it would a New Yorker who owned land in New York. Or if you got married in Maryland, every other state would recognize you as married. Usually "full faith and credit" among independent nations only comes about by treaty. But they were admitted rights under the Articles of Confederation.

Perhaps the closest analogy for the Articles of Confederation is to consider it a sort of treaty or a league of friendship among neighbors. It resembled a sort of treaty among independent powers. Each agreed to the terms of the treaty but without surrendering any of its "sovereignty, freedom and independence." Loosely joined together for some significant purposes, the member states retained their individual characteristics and their nationhood. A balancing act, to be sure, but one exactly suited to the purposes of the Revolution.

FROM CONFEDERATION TO CONSTITUTION

Issues in the Confederation Period

How did this infant nation deal with some of the problems inherited from Great Britain? Three stand out as prominent: Western Land Policy; The Relationship of the Parts to the Whole; and Winning a Place in the Family of Nations.

1 – Western Land Policy

The problem of western lands is first. American solutions to land issues were not enacted because Americans were smarter than the British ministers. But the bottom line was that in a most practical sense, perhaps out of self interest, most of the western land problems got themselves solved.

Remember that any number of states claimed land in the west which other states also claimed. What to do about those conflicts? In the first place the Articles of Confederation wasn't even ratified until 1781, nearly 5 years after independence was declared. The document had to be ratified unanimously, of course. But Maryland, a small, over-the-hill tobacco state with no western lands, blocked ratification until the big states agreed to allow their western claims to become part of the public domain. Maryland disliked the fact that big states were using their western lands to bring in huge revenues.

Now this behavior was not exactly high-minded – it is self-interest in its most obvious form. Your basic average everyday political blackmail. It worked, too! State claims remained until the war was over in 1783, for certainly the British did not think that these lands were American! The agreement was ultimately fulfilled. States ceded their western lands to the United States Government, to Congress. A problem that the British had been unable to solve for years, was concluded quickly because of the pressure of events.

Ah, but now the dilemma of what to do with the land after Congress had it? The problem of land use was also solved by the pressure of events. With no Proclamation Line to stop them, American settlers

poured into the area of the prohibited lands - west of the watershed of the Appalachians to the east bank of the Mississippi. That reality caused Congress to determine to sell land at auction to the public as a way of raising needed revenue (recall that Congress had no power to tax). Auction favored the big land companies, land developers who had capital and could afford to purchase large tracts of land. Individual settlers could still settle, but they would have to buy their land, not simply settle on it. We can understand why Congress would favor this revenue producing plan, but with the population pressure so severe, was this a farsighted policy decision?

Once the decision had been made to auction land, Congress authorized a land survey so that people would know what they were buying. The Crown had actually started this survey in 1774. Royal surveyors had gone in and started the survey. **The Land Ordinance of 1785** was thus not a new idea but a very good one it was, in any case. Even if they did it for revenue, not idealism.

The surveyed land was set up into seven ranges. Ranges were laid out in townships, each supposed to support four families on plots of 160 acres, about 25 families per square mile. A person could buy as little as 40 acres. Each section was six miles square. The land was then offered for sale. Each six mile square section also included a portion of land reserved for a public school. That is because these founders believed that public education was the key to informed citizen participation in republican government. One problem resolved.

2 – Relationship of Parts to the Whole: The Northwest Ordinance of 1787

Next is the relationship of the parts to the whole - and to the famous **Northwest Ordinance of 1787**. The Ordinance was clearly a brilliant piece of statesmanship for which Congress must get full praise - *summa cum laude*. The Norrthwest Ordinance solved once and for all the issue of what to do with areas under the control of the central government which were not states. All that Big Ten territory! Americans called these lands "territories" just as the British called them colonies. The Northwest Ordinance established a system of stages for creating new states out of these territories (or colonies). Over time a territory could became an equal partner with the original thirteen, or with the new American Mother Country, if you prefer.

In the first stage each organized territory would receive an appointed governor until it reached a certain level of inhabitants. Then at the

second stage it could elect its own territorial legislature and governor. And finally it could apply for statehood, once it had reached a mature stage of development. This progressive series of stages promised territories eventual equality with the original thirteen states. There would be no permanent subordinate colonies or territories within the American empire. A major issue which the British could never resolve was settled in a fair and satisfactory manner.

Ironically also, the Northwest Ordinance was illegal. The measure was passed by a majority of states, but not by the nine states or two-thirds that were needed for legislation to take effect. One of the first actions of the First Congress under the Constitution in 1789 was to re-ratify the Northwest Ordinance. It became a permanent part of the Federal system. It is without question the most significant contribution to governance under the Articles of Confederation.

3 – Winning a Place in the International Community

Sometimes we cannot see the forest for the trees. Obviously the most important achievement of government under the Articles was that the United States won a permanent place in the family of nations. It is easy to take for granted that America won the war against Great Britain and became, thereby an independent nation. How big was that? And there is more! The United States negotiated the most successful peace treaty in all of American history, a treaty hardly imaginable in 1776.

The principal treaty negotiators in 1783, **John Jay**, **Benjamin Franklin**, and **John Adams**, found willing ears in England. As with the war itself, it was not so much the brilliance of the American diplomats as it was the division of opinion in Great Britain that worked to America's success. The fact remains that the U.S. had friends in England. There had been a huge anti-war sentiment building against the war, not unlike American antiwar sentiment in Vietnam or Iraq.

Some Englishmen, including **Lord Shelbourne**, thought that over the long run Britain would be better off having the U.S. as an ally, rather than an enemy, and hence should not be tight-fisted about the Treaty. Others, such as **Lord Sheffield**, believed that England's interest lay in recapturing the American market. England was still the main source of manufactured goods for America. Britain would not need to own those markets as colonies. Indeed, it would take another war – the war of 1812 – before America gained her economic independence from Britain.

Under the **Treaty of Paris of 1783**, Great Britain recognized the independence of the United States as a sovereign nation. In addition, Britain ceded to the U.S. the huge terriroty just to the west of the thirteen original colonies. It was an enormous concession that included all the British territory south of Canada and east of the Mississippi.

FROM CONFEDERATION TO CONSTITUTION

So the Government under the Articles of Confederation should get a better grade than it usually does. A lot better grade. Yet major issues regarding the American Revolution remain in the roost!

Historians Disagree About the American Revolution

Essentially, the division among historians is about the motives for revolution, rather than the outcomes. Everyone agrees that the establishment of republican principles of government makes American actions revolutionary. The American Revolution was revolutionary, all right, but what sort of Revolution was it? Some attention has been noted regarding this matter in Chapter Four – page 65.

One congregation of historians interprets the American Revolution as restorative in nature. The Revolution reflected a conscious desire to restore the "good old days," the glory days prior to 1763, before London began to interfere with regulations designed to "reform" the empire. The days (as they imagined them) of genuine local autonomy. In the first state constitutions and in the Articles of Confederation Americans reenacted their ideals of local autonomy, garbed, of course, in republican political clothing. This position labels the Revolution conservative in its basic nature. It was an exercise in nostalgia, grounded in romanticized memory.

As evidence, say these historians, one need only examine the early state constitutions and the Articles of Confederation. Governmental powers were everywhere restrained, for the functions of government should be limited. These structures reestablished the doctrines that (1) government was best because it governed least, that (2) local government was more accountable to the governed than central government, and that (3) popular will found voice in legislative assemblies, rather in strong executives and powerful judiciaries. Least Government. Local Accountability. Legislative Supremacy. Free of British rule, these three principles could be implemented – or re-implemented. American local autonomy would flourish.

A different gaggle of historians emphasizes just how radical the intentions of the revolutionaries were. No mere romantic vision of past glories for them! These guys established a republic! At the end of the 18th century, when there had existed nary a major republic for centuries! [A few Swiss cantons and the miniscule Dutch republic seemed insufficiently relevant to be considered.] A republic represented ideological experimentation, a huge gamble. They dared to attempt a government with core values based on the consent of the governed

The radical interpretation of the Revolution, similarly requires explanation. Revolutionaries scrapped the entrenched (some claimed divine) European institutions based on heredity and tradition, in favor of a system in which individuals rose or fell based on their merits and talents. Individual abilities and honest efforts should matter. It didn't matter who your father was. For them the ingrained notions of class deference would dissipate until individuals could be recognized for their virtues, not their status.

This was hardly any sort of genuine egalitarianism; it is, cosmologically speaking, too early to expect real democracy. As earlier noted, democracy was a product of the 19th century and is still a work in progress. Nontheless, the revolution's instincts were democratic. Of course the revolutionaries recognized that the "few" had power and wealth and the "many" were poor and deprived. But no need to bow or courtsey in the street; you could shake hands and nod. You might have money and influence, the non-deferential view held, but down deep "you ain't no better than me!"

What fascinates Gerber is that the evidence for this more radical interpretation is precisely the same as that used to support the conservative position. Again, one need only examine the first state constitutions and the Articles of Confederation. (1) limited powers of government, (2) local accountability and (3) legislative supremacy were direct results of replacing the monarchy and hereditary aristocracy with overtly republican values and political structures. Free of British rule, the experiment in non-deferential self-government would flourish.

This dispute among historians continues. There can be little doubt that the American Revolution reflected the ideologies of the revolutionaries. The state constitutions and the Articles of Confederation embody their political values. What those ideals were remains unclear. Both arguments may have historial validity. The Confederation period from 1776 to the enactment of the Constitution may be rightly described as ambiguous.

Taking either interpretaion, or both interpretations, the revolutionaries succeeded in enacting their revolutionary aims. What, then, accounts for the Constitution of 1787?

CHAPTER SIX: THE CONSTITUTIONAL CONVENTION

What motivated the framers of the Constitution to commit what we must identify as a second revolutionary act? What explains scrapping the structure of government, so recently put into operation, one that so well reflected the political ideals and values of the Revolution just fought? Especially since, despite problems that remained unresolved, government seemed to function reasonably well? Why, then the abrupt shift from the Articles of Confederation to the Constitution?

The Traditional Explanation is Invalid

There is an old and traditional answer to this query. This old thesis we all learned in high school; even college textbooks repeat it to this very day. In a nutshell the idea was that weaknesses in the government structure established in the Articles of Confederation led to a drift toward anarchy and an incapacity to govern. Those weaknesses and that anarchy made it impossible to solve the problems faced by the new nation. Therefore, a new form of government was needed – hence the Constitution.

After all, the old thesis states, Congress could neither tax nor regulate interstate commerce. It couldn't even enforce the law it had permission to pass! Moreover, there was no strong national executive, nor any central judicial branch. How could any government so dependent on the states ever operate effectively? Nice theory, indeed.

The customary proof for that venerable thesis cites events such as **Shays' Rebellion** in western Massachusetts in 1786. That event, it is declared, became parlayed into evidence of just how much discontent there was in America under the Articles.

How valid is that old thesis? Was it indeed the weaknesses of the Articles of Confederation – the absence of powers of a central government – which caused the Constitution? In Gerber's opinion the old thesis is flat wrong! Indeed, the entire concept of weakness is a present-minded perception. We view the world with post-Constitution eyes. Most Americans cannot imagine, in the 21st century, a central government with such limited powers as those possessed by the Confederation Congress. We have, quite inappropriately, injected present-minded thinking into this entire explanation.

The alleged "weaknesses" of the Articles were hardly "weaknesses" in the minds of the framers of the Articles. The structure and function of government as established in the Articles deliberately reflected the purposes of the American Revolution. Local autonomy or state sovereignty was the order of the day. Americans were not willing to surrender back to a central government the powers they were fighting and dying to get out from under. They believed that government closest to the people was better than central government. That is why the Articles were deliberately decentralized. The Confederation most resembled a treaty of allies, loosely arranged to face the world, but with each member independent of the others. The United Nations analogy has validity in this instance.

The logic of the old thesis is that the framers of the Constitution were now willing to reverse themselves and give the new central authority the very powers they would not grant the Confederation. The framers therefore violated or subverted the purposes of the Revolution by scrapping the idea that local government was best for the people.

There is accuracy in the view that the framers wished to transfer power to the center. They understood local autonomy could be a two-sided sword. What is key is that they did in fact believe that the government closest to the people could harm the people more easily than central government, precisely because it was closer to them. They also believed that a central government was more responsive to popular needs than local government. They thought central government could respond better to national issues than a system of local governments. This was a different vision, to be sure. It was revolutionary.

Motivation of the Framers of the Constitution

The Constitution was written by men who possessed a combination of self-interests and ideals to promote and protect. The framers associated both their ideals and their interests with national or central government. The Constitution was a political document, a political process. The framers were political people who believed in a stronger national power, a central government, in large measure because they doubted the wisdom of their neighbors.

As do all politicians in time and space they identified their interests and ideals with the good of the nation. In politics there are no saints! Nobody's ideas are totally pure – unless one is Mother Teresa! It is high time we quit viewing the framers as divinities or demigods! It is time we raised the framers "from immortality to mortality," to borrow the felicitous phrase of historian Walton Hamilton.

It may be useful to note that the framers of the Constitution were an elite clique of young men; young lawyers, young merchants, young planters, young investors. Does the idea of young get through? Many of them were little children during the protest period of the 1760's. A full generation of twenty five years had elapsed from the Proclamation of 1763 to the writing of the Constitution!

Many of the framers did not remember the Stamp Act any more than many of you remember the Gulf War of 1990-1991! They grew to adulthood only during the War for Independence and did not recall with emotional power the dominant influences of British rule and the protests that led to Revolution. That generalization, just announced, did not apply to every delegate to the Constitutional Convention, certainly, but it does apply to more than many. They were the next generation. They had a different mind set, a cosmology not quite the same as those who resisted British central government and committed the American Revolution. These men set the tone of the Convention.

This distinction might serve. In the Articles of Confederation the local autonomy people had won out. If you prefer to label them state sovereignty people that also works. Patrick Henry, Samuel Adams, John Dickinson, for example. However, in writing the Constitution, the central government people, the national sovereignty people, if you wish, won out! James Madison, George Washington, Benjamin Franklin, Alexander Hamilton.

Nationalists did not want to turn the clock back to before 1763. They thought state-based government inadequate to solve the problems of a new nation in an era of big foreign powers. Because of the **sovereign powers of the states** – not the limitations on the Confederation – there was an absence of plenary power to deal with domestic problems. The Articles was not a weak reed. Rather the government had been built on outmoded political theories and institutional structures.

THE CONSTITUTIONAL CONVENTION

Recent scholarship demonstrates that the framers of the Constitution were gravely concerned about the behavior of many of the state governments established under the first state constitutions. State assemblies, often composed of uneducated men with no political experience, not infrequently passed measures to protect debtors (usually farmers) against their rightful creditors. Interest-based legislation of this type concerned the framers. If local interests could capture legislative majorities and thus override property rights, might they not also invade other individual rights in the name of majority will?

Continental Vision

More importantly, the framers held what we may call a **Continental Vision**. They envisioned a single republic, one nation, rather than thirteen independent republics held together loosely as by treaty. Thus they acted negatively against interest-based state sovereignty and positively in favor of their own continental vision. In order to dissolve the first and enact the second they had to stage their own revolution by writing the Constitution and getting it ratified. And they did it!! These men were ready to establish in 1787 what 20 years before their elders so bitterly resisted, namely a central government with the power to tax, regulate commerce and enforce its own laws. In their minds a centralized system was essential to national stability and welfare. To their welfare, too!

We must understand the ideological and psychological shift which was implied in the ability to accept such a central government. Most people maintained their loyalties to their particular States. Even John Adams said that Massachusetts was his country. The shift was enormous. It was as though the leaders of the major nations of the world today were to shift their allegiance from their respective countries to the United Nations. How many of us would be willing to surrender the powers of the United States government to the government of the United Nations? Imagine how that feels? How many of us could change our mind set to accept a change of that magnitude?

But that is precisely what the framers were willing to do. A global vision today; a Continental Vision in 1787! If there was any "miracle in Philadelphia," as historian Catherine Drinker Bowen deemed it, or if there was any "brilliant solution," as historian Carol Berkin labeled it, it was that quite amazing and improbable shift, not merely in government, but in perceptions, in psychology, in emotional loyalty, in cosmology.

THE CONSTITUTIONAL CONVENTION

The Constitutional Convention

Our examination of the Constitutional Convention begins with an understanding of the conversion of the original purpose of that conclave to a new and bolder purpose. The stated purpose of sending delegates to this convention was to rectify or remedy certain deficiencies in the Articles of Confederation. Perhaps some new taxing or regulatory powers would be given to the Confederation Congress. In any case it was certainly not the convention's original mandate to write a whole new form of government!

The convention was schedule to begin on the second Monday in May, 1787. By May 25 enough delegates had straggled in so that majorities of seven states had arrived; at that point a quorum was present. States could send as many delegates as they wished, but voting occurred by state: one state, one vote. Rhode Island never showed up at all.

Of the 74 delegates chosen, indeed only 55 ever arrived. The real work was done by a handful of men, maybe a dozen or so. They were the prominent and powerful men that we designate "the framers." Who were they? We cannot even speed through their resumés, but at least we ought to notice the people whose influence on us remains so significant.

George Washington of Virginia, whose health and financial conditions should have kept him at home, agreed to come to Philadelphia under the prodding of Hamilton and Madison. He was elected President of the Convention. He rarely spoke, but his presence kept the heat of argument under control.

James Madison of Virginia. Without doubt the Convention's brightest mind. It was Madison's **Virginia Plan** that first outlined the nature of the new national government. A brilliant scholar, if a poor speaker, Madison's notes of the proceedings form the major historical source for what we know about what happened there. Madison is sometimes called the "Father of the Constitution." He deserves the title.

James Wilson of Pennsylvania was America's foremost legal theorist. He believed in a completely national government founded on a popularly elected base. He was also the brains behind the Electoral College system, when he saw that direct popular election, the idea he preferred, would not pass.

THE CONSTITUTIONAL CONVENTION

Gouverneur Morris. This Pennsylvanian, an elitist by habit, was nonetheless a powerful proponent of strong national government. Morris was the person who put the Constitution into its final literary form. **Benjamin Franklin**, then 82, was as always a stabilizing presence. Franklin represented continuity from the revolutionary period to the Constitution. Very prestigious, this wise old man. He was surely the most famous American known to Europeans – because of his scientific achievements, of course. Did Franklin actually invent electricity? It was Franklin who said that he could not tell whether the half sun on the President's chair was a rising or a setting sun. When the document was written he said he knew that it was America's rising sun.

New York's outstanding person was **Alexander Hamilton**. An ardent nationalist, Hamilton was in the minority of his state's three-person delegation; consequently New York sometimes voted against nationalist proposals. Hamilton has been frequently misunderstood as being a closet monarchist. He clearly was not one. He was, however, strongly antislavery. Moreover, having been born in the West Indies (Nevis), he had no ardent loyalties to any state. That perspective permitted him to appreciate the continental republic that the Convention would create. Hamilton was a great American nationalist. Hamilton deserves a better reputation than he enjoys.

Oliver Ellesworth of Connecticut! This son of the Nutmeg State, was a brilliant lawyer, and Chief Justice of the Connecticut Supreme Court. He would write the **Judiciary Act of 1789**, which established the federal court structure that still exists. Ellesworth would become the second Chief Justice of the United States. **Roger Sherman,** also of Connecticut, had been a shoemaker, lawyer, and judge. Sherman signed everything, including the Declaration of Independence, the Articles of Confederation and then the Constitution. Sherman is best remembered as the engineer of the **Connecticut Compromise** – or the Great Compromise – Bowen's "miracle at Philadelphia." This conservative compromise on the problem of sovereignty severely weakened Madison's Virginia Plan, but it did permit the Convention to continue to function.

Charles Cotesworth Pinckney of South Carolina. Leader of a prominent family of Palmetto State Pinckneys, Charles Cotesworth had served as brigadier general in the War for Independence. He was John Adams's Federalist running mate in the election of 1800, only to lose to Thomas Jefferson and Aaron Burr. He later ran as Federalist candidate for President in 1804 and 1808 but lost first to Jefferson, then to Madison. Pinckney was a strong champion of the pro-slavery interests in the convention.

THE CONSTITUTIONAL CONVENTION

Luther Martin of Maryland. Nationalist sentiment held the clear majority in the Convention, but state sovereignty had its advocates as well. Martin fought tooth and nail against the nationalistic tendencies of the majority. What a terrible bore he was as a speaker; he sometimes held the floor for hours and drove his colleagues nearly ballistic. But at least he had two first names (reversed).

William Paterson of New Jersey. Paterson, an Irish immigrant, was a strong state sovereignty proponent. In the Convention he authored the **New Jersey Plan**, the so-called small state plan, as an alternative to Madison's Virginia Plan. In the end Paterson concluded that the Constitution was an acceptable bundle of compromises and signed it. President Washington appointed Paterson Associate Justice of the United States Supreme Court.

Elbridge Gerry of Massachusetts, was another strong states righter in this Convention of nationalists. He called the Constitution too monarchical and refused to sign. He later became Governor of Massachusetts and, perhaps ironically, James Madison's Vice President.

There were some notable powerful persons absent from the Constitutional Convention. **Thomas Jefferson** was serving as America's Ambassador to France. **John Adams** was in England, serving as Ambassador there. **Patrick Henry** was chosen as a delegate from Virginia. Henry harbored deep suspicions about what the Convention might do. He "smelt a rat," he said, and stayed home. **Samuel Adams** was not chosen as a delegate.

Altogether, this collection of delegates represented the cream of the intellectual and political crop in America. A talented group, to be sure! And also, to be sure, a group dominated by the nationalists.

The Revolutionary Constitution

The Constitution was indeed revolutionary in enacting the nationalist vision. How revolutionary was it? Right from the get-go, **Edmund Randolph** of Virginia, speaking for Madison, proposed that a *"national government"* ought to be established, consisting of a *"supreme legislature, executive, and judiciary!"* Randolph's simple-sounding resolution went way beyond anything the delegates were sent to Philadelphia to do. This was no mere proposal to patch up the Articles to give Congress some extra powers. Consider the contrast between

THE CONSTITUTIONAL CONVENTION

Randolph's words and those of Section #2 of the Articles of Confederation: *"each state retains its sovereignty, freedom and independence."* What did Madison mean by "national government?" Gouverneur Morris got it exactly right when he explained that the term "national" meant a complete and compulsive central operation, not simply a compact resting on the good faith of the states.

Yet ten states voted for Randolph's resolution. Only Connecticut voted no. The delegates knew that by erecting a national government they were obliterating state sovereignty. They knew exactly what they were doing! General Pinckney of South Carolina told the Convention that if they declared the government under the Articles inadequate, they must disband, because the Convention had no power to make such a declaration.

But they didn't disband! Instead, they closed the doors and windows, They locked themselves in -- and passed the resolution. Nobody went home. Nobody was particularly shocked by what they were doing! Nobody protested. Even Madison did not tell his pal Jefferson in Paris what was afoot!

What is more crucial is that even the states' rights minority in the Constitutional Convention accepted the fundamental purposes of the Convention. They did so even after the delegates passed Randolph's resolution! Anybody could have walked away and blown the whistle. Anyone could have told the newspapers what was going on. Had that happened, the whole enterprise would have collapsed. Instead, they returned day after day to argue in that hot sweaty Philadelphia summer heat. There was plenty of heated argument as well.

Compromises in the Constitution

First we must recall William Paterson's comment that the Constitution was a bundle of compromises. Paterson was right! Why did they compromise? It was because these delegates were realists. They knew very well that they were way out in front of the thinking of their fellow Americans. In current parlance they were the left wing of public opinion. They well understood that most Americans considered their own state as their country or nation. Whatever the virtues of a single national America, they appreciated that their position was clearly the minority position.

In short they recognized that their vision was too radical for most Americans of the late 18th century. They were very well aware that they would have to get the Constitution ratified by the very states whose power they were severely diminishing. Had they enacted their national principles intact, they would have stood not one remote chance of ratification. The delegates chose practical politics above overt ideology.

In five significant areas the nationalists chose to modify their ideological vision in favor of *realpolitik.*

1 - Sovereignty

First the crucial issue of **sovereignty.** Sovereignty refers to the most basic issue of governance: by whose authority is government permitted to govern? Who grants the government the power to govern? In a monarchy the king is sovereign. In the Articles of Confederation, it was the individual states which were sovereign. No majority of states could tell any single state what laws it must obey. The Philadelphia delegates who favored a "national government" wanted the people of the United States – not the states – to be sovereign. They wanted the majority will of the nation to prevail over state independence.

To enact such a huge change, states would have to surrender vast portions of their power. They would become subordinate to a central government based on the entire people. Would they do it? Especially after their experience with British central government! If the delegates could not solve this prime issue, the entire Convention would fail. The solution embedded in the Constitution was truly revolutionary.

It was Madison's idea that the national government would have power to make laws that would apply everywhere in the nation. The United States would have the power to enforce its own laws on each individual person. The national government would have its own officers, including its own legislative, executive and judicial branches. The U.S. would have its own courts, attorneys, marshals, even revenue officers. These officials would impose the will of the people – the majority will as expressed in Congress – on individuals. There is no way to square that idea with state sovereignty, is there? Popular sovereignty, through the national government, would revolutionize American governance.

Thus the Constitution would shift sovereignty away from the states and locate it in the people of the United States: a shift from state sovereignty to popular sovereignty. That would mean that the new national government would operate directly upon individuals. Laws of the government of the United States would apply directly to each individual person. States could not act as middlemen. States could not block the

THE CONSTITUTIONAL CONVENTION

implementation of laws of the government of the United States, nor prevent their enforcement.

We see this clearly in Madison's Virginia Plan. He envisioned a **bicameral Congress**, a **House of Representatives** and a **Senate**. He wanted both houses of Congress elected by the people. Members of the House would be chosen in each state by direct popular vote. Those representatives would then elect the Senators. Nationalists favored popular elections precisely because they would free the central government from control of the states, big or small. State legislatures, at least, would not elect the people's representatives!

Similarly, in the Virginia Plan, the President of the United States would be chosen by direct popular election. Whoever gets the most popular votes wins. It is sometimes argued that the Philadelphia folks were reluctant to trust the people. Madison's Plan certainly belies that viewpoint.

In the heat of debate, pious old Ben Franklin suggested that each meeting be opened with a prayer for divine guidance. It probably isn't true, but Alexander Hamilton, the ultimate **Deist**, supposedly answered that the U.S. didn't need any foreign aid.

Madison's plan for popular sovereignty (or national sovereignty, if you prefer) was significantly modified, in the so-called **Great Compromise** or **Connecticut Compromise.** In the U.S. Senate each state would have two senators, regardless of population, size, wealth or anything else. Delaware would have the same power in the Senate as New York. Virginia would be worth no more than Rhode Island. Senators, moreover, would be elected by the various State Legislatures, by whatever method each state determined. Popular election of Senators lasted until the 17th Amendment in 1913.

Why did the nationalists yield on this point? They certainly had the votes to pass the Virginia Plan or, indeed, anything they wished to pass. Once again the answer was political realism, a pragmatic sense that ratification lay ahead. It is true that Madison, Wilson and Morris all opposed the compromise. Even that much state sovereignty was too much for them to stomach. They were compelled to yield to the Convention's greater wisdom.

Ominously, in future years this very compromise led southern states to declare that the Constitution was merely a compact of states and that the states were still sovereign. That claim required 625,000 dead Civil War soldiers to disprove! In retrospect it might have been better if there had been no compromise. In the cosmology of 1787, however, even the most ardent nationalists knew they had to get the Constitution ratified.

Nevertheless, even with that compromise included, the preponderance of sovereignty now shifted from the states to the people. The Convention had enacted a revolutionary change in vision! Evidence for that view is warranted.

The new national Congress was given enormous powers of legislation. These included the power to tax, to regulate commerce, and to act in any case which required uniformity of purpose for the nation. Exactly what those contingencies would be remained undefined, but in Article 1, Section 8, Subsection 18, the "necessary and proper" clause, the United States Congress received the power to do what was "necessary and proper" to carry into effect any of the 17 enumerated powers in Article I, Section 8 and other powers listed elsewhere in the document. This famous "elastic clause" **did not confer** power to do anything Congress wanted. If it had held that meaning, none of the enumerated powers would have been necessary. Congress could do whatever was "necessary and proper" to implement any of the stated powers of Congress.

That power of the "necessary and proper" clause deliberately resurrected or renewed the general **prerogative power** in the supreme legislature. Parliament had possessed that very prerogative that the American revolutionaries had adamantly rejected. The "necessary and proper" clause would have made Lord North smile!

2 – Division of Power – National/State Relations

If the first issue of sovereignty was revolutionary, we can also see the revolutionary character of the Constitution – compromises and all – in the second crucial issue: the **Division of Powers**. Sometimes this issue is labeled "**federalism.**" Who would define the limits of national power in relation to the states? Where would the division be between state and national power? Who would ensure that the states did not emasculate the national power, as under the Articles of Confederation? Who would prevent the national government from shriveling the states down to mere administrative units?

The Virginia Plan awarded that power to a national agency; Congress would have authority to disallow state legislation. If so, the United States would serve as the monitor of its own jurisdiction. Parliament had possessed that power. However, Roger Sherman of Connecticut argued that if Congress exercised this power, they would spend all their time reviewing state laws and would not have time to govern. We might appreciate Sherman's point as a most sensible one.

Instead, Luther Martin of Maryland, perhaps the strongest states righter in the Convention, proposed that state courts should determine the line between national and state power. The state courts, if you please! A state agency! Of course Martin also agreed that state judges were not permitted to allow any state law to contradict the Constitution or a national law or a treaty, as had occurred so often under the Articles. Under the United States Constitution, national laws and treaties would be enforced in the state courts. The state judges were expected to give priority to any constitutional provision, congressional law or treaty provision that might be in conflict with any state law on the same subject.

Martin's idea became embedded into the Constitution in the famous national supremacy clause, or **King Bull clause: Article VI, Section 1**. The Constitution itself, all treaties and all acts of Congress would be the *supreme law of the land*. The judges in every state would be bound by them!

Thus, the issue of division of power was settled by providing that national law was superior to state law, in case of conflict between them. Even the judges in the state courts would have to be bound by that national supremacy. Quite a revolutionary shift in sovereignty in this provision, even though by virtue of a compromise state agencies would make the decision about whether state or federal law would be applied. Nationalists complied with the compromise, but they would change it in their favor early in the Washington Administration. Stay tuned for that one!

3 – Separation of Powers:
Checks and Balances Within the National Government

If the Constitution was revolutionary on questions of sovereignty and division of powers, then the solution to the issue of **separation of powers** also bears that same hallmark. Please do not confuse separation of powers with division of power. Separation of Powers is what we might call today checks and balances. The issue applies only to the national government, not to federal/state relations. Separation of Powers delineated the responsibilities and the limits of power among the three national branches of government: legislative, executive, judicial. It also resolved cases of conflict among those three branches. In case of conflict, which branch was superior?

THE CONSTITUTIONAL CONVENTION

The Articles of Confederation and the early state constitutions, please recall, rested on the doctrine of legislative supremacy. The framers of the Constitution scrapped that idea altogether. They replaced it with the idea of three separate, distinct, and independent (what they called "**coordinate**") branches. It would be the function of the legislature, the Congress, to make the laws. The Executive Branch would enforce or execute the laws. The Judiciary would interpret what the laws meant. We have already noted above the major expansion of the powers of the legislative branch, the Congress.

With regard to the judiciary, the judicial power of the United States was vested in one **Supreme Court** and such lower national courts as Congress would set up from time to time as they deemed wise or necessary. It is impossible to overestimate the impact of this decision on all our lives. Gerber's opinion is that the framers felt an elected legislature was incompetent to deal with any judicial problems of any magnitude or technical points of law.

There is plenty of evidence, moreover, that the national courts would have the power of **judicial review** over laws of Congress. Judicial review may be understood as the authority to decide whether a law was constitutional or unconstitutional. No provision empowering the federal courts (or any other courts) to exercise the power of judicial review was inserted into the Constitution, then or ever. Perhaps it was just an unspoken or implied power. Judicial review developed as a constitutional invention, an unwritten development. It grew from infancy to legitimacy largely as the contribution of **Chief Justice John Marshall**. But it did not take final root until the latter 19th century.

4 – The Executive Branch -- The Presidency
An Independent Executive

Most powers of the President were spelled out in Article II of the Constitution. The most significant roles and responsibilities include serving as Commander-in-Chief of the army, navy and state militias; the power to grant pardons and reprieves; the power to make treaties and appointments of ambassadors, officers of the United States, high ranking military officers and Justices of the Supreme Court (with advice and consent of the Senate); the discretion to recommend measures to Congress for their deliberation and to provide information about the state of the union; and the requirement to *"take care that the laws be faithfully executed."* The power to veto laws of Congress is located in Article I, Section 7. These powers represented dramatic grants of authority to this new executive officer, especially considering the absence of executive power under the Articles of Confederation and the state governors.

Immediately, however, the issue arose regarding how to elect this powerful independent Chief Executive. The Virginia Plan proposed to elect the President by direct popular vote. One voter, one vote! Whoever got the most votes wins the Presidency! For Madison, direct election would accomplish the objective of preventing state legislatures from electing the president. The Convention had granted state legislatures the power to elect United States Senators, but the nationalists were simply not going to permit state legislatures to elect the chief executive. Nationalists blocked that avenue of election.

But Madison could not garner a majority for direct popular election. States with few voters, generally small states, feared that power would flow to large (urban) population centers generally in large states. That is precisely what would have happened in a one man-one vote process. In Gerber's opinion it should have!

Some opponents of popular election wanted Congress to elect the President and make him responsible to Congress. A sort of parliamentary system, at least a legislative supremacy concept! The nationalists refused to make the new chief executive the puppet of any legislature and defeated that proposal. As Alexander Hamilton said, the President should function with "*energy, dispatch and responsibility.*"

With each of the three primary alternatives for electing the president unable to win a majority, there was a stalemate on this issue. Finally a Committee was set up led by James Wilson of Pennsylvania. What they invented toward the very end of the Convention was the **Electoral College** system which we still have today. In each state the eligible voters would choose **presidential electors**. The number of presidential electors in the various states would be determined by the size of the population of those states. Those electors, in turn, would choose the President by majority vote of the Electoral College.

Specifically, in the absence of political parties, and until passage of the 12th Amendment following the election of 1800, each presidential elector would cast two votes for president (but only one from his home state). Whoever received the highest number of electoral votes (assuming a majority) would become President. Whoever attained the second most electoral votes would become Vice President. Provisions were made for the House of Representatives to determine the winner in case no candidate received a majority of electoral votes or if candidates having a majority of electoral votes had the same number of votes.

THE CONSTITUTIONAL CONVENTION

Mythology tells us that the Electoral College was established to prevent the people from electing the President. Historical accuracy suggests instead that the Electoral College was a compromise devised, because the supporters of direct election could not gain a majority in the Convention. The Electoral College was never intended to prevent the people from electing the President, because that method was precisely what Madison wanted. It was designed to prevent the state legislatures from doing it! Or having Congress do it!

Has the Electoral College worked? The Electoral College had a huge impact on the election of 1800 and a significant impact in 1824 and again in 1876. There have also occurred several instances in which candidates won the presidency because they won the majority of electoral votes, even though they did not win the majority of popular votes; nearly all of those elections occurred the 19th century. It is notable that the Electoral College had no effect on any single election in the entire 20th century – until the Election of 2000! There are constant recommendations to revise the Electoral College process or to get rid of it altogether. What do you think about this issue?

5 – Slavery

There was a serious debate in the Constitutional Convention about the institution of slavery. Once again, compromise was the order of the day.

Many Northerners, including Alexander Hamilton, were powerfully opposed to the kind of private ownership of persons as property by which slaves were put to work like so many beasts of the field. Southerners threatened to walk out of the Convention, if any move should be made to abolish slavery in American in the new document. The Convention would thereby end; the chance for a continental vision gone along with the Southern delegates.

If any Constitution were to be adopted, what were antislavery Northerners to do? They had votes enough to abolish slavery in the new Constitution. Thus they could stand by their principles and eliminate slavery (even gradually) – and break up the Convention! Alternatively, they could let the issue alone to be settled later. This choice disturbed many Northern advocates of freedom, but not enough to risk the consequences. In the environment of 1787, with the fate of the new country at stake, with a need to get the continental vision enacted, Northerners decided not to throw away this chance for a new Constitution, even if it meant accepting slavery. At this moment in time other issues seemed more pressing. Not necessarily more important – just more immediate.

Again a compromise occurred: the notorious **three-fifths clause of Article I, Sec 2.** This meant that the population of a state would be decided by counting all the whites plus three-fifths of the slaves to reach a total number of persons. The number of representatives to the House of Representatives and thus also the number of presidential electors would be assigned as that total number.

Southerners, of course would have preferred to count slaves as whole persons, thus increasing their number of congressional representatives. That is even though slaves had no rights and obviously could not participate in the governance process in any manner whatever. Northerners, conversely, saw political advantage in counting only white persons and not counting slaves at all. Free blacks were counted as whole persons. This is a significant historical occurrence, because in the case of **Dred Scott v. Sanford (1857),** the United States Supreme Court would claim that even free blacks were not entitled to constitutional protection.

By virtue of the three-fifths compromise Southern states added some 14 delegates to their various congressional delegations. Two additional representatives were added to Northern states (one in New York; one in New Jersey) which had not yet abolished slavery and still contained substantial numbers of slaves in their midst.

Further, Congress could not prohibit the importation of slaves until 1808. This meant that slave trading, the importing of slaves from Africa, would be legal forever unless Congress acted to stop it. In 1808 Congress did in fact pass a law prohibiting any importation of slaves into the United States. In any event, with the issue of slavery swept safely under the rug, Southerners withdrew any opposition to the Constitution as proposed.

To summarize briefly: on the main issues of sovereignty, of division of powers, of separation of powers, of the election of the president, and (even of slavery, the solutions adopted by the Constitutional Convention reflected shrewd political compromises with a strong nationalist flavor!

The Constitution Made Final

Most of the delegates to the Constitutional Convention would likely have preferred the nationalist proposals in the Virginia Plan. Yet these framers recognized that they would be asking people who had not transcended their state loyalties to pledge allegiance to a new centralized form of government, extremely alien to their way of thinking. They knew that most Americans hardly shared their breadth of vision. So they diluted their positions in favor of solutions which would not sell out their objectives of national sovereignty, but would cater to the popular mind during the ratification process. These revolutionaries tempered their personal preferences to the times.

Perhaps Alexander Hamilton best typifies this position. Because Hamilton had been born in the West Indies (Nevis, but grew up in St. Croix), Hamilton was never handicapped by any of the state loyalties which restrained the thoughts of most of his countrymen. He blamed America's problems in the evils of local autonomy. Referring to state-based government he said, "*This pernicious mistake must be corrected.*"

Hamilton wanted to create a national government which would not be wrecked by the turbulence of local interest groups or the outbursts of popular mobs. He knew that different classes had different self-interests. He wished to avoid class conflict, precisely because he thought it would lead to civil war or anarchy, or the suppression of individual rights by local majorities. Thus Hamilton approved the economic clauses of the Constitution, which put restraints on state powers.

The economic provisions are located in Article I, Section 10. There were provisions to prohibit states from coining their own money or issuing Bills of Credit. States could not pay their debts in any tender but gold or silver. Perhaps most critical, states could not impair the obligation of contracts. That is, they could not change by legislation the terms of a legal contract.

Hamilton willingly gave up his pet ideas of a President and Senate elected for life, in favor of the compromises the Convention adopted. He was not a monarchist. He was a devout republican of the best kind.

At long last the draft of the proposed Constitution was submitted to the Convention president, George Washington, and put into final form. Having passed the Convention the document was duly signed. It is a notable point to understand that the document was then sent to the Confederation Congress – not for approval or revision – but only for transmission directly to the states for ratification.

That action once again confirms the assertion that the Constitutional Convention was a revolutionary body. Because the provisions of the

THE CONSTITUTIONAL CONVENTION

Articles of Confederation required that any amendment receive the approval of the Confederation Congress and then the unanimous approval of the state legislatures. The Constitution itself, by contrast, declared that only three-fourths of the states must ratify; nine states of the thirteen. This would be accomplished in ratifying conventions, moreover, not state legislatures. If those actions do not constitute a revolution, it is difficult to know what one is!

One final item: the framers intended the Constitution to bind the states in perpetuity. Ratifications were not conditional. They were not provisional. They were not temporary. They were permanent actions that could not be revoked! Many of Philadelphia conventioneers were not certain the nation would last under that document. But at least ratification was permanent, a way for the people of the United States to establish a form of government by consent. Southerners would later argue that the Constitution, much like the Articles of Confederation, was only a loose alliance which states, being sovereign, could dissolve at their will.

That was not the intent of the framers of the Constitution!

EPILOGUE: PURPOSES OF THE CONSTITUTION

The American Constitution may be said to embody a number of purposes. These are noted briefly next.

1 – The Constitution Established the Structure of Government.

One primary purpose of the U.S. Constitution was to establish the governance structure of the socio-political order. It established the outlines of the primary institutions of government. It declared their functions, roles and responsibilities. Put plainly, in any society there must be some definition of who will have power, what powers they will have, and how much power they will have. The Constitution did that and does it today.

Some filling out of that plan of governance would be implemented once the Constitution was ratified and took effect. Such supplementary action would take place by legislative mandate, such as the Judiciary Act of 1789 and its successor statutes. It also occurred by executive initiative, as with the establishment of the President's Cabinet, and later the Executive Ordinance, and even more recently the Executive Office of the President. It also occurred through common practice, custom, or usage, as through the congressional committee system or the establishment of judicial review.

THE CONSTITUTIONAL CONVENTION

2 – The Constitution Limited Power.

By setting forth the institutional structure of the government, the Constitution limited the power of government at every level: state, federal, local. It also limited the power of private institutions and, indeed, of individuals. It declared what each institution of government could do. This was a most significant purpose and its most prominent feature.

By expressing powers, however, the Constitution also defined what was not limited. Some historians observe in the Constitution a system which prevented the strong from exploiting the weak. Other analysts prefer to view the Constitution as setting the ground rules by which the strong could indeed exploit the weak!

One way the Constitution limited power was by distributing power. Power was distributed according to function. The American system of federalism, or more properly the "division of powers" between the United States (national government) and the states and/or local governments, provides a classic form of distribution. At the national level power was also distributed by function among the several branches (Legislative, Executive, and Judicial) in what is called "separation of powers."

States and local governments also distributed the powers they possess by employing a version of "separation of powers" at the state level. Once again it should be noticed that these are large areas of power which are not assigned to any governmental level or branch. That is, there are residual powers exercised by private individuals or groups – reservoirs of private power ungoverned by the sociopolitical order at any level.

3 – The Constitution Balanced Freedom and Order

The American community (and indeed societies everywhere) possesses a constant and legitimate need for social order and tranquility. Individuals, conversely, have a constant and legitimate interest in enlarging the sphere of personal liberty of action and expression. Nothing could be more American! At what point do the needs of society and the needs of individuals collide and become antagonistic? What government does or does not do – the activity level of the government at any moment – determines the balance between the individual freedom and social order. The nature of that balance is critical to understanding American constitutional development.

THE CONSTITUTIONAL CONVENTION

Perhaps this issue may be illustrated by placing varying degrees of government activity on a continuum. At one end of the continuum the minimal functions of government should produce the most personal liberties. The less government, the more freedom. Adding government functions beyond the minimal ones should, logically, result in less freedom. Totalitarian government, at the other end of the continuum, should result in total repression of liberty. But does it really work that way in America?

The most ardent advocates of limited government, beginning with **Thomas Carlyle** in the 18th century, suggested that at a minimum government must function as soldier, as police officer, and as judge. The first defends the nation or maintains external peace. The second maintains internal or civil peace. The third resolves problems among citizens.

In this minimal condition, government balances freedom and order, to be sure, but where is the balance? In this most *laissez faire* scenario the absence of layers of rules provides individuals with far more liberty than they would have if those rules existed; government will not abuse individual freedom. However, since government has no assigned responsibility to protect private individuals against encroachments on their liberties by their neighbors, weaker individuals may indeed be deprived of those liberties by their stronger neighbors. In this case it is the absence of government that results in restrictions of freedom, not the presence of it!

What happens if governmental functions are increased beyond the minimal three? As society adds to government's functional roles, what happens to the original balance? Does more government begin to thwart freedom? Or does one gain actual freedom by governmental protection of personal liberties?

What about government protection of individual rights and liberties against societal restrictions as in free speech, free press, petition and assembly, fair trial, due process of law, equal protection or protection of private property? What about enforcement of the civil rights laws? Are Americans freer because government protects individual rights? Or does the very assignment of protecting rights automatically limit liberty?

What about governmental functions beyond the protection of rights? Would taxation and the subsequent distribution of tax revenues for services ranging from roads, schools, and prisons, to student financial aid, medical care, and unemployment compensation shift the balance of freedom and order? What about stem cell research, the space program and subsidies to farmers? How is that balance affected by the military establishment, by warfare, homeland security, and veterans' pensions? Each person will have his or her own answer to these queries.

4 – The Constitution Provided a Basis for Continuing Allegiance.

Why should anyone beyond the generation which ratified the Constitution agree to live under the rules set down by its founding generation? Part of the reason Americans do so is pure convenience, of course. No society can rewrite its fundamental law every 25 or 30 years, can it? [Thomas Jefferson sometimes suggested that all laws expire after 18 years.]

A better reason is that the Constitution continues to embody America's core values, attitudes and ideological tenets. Those are learned, shared and transmitted to ensuing generations. The moral power of the principles located in the Constitution is real and tangible. It is embedded in the hearts and minds of Americans who have never read one syllable of the Constitution itself. We cannot fail to comprehend the validity of the Constitution as a symbol of our nation.

5 – The Constitution Accommodates Conflicting Interests inside the System

A final purpose of the Constitution, frequently overlooked, is to provide forums for resolving internal conflict among individuals, groups, or interests, without resorting to barricades, violence, or other significant disorder.

Does anyone doubt that the constitutional system reflects at any given moment the genuine power relationships in the nation. Said differently, the Constitution institutionalizes relative power in society. Hence the groups or interests with power can successfully oppose fundamental constitutional change and make it stick! Moreover, once the former "outs" muscle their way into the system they, too, become reluctant to abandon the structure which protects them.

What are the arenas in which power groups accommodate themselves to the realities of power? The major ones are fairly obvious: legislatures and courts at every level, administrative tribunals and agencies, the political process and political party platforms, local school boards, collective bargaining, protest demonstrations, college senates and every other species of participatory agency designed for conflict resolution.

THE CONSTITUTIONAL CONVENTION

In the absence of such institutions, the only resort against abuses or encroachments is to violence. Change may be conservative in these institutional settings, for the powerful rarely surrender power willingly. But it is peaceful and legitimate change!

Thus, the constitutional system is counter-revolutionary. The participatory devices established under it provide an alternative both to absolute or arbitrary power on one hand, and to riots and revolution on the other. Indeed, one of the strongest arguments for the extension of the privileges of full participation in society (voting, holding office, access to courts, equal justice, and integration) to racial minorities, women, or other groups excluded from that participation is precisely to permit redress of grievances without disorder.

Does this mean that people should gain rights so that they do not riot? Or does this mean that democracy contains the mechanisms for self-correction? Either way, or both ways, one characteristic of the Constitution is a capacity for constitutional homeostasis, a systemic flexibility to amend itself to accommodate shifts in power.

CHAPTER SEVEN: RATIFICATION AS REVOLUTION

Understanding Ratification

The process of ratifying the Constitution may be considered revolutionary in its nature.

Chapter Six demonstrated that the Constitution enacted a revolution in that it reversed the sovereignty in America from the states to the people. The framers erected powerful national institutions as the agencies of that popular sovereignty. Those actions, too, departed in revolutionary fashion from the idea that local government was best. That is even with all the compromises thrown in!

The framers clearly believed that central government, not local government, was the best government for America at this juncture in time! They also understood that most Americans would probably not agree with them; they would continue to believe that the closer government was to the people the more responsive was government to the needs of those people.

That viewpoint certainly raises a problem of what to think about the Constitution. If local accountability better represented the will of the community because it was strictly accountable to the people, then why did the framers of the Constitution think otherwise?

We address this issue by examining, all too briefly, the struggle to get the Constitution ratified. At this point every reader must understand something significant about American politics – a truth about how the American governance system functions.

This is the principle that the American system institutionalizes or internalizes conflict. That means that Americans translate our dreams and our interests into language that can be debated in forums which can resolve conflicts peacefully. Thus we can accept the results determined in those forums better than taking everything into the streets. That is, Americans do not talk in terms of naked self-interest. *"Wouldn't be prudent,"* as George Bush the First might say! Instead we translate our economic and social interests into legalistic, constitutional terms. Generally we take our interests into the political process or into the courts for peaceful resolution, instead of taking them to the streets for violent action.

We saw that process at work, for example, in the prior discussion of "taxation without representation." The same behavior is true about the Constitution, too. Once that document was sent out to the states, it became a political football. Of course the arguments for and against ratification revolved around details of the provisions of the proposed Constitution, about good government, the rights of the people, the powers of the states and powers of the United States. But make no mistake! These arguments disguised people's interests, people's fears about their future, and their sense of whether they would better off under the old system then in place or the new one under consideration.

The struggle over ratification should remind us about how people of various regions divided over the American Revolution. If the concept of "Who Should Rule At Home" operated in the decision to choose independence or to choose the Crown, that same process also operated in regard to ratification of the Constitution!

We might like to think that the Constitution got voted up or down on its own merits. But that would imply a totally unrealistic view of politics. People voted yes or no on practical considerations. Would their interests be protected better if the Constitution passed? Or would the power structure serve their interests better if it continued as it was? Look past the arguments. Look instead at the quality of people's vision of the future and their estimate, their gamble, about the success of their self interests in that future.

Criticisms of the Constitution

Generally, we can say that people who favored the Articles of Confederation also opposed the Constitution. The believers in local government opposed central or national government. Thus it is useful to examine the criticisms of the Constitution levelled by the anti-Constitution people. And how did the pro-Constitution framers respond to each significant criticism?

Criticism 1: The Country is Too Large For Any Central Government to Be Accountable to the People

RATIFICATION AS REVOLUTION

Anti-Constitution people thought no central government could govern a nation as huge as the United States. It was just too big. The very idea of local government assumed that no government could manage large areas and distant places without getting out of touch with the folks back home. The very size of the land mass of America required local government. In a large nation there was no way to make the government accountable. It would be too remote. How could anyone from New Hampshire possibly understand the issues of folks from South Carolina? How could rural people from western Virginia possibly be sensitive to the needs of urban Boston? America had already become a gigantic nation, a far flung one, too.

Implicit in this anti-Constitution criticism lurked the thought that representatives of the people who are not continually and instantly accountable to their constituents will yield to corruption. They will succumb to their personal self-interests, rather than the needs of the good people who put them into power. They will give in to pressure groups. They may even take bribes, steal, or otherwise fall victim to the blandishments of lobbyists and favor-seekers. Power corrupts, after all. Or so they said!!

How did James Madison answer that criticism? Consider the analysis of the Father of the Constitution. In **Federalist Paper #10** Madison argued that to enlarge the area governed by the nation would actually increase the likelihood that no one "**faction**," no one interest group, no single dominant point of view would capture public policy matters. In a small district, the dominant local interest – industry, family, church, even race – could rule without opposition. In a large nation, however, nobody could get control of policy except the majority point of view.

That was because, declared Madison, there were lots more interest groups or "factions" in a large area than existed in a small area. The more diverse the interest groups that were encompassed in the governing area, the better the chance there would be to play one off against the other. Interests would have to compete with each other. They would neutralize each other's power. The coal industry in West Virginia, to use a contemporary example, could dominate the policies of that state. But in a national setting they would have to compete with environmentalists in California and oil producers in Texas.

In a large area, Madison averred, no one interest group could control government decisions; only the majority. Legislation would thus not favor interests but rather the whole populace. The Constitution, presiding over all local divisions, would be more representative of everyone's needs than any local government or state government possibly could. One might hear Madison's earlier arguments against state-based power echoing in

RATIFICATION AS REVOLUTION

Federalist #10. That essay remains one of the most significant American contributions to western political thought.

Criticism 2: Terms of Office Too Long

A second criticism leveled by opponents of the Constitution, whom we may now call **Antifederalists,** was that the terms of office, especially for United States Senators and President were too long. Worse, there were no guarantees of rotation in office. The same people could get reelected over and over! There were no term limits. Some Antifederalists even took the idea of local accountability to the degree that they wanted to be able to instruct their representatives how to vote on issues before Congress.

Why did Antifederalists want short terms and term limits? They argued that government officers would tyrannize, or become corrupt. People fear what will happen the minute their representatives are out of sight. Historian **Cecelia Kenyon** originated the analysis that such a skeptical and suspicious viewpoint is simply not a democratic attitude. "Men of Little Faith," she designated them. Gerber agrees whole-heartedly with her perspective. Distrust stiffles delegate responsibility, that precious deliberative function of government, and discounts the wisdom and experience gained in government service. Isn't it far more democratic to trust the people you elect to speak and act for you than to hamstring them at every turn? If Americans want a person to be President four times in a row, why should we not have the right to elect him? Or her? To act otherwise denies the majority its will! And being opposed to majority will is quite the reverse of being democratic.

Criticism 3 – The National Government Should Not Use the Militia to Enforce National Laws

Anti-Constitution forces also opposed the use of the militia by the national government to enforce national laws. Why? The law and the militia that enforces the law act on individuals, please remember, who refuse to accept the law as made by the representatives of the majority. They could be Whiskey Rebels. Or they could be Governor George Wallace of Alabama, standing in the schoolhouse door to keep African-American children from integrating the schools. Or they could be the Ku Klux Klan. Or they could be (and were) Southern secessionists. The point is that coercion of recalcitrant persons opposed to majority will could only be rejected by people who did not want the majority will to be enforced. Once again, Kenyon and Gerber observe, if you are opposed to majority will, then you are one who is undemocratic.

Criticism 4 – The National Government Should Not Have Power to Tax

RATIFICATION AS REVOLUTION

Similarly, anti-Constitution people opposed the government's power to tax. Why? It is the same reason as they gave in criticisms 2 and 3 above. The decisions about who pays what taxes and also about the use of the money collected by taxation is a majority decision. And only fear of what the majority will do through their representatives lies behind this opposition. Again, an undemocratic attitude.

Criticism 5 – Why No Opposition to the Supreme Court?

If the local government people were so concerned about accountability to the folks back home, why didn't they oppose the Supreme Court? It is absolutely fascinating that they only very rarely did not do so. The Court was and remains the one agency of American national government which is the least responsive to local control and popular will. It was deliberately set up to be exempt from popular attitudes and shifting public opinion. The framers established an indep[endent judiciary. On purpose. Every confirmation hearing from John Jay to most recent Samuel Alito underscores that judicial independence.

It is perhaps astonishing that Antifederalists remained mostly silent about this most non-accountable national agency. It is possible that they did not foresee the Supreme Court's role in the constitutional system as particularly significant; even some framers felt the Court would be "the least dangerous branch." Nontheless, for people whose prime concern was about holding government officials accountable for their actions in office, the absence of comment about the Court certainly appears inconsistent with their stated principles.

Criticism 6 – No Bill of Rights

In one area the anti-Constitution movement did make headway. That was in extracting a promise of a Bill of Rights. They had severely criticized the Constitution for failing to provide any Bill of Rights. Without such a written Bill, they said, the new government would encroach on the liberties of the people.

Why had the framers not included a bill of rights? The best answer to this charge came from George Washington and from James Wilson of Pennsylvania. They answered that to enumerate the rights in a list of the Rights of the people was to limit them to the rights on the list.

In **Common Law** practice, if one wrote a list of rights and left something out, then it was assumed that the omission was intentional and deliberate, that one meant to leave that item off the list. Moreover, they argued, if rights were natural, then the Bill of Rights was unnecessary, because government could not take away natural rights even if they were not written down.

A little Latin phrase, **_expressio unius est exclusio alterius_**, captures this idea. It translates as *"the expression of one thing is the exclusion of other things not expressed."* Washington and Wilson were saying that they did not want to put any limits on individual rights by making a list and risk leaving any off. James Madison would resolve this problem by constructing the **Ninth Amendment**, which in essence declared that just in case any right had been omitted, Americans had them anyhow!

Actually, the absence of a Bill of Rights worked to the framers' advantage, because it allowed them to pledge that they would adopt such a document when the new government went into effect. This commitment was apparently a convincing argument in several state ratifying conventions.

The AntiFederalist [Anti-Constitution] Argument

Of all the anti-Constitution literature the most effective was penned by **Richard Henry Lee** of Virginia. Lee. It may be recalled, had proposed revolution in the Second Continental Congress in 1776. Lee was consistent. He argued that the Constitution aimed too strongly at one consolidated government. Lee thought centralized government dangerous to liberty. It subordinated majority will to minority will. The House of Representatives could not possibly represent everyone, because it was too small. Equal representation in the Senate was bad for the big states. Lee awaited a Bill of Rights.

Patrick Henry of Virginia summed up the matter just as well when he said: *"Who told them they could say 'We the People' Instead of We the States?"* And of course Henry was right. No one had told them. They just enacted a *coup.* The Constitution was a revolution.

Lots of additional evidence exists that anti-Constitution forces distrusted the democratic instincts of the American people. To be sure the framers were wary of majority will. They were especially concerned about interest group pressure that would threaten individual rights. At least, however, they believed that people could select wisely and well, if they were well-informed. The anti-Constitution people, conversely, were

much more fearful of the democratic instincts of the people than the framers ever were. The signers of the Declaration of Independence voted 6 to 1 in favor of the new document. Apparently they did not see any confict or inconsistency in doing that.

RATIFICATION AS REVOLUTION

It is also useful to recognize that the anti-constitutionalists were local leaders, not national ones, who stood to lose power in their communities if the Constituton passed. **George Clinton** in New York, **Patrick Henry** in Virginia, **Wyllie Jones** in North Carolina come to mind. They included folks who were occasionally rural-minded and more than occasionally anti-intellectual.

Thus the Constitution became a local issue as well as a national one. It was rarely voted up or down according to its intrinsic merits, despite all the rhetoric of the debates. A person's decision to favor ratification or not largely depended on what would happen to him and his interests if it passed or failed.

Who then, were the little "d" democrats in this ratification fight? Clearly, there were none and, indeed, there should be none! The Constitution was an 18th century document. Democracy in our sense of the word is a 19th century, and in some respects even a 21st century idea in that it is not perfected yet!   In comparing the two groups, however, the framers appear far more modern and less anti-democratic than the advocates of local government and state sovereignty. That remains the case despite the surface shine that local government is more democratic than central government.

Why Did the Constitution Pass?

Given the stark differences between the Articles of Confederation and the Constitution, and given the state of popular opinion in 1787, how did the Constitution survive the ratification process? Four primary reasons may be offered.

1 – Political Savvy

The first reason was political experience or savvy. The pro-Constitution nationalists put themselves in the position of assuring the American people that the nation and they themselves would be safe under the Constitution. They were simply brilliant at making this case! Nowhere is this brilliance better portrayed than in the **Federalist Papers**. These documents examined every nook and cranny of the new Constitution and expounded some of the most intelligent political theory ever produced.

The Federalist Papers were 85 long editorials written for the people of New York State to try to persuade them to ratify the new Constitution. **James Madison** wrote 29 of these, including that critical #10. **Alexander** Hamilton wrote 51. If you ever read them, you will never think of him as a closet monarchist again! **John Jay** wrote 5. That does add up to 85. Jay would become America's first Chief Justice. Does the evolution of the Supreme Court from Chief Justice John Jay to Chief Justice John Roberts suggest that Darwin was wrong?

The central thesis of the Federalist Papers, taken together, was that the rights of individual citizens were best protected by national government. Not by state or local government. The government closest to the people could most easily harm them. National government, acting uniformly on everyone everywhere, would protect rights which local majorities might deny their neighbors. The national government provided more rights as well.

That principle is still true today. The United States government has been the progressive force in expanding individual rights throughout the span of American history. It continues so today. Who lynches people, local mobs or the national government? Who denies rights based on race or religion or gender or age or other arbitrary differences? The United States or the states? If you get caught speeding in the sticks what rights will you have? You have whatever they give you. Remember the movie, "My Cousin Vinny?" Go into federal court, however, and you have every right under the Constitution. That can be in Montana or Alabama or even Connecticut.

The old argument that local government was best was precisely what Madison wished to protect against when he argued in Federalist #10 that for majority will to work one faction must be countered by another, so that no geographical position, or class position, or moneyed position, or racial position, would dominate. One would hardly argue that the national government was never guilty of abuse of individual rights; the record is replete with instances of bad behavior, from the **Alien and Sedition Acts** of the Adams administration to the invasions of privacy under the current **USA PATRIOT Act**. Uncle Sam has been responsible for his share of abuses. But compared to abuses of rights at the state government level or the local level, the United States government has been a veritable saint!

2 – The Nationalists Had a Positive Program

Second, the nationalists had a positive program to offer, namely, the Constitution. They drew a terrifying picture of the results of rejection: monetary chaos, national bankruptcy, division of the Confederation into parts, easily swallowed up by Britain or some other foreign power or allied to different foreign powers. The anti-Consitution people had no tangible response to the proposed Constitution. They had no alternative program to offer, except some patchwork for the Articles of

RATIFICATION AS REVOLUTION

Confederation. The pro-Constitution "Federalists" had seized the momentum.

3 – Method of Ratification Favored Ratification

Third, the method of ratification, the procedure set up for ratification, also favored ratification. Constitutional conventions were elected the same way as state legislatures. Remember that in state legislatures the western areas, the backcountry, were under-represented. Yet that is where so many Antifederalists came from. That under-representation now carried over to the ratifying conventions. This gave the folks in the tidewater, where pro-Constitution Federalists came from, more weight in those conventions than their numbers may have deserved.

Similarly, property requirements for voting sometimes disqualified the landless and propertyless groups, among whom sentiment against the Constitution was also strong. Again that was because the suffrage qualifications for the constitutional ratifying conventions remained the same as state legislatures.

Nobody rigged this process. It was simply the most convenient way to handle the situation. Please note also that only one-fourth of those who could vote for delegates to the ratifying conclaves, took the trouble to do so. Were they apathetic even in the face of such a momentous decision? Why would they be?

4 – Prestige of the Pro-Constitution Proponents

Fourth, and finally, the prestige of proponents of the Constitution, including most of the framers themselves, was a major factor. People said if the Constitution was good enough for Washington or Franklin or Madison or Jay, then it's good enough for me! Apparently many Americans held significant public figures in high esteem. Their endorsement persuaded many a fence-sitter to take a chance on the new document.

State Ratifications

Delaware was the first state to ratify the Constitution, on December 7, 1787. Then came Pennsylvania. That state was significant, because of the power and size of the Keystone State. Then New Jersey, Georgia and Connecticut. However, key states had still not yet ratified. Massachusetts, Virginia, and New York. The nine needed states could have ratified the Constitution, but without any one of these big three, the entire enterprise would likely have collapsed. America could not truly be a country without Virginia or Massachusetts or New York.

In Massachusetts the main opponents were two powerful revolutionary period characters John Hancock and Samuel Adams. The nationalists won Hancock over by promising him the Governorship. He decided that well, maybe, the Constitution might not be so bad after all. Politician all the way! Adams caved in with the promise of a Bill of Rights, a tribute to his growth and the political realism that was always his trademark.

In Virginia, there were three major opponents. Patrick Henry, as one might expect, given his previous attitudes about the convention and its outcomes opposed the Constitution and could not be won over. Richard Henry Lee, whose anti-Constitution comments have been noted, also opposed the new Constitution. Strangely, **Edmund Randolph**, who had been Madison's spokesman in the Constitutional Convention also now opposed ratification. However, the nationalists had even more powerful figures on their side.

They had everybody's father-figure, **George Washington**. Washington represented continuous leadership from the War for Independence, through the Confederation period, to the presidency of the Philadelphia Convention. Americans generally thought that Washington would be the first President of the United States, if the Constitution passed. For many that thought comforted them into voting for the document. Everywhere he traveled, people placed signs, "George Washington Slept Here!" If he had, indeed, slept in all those beds, he really might have been the father of our country. "First in War, First in Peace, First in the Hearts of His Countrymen," the saying about Washington was spoken. But Washington wasn't always first; he married a widow!

The pro-Constitution side also had James Madison, the head framer, perhaps the brainiest of all. They also had a youngster named **John Marshall,** who, as Chief Justice, would have as much to say about the content of the Constitution as any of them. In Virginia, the promised Bill of Rights seemed to do the trick. And thus the Constitution passed in Virginia. Close vote, but they ratified it!

In New York the struggle boiled down to a personal contest between George Clinton versus and Alexander Hamilton. Hamilton used his political talent to stall the ratifying vote until just the right instant, until the news of Virginia's ratification arrived. Then he somhow compelled a vote. New York ratified the Constitution by a vote of 30 - 27. A masterful feat. A mere two votes cast the other way and New York would have failed to ratify and there would have been no viable Constitution. The Empire State's ratification insured not just the majority, but the solidity of the significant states behind the new document. New York was actually the 11th state to ratify, but there would have been no nation without New York in it, no matter what the others did. It was an occasion to rejoice.

Rhode Island voted the Constitution down! It was not until the state was threatened with permanent exclusion from the new nation and a trade boycott to boot that they finally caved in and voted yes.

A careful analysis of the distribution of votes throughout each of the thirteen state reflects the political prowess of the pro-Constitution nationalists. They succeeded in polling their votes in just the right places. Passage of the Constitution was a remarkable achievement. The nationalists won ratification of a document whose principles would have been unthinkable to most Americans.

The Constitution Takes Effect

In January of 1789 George Washington of Virginia was chosen by the first set of presidential electors as the first president of the United States. It was a unanimous vote; every elector voted for Washington. John Adams, who received far fewer votes than Washington, but enough to claim a majority, was elected Vice President. Washington was inaugurated on April 30, 1789. The duly elected Congress had opened its inaugural session during the first week of April.

It might be noted that on November 1, 1788, with enough states having ratified the Constitution, the old Congress of the Confederation adjourned for the final time. This means that from November 1788 until April 1789, the United States had no central government at all! Did anyone notice?

The Constitution went into effect amid great rejoicing around the country. A revolution if there ever was one had been pulled off! It is significant that this revolution from local autonomy to continental vision had occurred peacefully. Once in place the new Constitution seemed to be accepted by just about everybody. Even amid the party wars of the Jeffersonian era, when political tempers were at their hottest, nobody proposed scrapping the document. Not until 1861 anyhow.

To sum up: the Constitution overturned those objectives of the American Revolution that harked backward to the pre-1763 period of local autonomy. The Constitution was not backward-yearning. It was not nostalgic, like the Articles of Confederation.

The Constitution was instead a document in tune with its times. It retained the republican thrust of the revolution. Simultaneously   it responded to real problems posed by the issues of the moment. As with all constitutions this one embodied the interests of the those who held power. Over time those interests – grounded in individual rights and liberties – would become the interests of every American.

Of course the Constitution could hardly cover every contingency. No provisions was made, for example, for emergency conditions. This author finds agreement with historians who say that the Constitution was deliberately made flexible to cover future changes. Immediately, the issues of the early republic would test that flexibility. Could the constitutional system called into being by the newly ratified document cover new contingencies and still continue the original intent of the framers?

CHAPTER EIGHT: COMPLETING THE AMERICAN REVOLUTION

The American Revolution did not end with formal independence from Great Britain. The War for Independence certainly resulted in nationhood, but the full establishment of republican principles would take nearly another generation. The Revolution did not end with the enactment of the Constitution, either. Some even contend that the Revolution will never be fulfilled until every American is guaranteed the justice of individual rights. This chapter takes a somewhat shorter perspective. The implementation of majoritarian governance following the election of Thomas Jefferson in 1800 offers a convenient moment to consider the Founders' revolution concluded.

Three significant milestones following ratification convey us to the completion of the American Revolution: (1) the **Judiciary Act of 1789 and Judicial Review**; (2) the **Bill of Rights of 1791**; and (3) the **Election of 1800,** in what historian Susan Dunn calls "Jefferson's Second Revolution."

1 – The Judiciary Act of 1789 and Judicial Review

The powers of the Supreme Court are both written and unwritten. The written or stated powers of the Supreme Court are enumerated – and hence limited – in Article III of the Constitution. They may be examined by any reader; they need not be reiterated in this chapter. Because the Supreme Court serves as the arbiter of the individual rights of Americans, the development of the Court is integral to the fulfillment of the concept of the American Revolution.

As to unwritten powers it should be observed that the Supreme Court changes constitutional law only very slowly and deliberately. The Court only hears what comes to it. There must be a real issue with real persons involved. There are no trumped up cases to be decided because the Justices wish to make a ruling. Thus Supreme Court decisions are for specific instances. They do not automatically cover similar circumstances,

112

unless the Court says they do. Consequently, there is very slow progress in changing constitutional law. Moreover, if the Supreme Court can find some way to decide a case on grounds other than by interpreting a constitutional provision, it will do so. That also means that there is very slow progress in changing the law.

Further, the Court uses the doctrine of precedent, technically *stare decisis*, the Latin phrase that means "let the decision stand." Once the high Court makes a ruling, that ruling binds every single Court in the United States, including the Supreme Court itself. In order to overturn a precedent, cases with slightly different fact situations must be heard and slight alterations made, until the original ruling has been reversed. This is another reason that constitutional law changes so slowly. There are exceptions, of course: *West Coast Hotel v. Parrish* (1937) is a clear one, as is *Brown v. Board of Education* (1954) – are rare birds, indeed.

The prime reason for this piecemeal, sometimes even imperceptible, rate of change is that the Supreme Court has no enforcement power. It has no credibility beyond the moral acceptance of the American people. Americans accept Court rulings essentially because of their faith in the constitutional system. That is true even if we detest particular decisions.

The Unwritten Power – Judicial Review

The primary unwritten power of the Supreme Court is the power of **judicial review of legislation**. Or just judicial review! Is a law of a state or a law of Congress constitutional? The notion of judicial review is the process for making that determination. There is no mention of judicial review anywhere in the Constitution. It is quite possible that the Framers simply assumed by implication that the Supreme Court would exercise this certainly customary practice. In any event the Court began to exercise judicial review in the early days of the new nation.

The authority of the Court to match state or federal law against a provision of the Constitution and hence to determine the consistency or inconsistency of the two has over the course of American history become the plenary power of the Supreme Court. The Supreme Court determines if a law is constitutional or not. This power extends both to state and local laws and to congressional statutes.

English precedent for the process of judicial review was well known to the Framers (and indeed it was well known in the colonial period and during the years of the Confederation). **Sir Edward Coke** (pronounced Cook), as Chief Justice of the **Court of King's Bench**, the highest English criminal court, early in the 17th century had been the first to claim the judicial liberty of declaring a law unconstitutional. This was in the famous *Dr. Bonham's Case* of 1610. American jurists were familiar with the Bonham precedent and those English precedents that followed. American lawyers studied Coke's decisions and knew well the notion of judicial review.

In the early years of the republic there was a competitor for determining constitutionality. Presidential veto was originally anticipated by the framers for use in cases in which the Chief Executive believed a law unconstitutional. Washington used the veto once. Neither John Adams nor Thomas Jefferson ever exercised the veto. The idea of vetoing a law because it was unconstitutional has since fallen into total oblivion once President **Andrew Jackson** converted the constitutional veto into a policy veto in the 1830s. Today the veto is used only because a President disagrees with a statute – never because he thinks it unconstitutional. It took until the end of the nineteenth century before the Supreme Court was deemed to be the sole and exclusive interpreter of the Constitution through the exercise of judicial review. Today that power is unchallenged.

Supreme Court Appellate Jurisdiction

The other primary power of the Court is in fact written, but not in the Constitution. Instead it is located in the **Judiciary Act of 1789**, arguably the most significant law ever passed by Congress. In **Section 25** of the Judiciary Act, Congress permitted appeals from the Supreme Courts of the several States into the federal court system and ultimately to the United State Supreme Court.

This appellate power shifted power away from the states, as noted in Article VI of the Constitution, into the United States. The judges in every state would now be subject to having their decisions reviewed by the Supreme Court. Section 25 thereby created a single uniform interpretation of the Constitution, applicable in every state. It converted thirteen – now fifty – state interpretations of a constitutional provision which might vary widely from state to state into one interpretation to be followed in every judicial jurisdiction under the Constitution.

With some irony the Supreme Court upheld the constitutionality of Section 25, the Court's appellate jurisdiction, in the case of *Cohens v. Virginia* (1821). Can anyone imagine the Supreme Court denying Congress's power to grant that very Supreme Court the power to hear appeals from the state courts? Gerber cannot. Neither could Chief Justice John Marshall.

COMPLETING THE AMERICAN REVOLUTION

Theories of Interpreting the Constitution

There are several ways in which the Supreme Court interprets the Constitution. Some Justices prefer the doctrine of "**original intent**." One can determine whether a law is constitutional by examining just what the Framers originally intended by a particular clause when they wrote the Constitution. In this view changing conditions, not even significant issues needing constitutional solutions, do not affect the literal meaning of what the framers ordained.

By this strict definition only oral or written statements would be considered free speech. Interstate Commerce would be defined to shipping only. Of course the Constitution may be changed by amendment, but not by reinterpreting or altering the meaning of the words of the document to meet current circumstances. Could it occur that if the Constitution retained only its 18th century meaning, and lost its flexibility, that it would have to be trashed in favor of a new document that would appreciate current times?

The opposite view may be called "**judicial pragmatism**." This viewpoint holds that the words of the Constitution, even in the absence of formal amendments, must from time to time be revised to meet circumstances. In our own day the invention of symbolic speech is such an example. The interpretation of the Interstate Commerce clause includes banning racial discrimination in businesses open to the public. How far the Justices should go in this process of reinterpretation remains an open question. Might a moment arrive when the original Constitution has been so totally reinterpreted that it no longer means anything the framers had in mind?

However it occurred, today the United States Supreme Court is the exclusive interpreter of the Constitution. The American public no longer challenges the Court's jurisdiction. Americans of the 21st century cannot imagine it any other way.

Early Instances of Judicial Review

The first instance under the Constitution of the exercise of judicial review brought upon appeal from a state Supreme Court occurred in 1792. When the legislature of Rhode Island, pressured by poor farmers, passed a law that permitted debtors three extra years to repay their debts, the U.S. Circuit Court for that region declared that state law invalid in *Champion v. Casey (1792).* The state law, the Court ruled, violated Article I, Section

10 of the Constitution. That clause expressly prohibits any state from impairing the obligation of a contract. The government of Rhode Island could not interfere with contracts made between debtors and creditors. That law was unconstitutional.

The initial instance in which a congressional statute was declared unconstitutional occurred in the famous case of *Marbury v. Madison (1803).* Without reciting the familiar facts of *Marbury*, we note that the Marshall Court invalidated **Section 13 of the Judiciary Act of 1789** because Section 13 gave the Court authority to perform judicial functions not specified in Article III, Section 2 of the Constitution.

It is a common myth to think that the *Marbury* decision was the first case of judicial review. It was not. It certainly was the first instance of **negative** congressional judicial review. However, the Supreme Court had already declared several statutes passed by Congress to be constitutional. *Hylton v. U.S.* (1796) was one prime example.

The Rise of Judicial Review

The spectacular rise of negative judicial review – the cases in which the Supreme Court declared laws unconstitutional – deserves mention. Between 1789 and 1864 the Court invalidated only two laws of Congress and thirty nine state laws. Between 1864 and 1954, some sixty nine federal statutes failed constitutional muster, while 413 state laws were declared unconstitutional. Since 1954 there have been 95 congressional statutes and 1125 state laws declared unconstitutional. Please note that this total of 1301 does not include the huge majority of cases in which the Supreme Court held state and federal statute to be constitutional. As you read this, the numbers may have already changed.

One issue can be raised about this judicial takeover of the role of the Supreme Court as exclusive constitutional interpreter. What if the Court makes decisions dramatically in conflict with the will of the American people? This is not to suggest that they would or that they do; constitutional law moves but slowly, as noted. But raising a constitutional "what if" is certainly appropriate. Is there a remedy for judicial over-reaching within the scope of the Constitution? Or would "we the people" be stuck with a form of judicial tyranny that we would never accept from an arbitrary President? Perhaps we might phrase this query by asking whether the agencies of the government, established by the consent of the governed to defend our rights and freedoms, can take precedence over the will of the American people. If so, what can we do about it?

COMPLETING THE AMERICAN REVOLUTION

Conclusions

Two brief conclusions may be drawn from this discussion of the role of the Supreme Court in the American constitutional system:

1 – The Supreme Court is the exclusive interpreter of the Constitution. While this development reached fulfillment only in the late nineteenth century, that role is challenged today only most rarely and without effect. Americans continue to view the Justices as black-robed moguls, above the fray of political battle, and acting in accord with constitutional principles. To imagine that Supreme Court Justices have no ideologies, however, is incomprehensible. Justices may cloak their ideas in judicial reasoning but they have political agendas, even if they are not overtly Republicans or Democrats, in their decision-making.

The Court has acquired tremendous power. The Framers would have shaken their heads in disbelief! They expected Congress to be the dominant branch of government in the constitutional system. Thus the Constitution means what the Supreme Court says it means. The document says what the Justices say it says. The Court's interpretations can remain moored to the literal words of the Constitution or the Justices can fashion it according to current circumstances as they determine. But what they decide is the constitutional law of America.

2 – Supreme Court decisions have extended individual rights to Americans from 1789 to the current day. Of course the Bill of Rights – to be examined next – had to be in place for this extension to occur. From the early days under the Constitution, when only white male property owners possessed rights, the Court has constantly extended liberties to additional groups of Americans. The Court has made frequent decisions that uphold congressional statutes which confer rights, such as the Civil Rights Act of 1866 or the Civil Rights Act of 1964. The Justices have also decided cases that protect the rights of individuals against the wishes of state legislatures. Despite some backsliding, the Supreme Court has been the primary bulwark against arbitrary and discriminatory acts by state governments.

For example, the high Court has extended the protection of property rights, broadened the definitions of free speech, strengthened due process of law, and defined expansively the equal protection of the laws. It has expanded freedom of religion, the rights of persons accused of crimes, the rights of women, and surely the rights of racial minorities. Therefore, the rise of the Supreme Court's power to protect the rights of

117

COMPLETING THE AMERICAN REVOLUTION

Americans deserves to be included in one of the milestones in the completion of the American Revolution.

There is delicious irony in that the branch of government least accountable to the American public, and deliberately structured so, has emerged as the protector of our sacred individual rights.

2 – The Bill of Rights (1791)

The anti-Constitution forces have earlier been described as distrustful of representative government. Their fear of the new central government and their devotion to local government came from the same suspicion of what their representatives would do the moment they got out of sight. They had demanded a written **Bill of Rights** as a condition of ratification of the Constitution, to protect the civil liberties -- or shall we say "natural rights" of the people.

It may also be recalled that the Framers had thought a list of written guarantees would limit the people's liberties only to those listed. By Common Law practice, if a right were omitted, it would be assumed that the omission was deliberate and that the right did not exist. No "whoops, we forgot" would be allowed!

In any event following ratification of the Constitution **states' rights** advocates (we can now use that term) renewed their demands for a written Bill of Rights. They claimed they wished for a list of rights and liberties. And that is precisely what they got. The Washington Administration now delivered on its promise.

But were individual rights what the states' rights folks really wanted? The various state ratifying conventions submitted some 210 constitutional amendment proposals to Congress, of which approximately 80 were left after all the duplicates were deleted. Most of these tried to weaken the Constitution by diluting national power, because the local autonomy forces (we can still use that term) were hardly ready to roll over and play dead. Many others masked some illiberality, even outright bigotry, in the name of local government and civil liberties.

As one example, liberty-loving New Englanders proposed to remove the constitutional prohibition against religious tests for holding office, because, they claimed, the provision opened the door "to Jews, Turks and infidels" to infiltrate the government. Echoes of those views can still be heard in the more strident right-wing fundamentalist political movements of the 21st century.

COMPLETING THE AMERICAN REVOLUTION

Indeed, most amendments suggested by the state conventions were not even remotely related to the issues of civil liberties, but were another attempt to damage the kind of government they had been unable to defeat at ratification. Every state convention, for example, recommended restrictions on the new government's power to tax. Every state proposed that powers not delegated to the central government be reserved to the states. There were proposals for state control of the militia, proposals for increasing the number of members of Congress, proposals for curtailing the power of the national judiciary, and so on.

Some of these proposals may have been legitimate positions. Some even good ideas. But they have nothing to do with rights and liberties. They were unrelated to free speech, freedom of religion, free press, due process of law, trial by jury, the right against self-incrimination, the right to counsel, or any of the other guarantees one thinks about as civil liberties or natural rights.

In Congress, Representative James Madison of Virginia again took the leadership for steering a genuine Bill of Rights through the legislative process. Madison was resolved that no set of amendments would weaken the anatomy of the new system. As prime architect of that system, through the Virginia Plan, he would have been inconsistent if he now altered his stance or narrowed his vision about the transfer of sovereignty to the national regime or the specific construction of the government under the Constitution. He saw his task as reconciling liberty and authority, or, if one prefers, freedom and order. Madison determined to confine the amendments to the relatively harmless subject of rights and liberties.

From the **Virginia Bill of Rights of 1776**, written by **George Mason**, Madison drew eight amendments which constitute the original eight of the Constitution's Bill of Rights. He said he intended to guarantee the "inalienable rights of man" without impairing the necessary powers of the national government. In addition, Madison also proposed what are now the 9th and 10th amendments to the Constitution. These do not properly belong to the Bill of Rights, but we have gotten used to thinking of the first ten amendments under that title. Every reader should have a clear grasp of the guarantees contained in those amendments.

It should be noted that the rights located in the Bill of Rights were directed only at the U.S. government, not the states. "Congress shall make no law respecting the establishment of religion..." declared the First Amendment, for example. But presumably a state could make such a law. The U.S. government cannot deprive a person of "life, liberty or property," says the Fifth Amendment, but a state could deprive someone, if it chose to do so. An analogous parallel may be made for the others as well. The guarantees of the Bill of Rights were finally made applicable to the states by judicial rulings only in the 1960s!

The 9th Amendment

The 9th Amendment was designed to avoid the possibility that any liberty not written would be lost, that any right not listed or enumerated would cease to be a right. The amendment declares that "the enumeration in this Constitution, of certain rights, shall not be construed to deny or disparage others retained by the people." Or, more colloquially, just in case we forgot any rights, we still have them! Madison knew that not all rights would or could be written. The 9th Amendment has never, or almost never, been used in the long history of cases coming before the Supreme Court, perhaps vindicating the framers in their belief that unwritten rights were nevertheless enforceable rights. The 9th Amendment remains the written repository of unwritten rights.

The 10th Amendment

There is considerable confusion about the 10th Amendment -- the so-called **Reserve Clause**: "Powers not delegated to the United States by the Constitution, nor prohibited to it by the states, are reserved to the states, respectively, or to the people." The Amendment was simply intended to contain the national government inside its allotted jurisdiction. But it was **not** intended to confine that sphere to only those stated powers originally granted under the Constitution. The author of the Virginia plan and his nationalistic colleagues of 1791 would not have reversed their intellectual position suddenly to favor states' rights.

It is a product of historical development that as sectional issues grew to dominate American politics through the course of the pre-Civil War America, the 10th Amendment became a keystone of the states' rights interpretation of the Constitution. As originally written Congress had no intention that the amendment give states new powers or weaken those of the national government. It would have been totally inconsistent with the idea of implied power, for example, if they had.

The 10th amendment does not (and cannot) answer the critical question of whether a particular power (whether enumerated or implied) had been "delegated" to the national government. It says only that whatever those powers were, the other powers were reserved. And, let us note, they were reserved not merely to the states, but also to the people. We may be used to hearing states' rights advocates insist that the 10th amendment made implied powers illegal so frequently that we may forget that the original conception contradicts their interpretation entirely.

Conclusions

It is critical to recall that Madison and Congress believed in inherent national power. They had struggled long and hard to achieve that goal in the Constitution. They were not likely to throw it away by any misplaced phrase in any amendment, or by approving proposals to weaken national power.

When the amendments passed through Congress, states' rights proponents who had made a Bill of Rights their good reason, but not their real reason, for opposing the Constitution and the new government, now found themselves embarrassed to discover that the new Bill of Rights did indeed deal with rights and liberties. They had been outflanked, outmaneuvered by Madison. Without curtailing any of the sovereign powers of the national government, Madison had taken away their most potent weapon against the implementation of the Constitution.

Perhaps it might be suggested that the Bill of Rights did not genuinely change anything of substance. To have written guarantees made those rights no more substantial than had they remained unwritten. The liberties of the Bill of Rights were taken for granted, whatever anxieties Americans may have about them in the absence of written documents. As a political ploy the Bill of Rights was brilliant. Writing down fundamental rights made people feel better – then and now. The Bill of Rights qualifies as a major milestone in completing the American Revolution.

3 – The Election of 1800

This analysis of the election of 1800 raises issues about the effectiveness of the political process, the role of the **Electoral College**, and the impact of this significant and pivotal election in completing the objectives of the American Revolution. Because that election resulted in implanting the idea of majority government – perhaps planting the seeds of the idea of democracy – it makes it into the milestone category.

Americans frequently feel disappointed by the quality of our Presidents. Why don't we elect noble, experienced, principled Chief Executives? It is Gerber's contention that a large reason for this is that there is a huge mismatch between the constitutional ideals of the framers and our current political process.

The vision of the American revolutionaries, that precious ideal of the establishment of a republic, was continued and strengthened by the framers of the Constitution. Republicanism, however, was more than merely a substitution of an elective system for kingship. It was more than scrapping the Crown, the hereditary aristocracy, the standing army, and the established religious hierarchy.

There was a moral dimension to the constitutional process. The original intent of the Framers anticipated that elected Presidents would be able to rise above their personal self-interest, rise above state and local and regional interests, rise even above the interests of those who voted for them. Presidents would be "disinterested" [not "uninterested"]. They would act for the benefit of the entire nation, not their popularity. Presidents would act on wisdom, on virtue, on high-mindedness, on principles, with vision, and with the values of good character and integrity.

Moreover, the Philadelphia conventioneers absolutely never envisioned presidents as leaders of political parties. They did not anticipate large organizations, representing shifting majorities, with interest-oriented programs to enact on behalf of the majority of American public. The adversarial nature of political parties, the Framers believed, would only divide the nation, not unify it. The Constitution, as a consequence, does not account for political parties.

The Electoral College and Political Parties

Would the Framers have constructed the Electoral College if they anticipated the power of political parties? Was that an oversight? Or was it a "Founding Blunder" as Yale Law Professor Bruce Ackerman calls it? Or were they, as Gerber believes, enacting their ideal, their vision?

Our current political process, by contrast, is built precisely on serving the will of the majority interests, the majority party, in any presidential election. Elections are deliberately adversarial. The collective interests of the majority party rules! Presidents who emerge from this political process are the products of compromises, deals, and political coalitions that must be satisfied. Redeeming campaign pledges for the voters who elected them frequently trumps principles and national needs. Political parties, of course, are the life-blood of our political system. We could hardly do without them today. Surely, however, they stand in stark contrast to the original views of the framers.

COMPLETING THE AMERICAN REVOLUTION

When and how did this conversion in the constitutional process occur? How did it happen that the constitutional system shifted from what Gerber calls a "government of public virtue" to what he calls "a government of majority interests?" This chapter contends that the conversion occurred with the Election of 1800. That election revolutionized the system from "a government of public virtue" to "a government of majority interests."

Before examining that election we need to dwell briefly on the Electoral College. Because of the current common and persistent claims of dissatisfaction with the Electoral College, one critical point must be made: that device was created because the nationalists in the Constitutional Convention could not get a majority of states to support direct popular election of the President. Direct elections, as in Madison's Virginia Plan, would have given the preponderance of power to the most populous states at the expense of states with sparse populations.

The Electoral College was also a method of preventing Congress from electing the President, or even worse from the Framers' viewpoint, of having the state legislatures do it! The Electoral College was the second choice of people attempting to settle this thorny constitutional issue. It was never designed to prevent the people of the United States from electing the President, because a straight popular vote is exactly what Madison had wanted. We must finally abandon that choice fiction.

Nonetheless, the Electoral College provisions would cause electoral complications once political parties came into being, particularly in the Election of 1800.

In the original Electoral College each elector would cast two votes for President. Only one vote could be cast for a candidate from the elector's home state. The second vote would overcome the problem of multiple favorite-sons. Whoever received the most electoral votes – assuming that someone received a majority of votes cast -- would be President. The second biggest vote-getter would be Vice President. No political parties – no problem!

But with political parties in operation the Vice President would very likely be the defeated candidate of the opposite party, a circumstance hardly calculated to bring about a government of "public virtue." Thus, the Republican Thomas Jefferson became the Federalist John Adams's Vice President in the election of 1796. This situation could prove most troublesome if a President should die in office, troublesome in terms of the continuity of administration and policy, to say nothing of the wishes of the voting public.

Furthermore, the Constitution charged the President of the Senate, officially the Vice President of the U.S., to receive and count the electoral votes. Jefferson would count his own votes in 1800. Al Gore would count his in 2000. Would anyone today establish a system in which a candidate for President counted his own and his opponent's electoral votes? Certainly not if there were political parties to factor in!

The procedure for breaking tie votes was also unusual. Tied votes required the House of Representatives to break the tie by a vote by state: one state, one vote. How curious for the "Peoples' House," where congressmen were elected on the basis of population! If presidential candidates tied with a majority of the votes needed for election, the run-off in the House would be only for the top two. If candidates were tied without a majority, or if no one had a majority, the House could consider the top five candidates.

Whether to count two candidates or five would also emerge as a problem in 1800. The Constitution bids the House of Representatives to act immediately upon notification of the results of the vote. Thus a further complication arose, because of the constitutional provision by which the new Congress did not meet until roughly thirteen months after its election. The House of Representatives breaking the tie was the outgoing House, the **Lame Duck** House, not the House elected with the next President, whoever that was. Should a run-off include five candidates, the House majority of states could quite possibly elect someone with very little support in the popular election They could even elect the defeated candidate of their own defeated party. This, too, nearly occurred in 1800.

The Election of 1800

At last to the Election of 1800! Again, that contest should be understood as a defining moment in American constitutional history. Thomas Jefferson had won a convincing popular majority, but the electoral vote was much closer. Jefferson and his running mate, **Aaron Burr** of New York, won the same number of electoral votes. Each supposedly had 73 electoral votes. 71 electoral votes were needed for victory.

Jefferson and Burr ended in a tie, because, incomprehensibly, the Republican managers neglected to tell some elector to turn in a blank ballot or vote for some third Republican. For their part the Federalists had managed their tallies so that Adams, with 65 votes, had one more vote than **Charles Cotesworth Pinckney** of South Carolina, the vice presidential candidate, who received 64 votes. One vote that might have gone to Pinckney was cast for former **Chief Justice John Jay** of New York.

Ah, but did Jefferson and Burr actually have 73 votes? The clerks of the House opened the votes of the electors. Each must be signed, certified and transmitted sealed to the President of the Senate as the Constitution requires in Article II, Section 3. However, the four votes from Georgia, all cast for Jefferson and Burr, were considerably irregular in form. They did not conform to the requirements of the Constitution. The clerks submitted them to Jefferson, as President of the Senate, to determine whether they were legal and should be counted. Or discarded as irregular!

Jefferson, thus, was faced with the monumental choice of accepting those votes and placing them in his column, or else discarding them because of their irregularities. If he did the right thing and the legal thing, and refuse to count the Georgia votes, he and Burr would still be tied with 69 votes. But they would not possess an electoral majority. Then the House of Representatives could consider the five highest vote-getters. Since there were more Federalist states than Republican states in the lame duck House, quite possibly Adams, or possibly Pinckney, or conceivably John Jay, could be chosen President. The candidate clearly chosen by the people by substantial popular vote in 1800 could lose the election.

Alternatively, Jefferson, his constitutional role as the President of the Senate notwithstanding, could behave as a politician. He could overlook the irregularities and tally the Georgia votes for himself and Burr. To do that would give the Republicans an electoral majority of 73 votes, thus limiting the House tie-breaker to the two Republicans. No Federalist candidates could be considered.

Jefferson did not hesitate for an instant. He declared that four votes from Georgia had been cast for Jefferson and Burr. It is Prof. Ackerman's contention, as it is Gerber's, that this decision was the moment when the original constitutional vision of republicanism, so dear to the Framers, changed forever into a party-based political system.

Jefferson's decision to count the Georgia votes had transformed the ideal of a government of public virtue, placing the national welfare above self-interest, into a government of majority interest that reflected the shifting popular will. Certainly it is difficult to imagine any presidential candidate taking the moral high road and trashing his own election chances in favor of constitutional principles. Perhaps John Adams might have acted with such courage and commitment. Certainly not the Sage of Monticello!

COMPLETING THE AMERICAN REVOLUTION

The tied contest was thrown into the House of Representatives. Since each state cast one vote in this particular process, it was suddenly up to the Federalists to choose their successors from among the two Republican front runners. Most Federalists, perhaps with good reason, detested Jefferson more than they hated Burr – they reluctantly agreed to support Burr for President to prevent Jefferson's victory. Nine of 16 states were required for a majority. Jefferson had 8 states but not the 9th state that would elect him.

Historians now know something of the horse trading that occurred in the Federalist caucus and between the candidates. Over the course of an entire week some 36 ballots were cast without breaking the tie. Finally, Jefferson emerged the victor by the votes of 10 states to 4 for Burr. In 2 states the delegates split dead even for Jefferson and for Burr and thus those states could cast their votes and abstained.

Federalist **James Bayard** of Delaware, the lone Congressman from his state, agreed to abandon Burr for Jefferson by abstaining from the next ballot. In that occurrence, Jefferson would need only eight states to win, which he already had. In return Bayard received the Virginian's pledge to leave intact many Federalist policies, including the National Bank, after he became President. Bayard's announcement led directly to a split vote in Vermont and Maryland, and their consequent abstentions on the final ballot. With only 14 states voting, the deadlock was broken in Jefferson's favor. Actually, Bayard's Delaware did not have to abstain. Thomas Jefferson thus became the third president of the United States. Aaron Burr became Vice President.

The election of 1800 – and the realities of political parties – led directly to the **12th Amendment** to the Constitution. That Article revised the electoral system so that each presidential elector would cast only one ballot, not two. The ballot would contain the names of President and Vice-President each designated as such. Thus the two candidates ran as a team or a slate with their positions clearly indicated. Only one slate could win, of course. The Amendment proposal was rushed through the Jeffersonian - controlled state legislatures. It was ratified in time for the 1804 election. Jefferson was returned to office with comparative ease.

Conclusions

1 - The election of 1800 substituted the original principles of a republic of moral virtue for a republic of majority interests. That shift was caused by the invention of political parties in America. The Federalists and the Republicans had diametrically opposite visions for America's future. From 1800 to the current moment political parties have been composed

of coalitions of interest groups most likely to benefit from the enactment of that party's vision and the agenda that supported it. Perhaps parties were inevitable, perhaps not, but they were a fixed reality by 1800.

It may well be argued that it is precisely the adversarial relationship between the two major parties that gives the American political system its strength and productivity. The competition between candidates, ideas and policies represented by the opposing parties, is what sharpens the debate and ultimately produces legitimacy. However bruising presidential contests may be, the partisan nature of the election process provides opportunity for ideas to compete in the marketplace for the votes of the American people.

2 – The election of 1800 ushered in the political principle that the majority will must prevail in the American governmental system. To the original concept of American republicanism, based on individual rights and liberties, the election of 1800 invented the basic notion that the majority viewpoint must rule! What the majority wishes, whether enlightened or whimsical, whether valid policy for the United States or destructive to its future, ultimately does not matter. What does matter is that some form of democratic process is employed to make the decisions. After all, a majority cannot misgovern itself for very long without feeling harmful effects.

Thus, the election of 1800 must be counted as completing the American Revolution. The notion of majority will is a bedrock principle of our governmental system. Thomas Jefferson must get his due!

PART TWO

UNION

CHAPTER NINE: SLAVERY IN THE TERRITORIES
1787 - 1856

The issues related to **slavery in the American territories** may properly be considered the primary cause of the Civil War. It was not slavery as an institution, nor slavery as a moral question, that rises to such a momentous cause. But whether the territories should be free or slave certainly does. The argument between North and South during the turbulent 1850s over slavery in the territories opened divisions that could not be reconciled. Compromises were enacted. They failed. The conflict could not be stopped. By 1861 there was nothing left but secession. And war!

This chapter analyzes the issues of slavery in the territories from the formation of the Constitution through the election of President James Buchanan in 1856. The ensuing chapter [#10] commences with the Dred Scott decision of 1857 and continues through the development of Emancipation to the Thirteenth Amendment in 1865.

Slavery and the Law

Slavery may be described as the total subjection of one will to another by force. In the Southern states, state laws encased this subjection in the skin of legality and gave it legitimacy. Wherever that force should be broken, or where there was no such force, people were free. American slavery was a full fledged system of private relationships between master and slave which degraded African Americans during the time in which it existed, and has ever since created a climate in which African Americans still face racism and discrimination.

The core premise upon which American slavery existed was the theory that black people were biologically and mentally inferior to whites. Therefore the superior white race could do anything it chose with its inferiors -- including owning them as chattel property. Southerners argued that slavery was benevolent, that it was good for the slave, an idea that smacks of the vilest form of paternalism. One cannot erase the basic blunt fact that one human being was held in absolute subjection to the pure whim of another.

The law in the slaveholding states ignored the informal – the private – relationships between master and slave. There were almost no state regulations about how slaves should be treated. Slave holders, after all, controlled southern state legislatures, too.

Slaves had absolutely no rights in the law. They belonged to their masters body and soul as much as a machine or a fence! A slave might have some privileges, but there were no uniform standards a master had to meet. He provided the necessities of life – or not – as he chose. He could allow slaves to marry and have a family relationship, or he could destroy the family by sale of one of the partners, or by murder, or even simply by order! The master could do what he chose. Slaves were sold in the marketplace, according to law, for debt, or for profit. Or for any reason!

Following the Nat Turner rebellion of 1831 in Virginia Southern states enacted heavy penalties on those who taught slaves to read or to write. There were equally heavy penalties for teaching slaves Christianity. While those provisions were often ignored in practice, they were the law. Most masters believed that literate slaves, especially if they could read the Bible, would question authority. That was unacceptable. Slaves did not have the right of assembly. There was always a white person around at all of their gatherings, just to see to it that no insurrections were planned. Slaves could not even defend themselves or their families against the actions of the master, or any white person for that matter.

Sometimes masters were kind to their slaves; kindness was not uncommon in the cotton South. Often kindness confirmed the self-interest of the owner, because slaves were expensive. Prime field hands cost $2000. Better to feed them and make them comfortable, so as to get a better day's work out of them. Always better to change your car's oil every 3000 miles!

There was no organization to which a slave could appeal injustice, no agency which he or she could appeal for protection. The law protected society, which is to say the owners, not the source of labor. Slaves were denied access to the courts. They could not testify to anyone against whites. As chattel property, the women were absolutely helpless against the loss of their virtue – against rape – by any white male. They had no protection against rape unless the owner sued the offender for trespass upon his property! The whole point was that the law, which reflected the thinking of the slave owners, victimized the entire black race.

SLAVERY IN THE TERRITORIES 1787 - 1856

With that blink of an introduction we may travel, albeit briefly, through a series of significant constitutional events and issues related in some way to slavery with emphasis on those relating to the territories.

Milestones Related to Slavery Prior to 1848

1 – The Constitutional Convention of 1787

There was serious debate in the Convention, we recall, about the abolition of slavery. Many Northerners powerfully opposed the private ownership of persons as property. Southerners threatened to walk out of the Convention if Northerners made any move to abolish slavery in the new document. For them slavery was a life and death issue even in the 18th century. If any Constitution was to be adopted, what were Northerners to do? They had the votes. They could eliminate slavery -- and break up the Convention, or they could defer to the South and postpone the matter of slavery to a later date once the Constitution was safely ratified and the new national government established.

In the environment of 1787, with the fate of the new country at stake, Northerners decided not to throw away this chance for a new Constitution, even if it meant accepting slavery. At this moment in time other issues seemed more pressing. Not more important – just more immediate. Were they right? It is difficult to see how abolishing slavery and then defeating the Constitution would have helped Southern slaves unless the North was willing to fight the Civil War in 1787!!

We have also already noted that slaves would be counted, for purposes of congressional representation, as three-fifths of a whole person. The population of a southern state would be decided by counting all the whites plus three-fifths of the slaves to reach a total number of persons. Representatives to Congress would be assigned that augmented number, even though slaves had no rights and obviously would never be permitted to participate in governance in any manner whatever.

Moreover, Congress could not prohibit the importation of slaves until 1808. Slave trading would remain legal unless Congress acted to stop it. In 1808, we remind ourselves, that Congress did pass a law prohibiting any importation of slaves into the U.S. That law had the unintended consequence of granting slave breeders in Virginia a virtual monopoly of providing spare parts for the slave system.

SLAVERY IN THE TERRITORIES 1787 - 1856

2 – The Purchase of Louisiana

The Purchase of Louisiana from France on April 30, 1803, brings us to the issue of slavery in the territories. Need we be concerned about President Jefferson's quibbles about his constitutional authority to acquire this new territory? We have only the opportunism of a President who rose to power by denying the Federalist doctrine of implied powers but who then trashed his own precious doctrine of enumerated powers when faced with this stunning opportunity vastly to expand America's borders.

The acquisition of the Louisiana territory would essentially double the size of the United States. The Louisiana territory contained about 828,000 square miles within its dimensions. Jefferson signed the Louisiana Purchase agreement without hesitation. He admitted that the Treaty made "blank paper of the constitution." Congress would have to accept what the President labeled "metaphysical subtleties."

For the lower portion of the territory, which includes the current state of Louisiana, Congress set up a government of stages, much like that of the Northwest Territory, except that slavery was legal there! The rest of the territory was attached to reserved Indian land for purposes of administration. In 1812 Louisiana became a state, a slave state.

3 - The Missouri Compromise 1820

The next major moment to note is the **Compromise of 1820** or the **Missouri Compromise**, particularly the portion of the compromise plan regarding slavery in the territories. Before 1820 no practical solution had been determined about whether slavery would be allowed in the upper portion of the Louisiana Purchase territory.

An expanding South wished another slave state to be added to the Union, to be carved out of Louisiana Purchase territory. In 1820 there were 11 slave states in the United States and 11 free states. Southerners wanted the extra two votes in the U.S. Senate that would give the South a majority, if states voted as blocs: South versus North. The South could then control legislation, even though the Northern population increased the number of Northern members in the House of Representatives.

The Territory of Missouri had proceeded through the appropriate territorial stages and was ready to be admitted to the Union as a state. Northerners, however, objected to the additional power the slave holding states would have if Missouri were admitted.

SLAVERY IN THE TERRITORIES 1787 - 1856

Senator **Henry Clay** of Kentucky, always the zealous nationalist, did not wish to see the nation divided by the slavery issue. At this juncture he stepped up, as he would do on several occasions. Clay proposed what became the Missouri Compromise.

The compromise consisted of three parts. First, Missouri was admitted as a slave state. Second, that admission would be balanced by the admission of Maine as a free state. Maine had previously belonged to Massachusetts and was also ready for statehood. Third, the critical item for this discussion, Congress drew an east-west line at **36° 30'** through the Louisiana Purchase territory. North of that line slavery was prohibited (except for Missouri). South of that line it was not. Clearly, slavery in the territories had already become an explosive issue. This time the nation skidded past conflagration. An elderly Jefferson called slavery in the territories a "fire bell in the night."

4 – The 1830s: Slavery Polarizes the Nation

The development of North/South sectionalism, particularly the growing consciousness of the South as a distinct culture, would polarize the nation. The south would spend its considerable talent and energy defending what even Southerners called **"The Peculiar Institution."**

One defense of slavery by the slaveholding aristocracy took the form of repression of dissent. The South doggedly took whatever steps it needed to take to prevent outside influences from disrupting the status quo. Three examples of evidence may suffice:

1 - Southern states placed heavy penalties on persons who disseminated or received antislavery literature. Even worse, United States postmasters were ordered to sort the mail and destroy whatever they considered dangerous. That action made every ignorant red-neck postmaster in the South the guardian of the minds of his communities through out-and-out censorship.

2 - Mob violence was also a factor. Antislavery whites, ranging from outright abolitionists to moderate gradualists were kicked out of their homes by mobs. They either fled north - or shut up! The repression of dissent also included the breaking up of abolitionist meetings by force. Abolitionist meetings disappeared from the South after 1830. Southern mobs also attacked the press of antislavery publisher Elijah Lovejoy - in southern Illinois! They destroyed it - and Lovejoy along with it! So much for a free press! And even in faraway Canterbury, Connecticut, Prudence Crandall's school for African American girls was burned to the ground by her neighborly southern sympathizers.

135

3 - Then in 1836 Southerners forced through Congress the so-called **"Gag Resolution."** This resolution prohibited Congress from hearing or accepting any antislavery petitions. Petitions, of course, were printed in the **Congressional Globe** (now the Congressional Record), the official record of the proceedings of Congress. The Globe of course circulated throughout the South. Not even Southerners dared censor the official publication of Congress. Instead, they silenced antislavery petitions before they could ever be presented and heard in Congress.

Thus between 1830 and 1861 the South insulated itself from anything that could be interpreted as antislavery. They established a sort of **"intellectual blockade,"** a phrase coined by historian **Clement Eaton.** All antislavery attitudes external to the South were effectively sealed off. Any internal dissent was repressed. Every guarantee of the Bill of Rights was silenced in practice. The South became a proslavery police state.

The following comment from one prominent Southerner on the eve of the Civil War perhaps expressed best the position of the South regarding the protection of slavery:

> *Books written in the whole range of moral science...* [that means politics, history, literature, philosophy, economics, religion, ethics] *... if not written by Southern authors within the last 20 or 30 years, inculcate abolition either directly or indirectly. If written before that time, even by Southern authors, they are likely to be as dangerous and as absurd as the Declaration of Independence or the Virginia Bill of Rights.*

1848 and Beyond

The period beginning with the crucial year of 1848 sealed the fate of the Union. The 1850s witnessed a decade-long showdown over slavery in the territories. That issue led without interruption to Civil War. Nothing in our lifetimes – not abortion – not Vietnam – nothing – has been as explosive an issue as slavery in the territories.

Once again we take pains to observe that it was not the moral issue about slavery that was at stake in the 1850's. Abolitionists were generally condemned in the North as in the South. They could command only a tiny fraction of Northern support, however vocal they might be. To Northerners, even those most revolted by slavery, that institution fell beyond the reach of United States government power. The internal institutions of each state were the sole business of each state. In the 19th century interpretation of the federal system, the national government could not interfere with institutions which existed by virtue of state constitutions. Thus even antislavery Northerners were compelled to accept the reality of slavery in the states in which it existed.

However, the one key vital issue throughout the entirety of the 1850's, revolved around the extension of slavery to areas which were not yet states, namely the territories. The issue of slavery extension would produce Civil War in America.

The American territories in 1848 were vast and sprawling. South of Oregon and west of the Louisiana Purchase lay the huge acreage just acquired from Mexico in 1848 in the **Treaty of Guadeloupe-Hidalgo**. California, of course, was included, along with two huge areas that would become the Utah and New Mexico territories.

For these areas Southerners demanded John C. Calhoun's formula. The South Carolina Senator had insisted that the number of free states must always be balanced by an equal number of slaves states, and their U.S. Senators. If that balance were once upset to favor the North in the Senate, Northerners, Calhoun reasoned, would vote into the Union one new free state after another, until there were enough free states to abolish slavery by constitutional amendment. This must never be allowed to occur. The South must therefore expand in order to survive. The extension of slavery to the territories became as vital as maintaining slavery at home! Southerners sloganized that idea by saying that the South must "expand or expire."

No longer content with the Missouri Compromise formula, Southerners claimed that wherever there was American territory – wherever the United States flag was planted, as distinct from a state flag – there a person could take his property. He could take his horse. He could take his cell phone. He could take his slave. Property must be protected by law.

That law, of course, was the 5th Amendment to the Constitution. That document says: "No Person...shall be deprived of life, liberty, or property without due process of law." Congress, Southerners argued, could not prevent property from being taken to any territory. Rather, Congress must protect property rights, including slave property, under the 5th Amendment. The key to understanding the Southern position is to appreciate how dedicated Southerners were to the little slogan that demanded that **"Slavery Follows the Flag."** This was an extreme Southern position. If accepted, it would open up to slavery every single one of the American territories, north and south, old and new.

Indeed, any future territories (perhaps Cuba) would also be open to the influx of slavery. All of the Louisiana Purchase territory would become slave territory, the ban on slavery north of 36° 30' notwithstanding. The new territories taken from Mexico would become slave territories. Even the recently acquired Oregon territory would be open to slavery.

It bears repeating that most pre-war northerners were not abolitionists. Most, including future President **Abraham Lincoln**, had little concept of racial equality as we understand that idea. They opposed the extension of slavery because slavery was in conflict with the basic democratic faith in individual self-help and opportunity. The territories must be free for Northern wage-earners and farmers – white wage earners and farmers – to work out their destiny without the polluting air of slavery to corrupt the doctrine of freedom. Thus, they could maintain that, however evil it was, slavery could exist in the Southern states. They could nonetheless oppose the extension of slavery into any free areas. That was certainly Abraham Lincoln's position.

Northerners clung to the constitutional provision that "Congress can make all needful rules for the territories," from Article 4, Section 3 of the Constitution. About that provision Southerners just yawned. A "needful rule," Southerners said, could never include emancipation, since that would take property without due process of law. No congressional policy, not even emancipation, could be a higher law than the Bill of Rights.

This extreme Southern position, that slavery was legal in every territory, would eventually become the constitutional law of the land. Despite all northern fulminations against it, the Southern view that property must be protected by the Constitution in every territory under the American flag emerged victorious. By the time of Abraham Lincoln's election in 1860, the Southern position had been hammered into the Constitution by Southern victory in one event after the next. From 1848 to 1860 that position grew stronger and stronger. It eventually triumphed totally. What evidence exists for this point of view? The place to begin is with the so-called Compromise of 1850!

Southern Victory #1: The Compromise of 1850

The Compromise of 1850 was intended to be the final compromise on slavery extension, given the explosive emotions surrounding the extension of slavery to the territories. The Compromise had the notable effect of preventing civil war in 1850. Most historians consider the Compromise of 1850 a genuine compromise, a balanced affair in which both sides won and lost something. Some even think the North gained the advantage.

SLAVERY IN THE TERRITORIES 1787 - 1856

On reexamination, however, we can determine that the Compromise of 1850 was a clear Southern victory, a Southern triumph. We can examine the provisions. First, the admission of California to the Union as a free state! A free California would give the North a slim edge in the U.S. Senate. There would now be 16 free states and only 15 slave states. Calhoun's precious balance would be upset! One might normally view that action as a major northern victory and a southern defeat.

However, that perspective may be too simple. The vote in California on the question of slavery was approximately 12,500 for admission as a free state, to only about 800 for admission as a slave state. This vote was so overwhelmingly anti-slavery that it meant that California would have to be admitted as a free state or not admitted at all. There was nothing Southerners could do to stop a free California.

Even had Southerners compelled California to seek admission as a slave state, Californians would have reversed that position the instant the territory joined the Union and became a state. Not even Southerners ever argued that every state (as opposed to a territory) had to have slavery! Southern theory held that each state was sovereign. States could make up their own minds! Ergo, since the admission of free California was inevitable, why is it considered part of the Compromise of 1850 at all? It was going to happen anyhow! Consequently, anything the South got in return for the admission of California was an outright gift.

What the South received was a new and stringent Fugitive Slave Law, the **Fugitive Slave Act of 1850**. We may be reminded that there had been a Fugitive Slave law passed in 1793, but it had been mild and rarely enforced. There had been frequent runaways from plantations along the **"underground railroad."** Southerners wanted this stopped. Runaways were dangerous to the slave system – and besides they were expensive to replace. The Fugitive Slave Act went a long way in redressing Southern grievances.

Under the 1850 law Federal Marshals and their deputies were ordered to assist the slave-catchers in tracking and capturing alleged fugitives. All citizens were urged to aid in the pursuit. There were severe penalties – fines and jail time – if a private citizen aided a runaway or hid a runaway, or harbored fugitive slaves in any manner. Once a black person was seized by the owner, or by some goon the owner hired to find his slave, or by United States officials, the person seized would be "tried" before a special Federal commissioner or judge – without a jury! At such a trial, more properly a hearing, the only evidence needed to determine that the person seized was the runaway fugitive was a statement from the owner or agent that this was the slave! Persons seized – whoever they were – could not testify on their own behalf. In practice the Act amounted to seizing any black person in the North, slave or not, and hauling him off! The only chance any black person had was if local whites vouched for him or her. Of course whites had to be most careful, because of the penalties for aiding runaways. The passage of the Fugitive Slave Act was a significant pro-Southern provision of the Compromise of 1850. What did the South give up in return?

The abolition of the slave trade in the District of Columbia – not even slavery itself! The slave trade! Slaves could no longer be bought or sold at auction in the nation's capital. It is useful to observe that the D.C. slave trade was only a minimal factor in the operation of the slave system. That is because the leadership of the slave states had shifted from the coastal tidewater into the deep South. Indeed, Maryland and Virginia slave traders were only too glad to get rid of their competitors in the city of Washington. To give up that trade changed very little. That is why the Fugitive Slave Act was so powerful a Southern advantage.

What of Northern responses to the Fugitive Slave Act? We may be certain that it was the one aspect of the entire compromise package that stuck in Northern throats! Northerners hated this law. If the South could have realized that the only hope for slavery was to let the North forget about it, the end result might possibly have been different. Instead, they rubbed Northern noses in it! When **Ralph Waldo Emerson** read the Fugitive Slave Act he declared, "This filthy enactment was made in the middle of the 19th century by men who could read and write! I will not obey it, by God!" More than occasionally it took protective cordons of police to prevent Northern mobs from attacking marshals and setting fugitives loose.

Some Northern states went so far as to pass what were called **Personal Liberty Laws.** These state laws instructed state courts to issue a *writ of habeas corpus* on behalf of anyone detained as a fugitive. They also prohibited state and local officials from aiding in the capture of a fugitive, in open defiance of the Fugitive Slave Act. Personal Liberty Laws had the effect of interposing state authority between the fugitives and the enforcement of federal law – a sort of Northern version of nullification.

It was with the utmost irony that the United States Supreme Court, Chief Justice Roger B. Taney's Supreme Court, declared Personal Liberty Laws unconstitutional in the case of *Ableman v. Booth* in 1859. Those laws were unconstitutional, of course, because they interfered with the federal judicial system. National jurisdiction was the supreme law of the land, after all, and in this case the Court said so clearly.

SLAVERY IN THE TERRITORIES 1787 - 1856

To compound the irony, Southerners also reversed their position. They applauded the Court's decision to void those laws, regardless of their real opinions about states' rights. Ergo, not only was the Fugitive Slave Act of 1850 a Southern advantage, but Northern attempts to block it by law were also defeated.

The other significant provision of the Compromise of 1850 was the organization of the huge Utah Territory and the huge New Mexico Territory into governments. Organization of a territory starts them on the road to eventual statehood. Please understand that not one word was said in the two bills that established administrations for these gigantic areas about slavery! Silence! Nada!

This part of the Compromise was another big victory for the South. Why? In the first place New Mexico had proposed a state constitution banning slavery, but the South refused to accept it and blocked approval of that document in the Senate. The stated wish of the people of New Mexico to enter the Union as a free state was simply overruled.

More important, silence regarding slavery in these territories was taken by both North and South to mean that the status of slavery in the territories would be decided by the principle of what was called **Popular Sovereignty** or sometimes **Squatter Sovereignty.** Popular Sovereignty was the brainchild of Democratic Senator **Stephen A. Douglas** of Illinois.

Thus there were three positions on the matter of slavery in the territories. The Southern position held that "slavery follows the American flag" to every territory. The Northern position, the Wilmot Proviso position, declared that Congress must outlaw slavery in the territories. And now the middle position, that would permit the people of the territory to decide the matter for themselves.

By Popular Sovereignty Douglas meant explicitly that the territorial legislature, representing the people of the territory, would by some vote settle the question of slavery for that territory. Douglas even once said that he didn't care if slavery were voted up or if it were voted down, as long as the people of the territory decided the issue for themselves. Under questioning from other Senators, Douglas emphasized that slave-owners could take slaves into a territory *before* the territorial legislature decided. How could there be two sides to the question otherwise!

After all it might take some years, perhaps a decade or more, before the territory reached the appropriate number of residents to get the territorial legislature in place and before that legislature was ready to tackle the slavery issue. What happened in the interim between territorial organization and the legislative vote?

The problem is this: if a slave owner could take his slaves into a territory *before* the territorial legislature voted, where did he get the right to do so? That right must come from written law. But there was no local or territorial law yet, because the territorial legislature hadn't yet acted. And there was no Congressional law, obviously! The only place that right could come from was the United States Constitution. Southerners argued that the 5th Amendment gave slave owners the right to take slaves to the territory *prior* to the vote. "No person...shall be deprived of life, liberty, or property without due process of law." If property was to be protected, slavery could exist in the territories by constitutional right *before* any territorial vote! But wait! There's more!

Play out the scenario. Suppose the territorial legislature voted to outlaw slavery in the territory. Now what happens? Southerners would immediately take the case to the Supreme Court. Now we have a territorial law in conflict with the Constitution – in conflict with the 5th Amendment. The Court would have no choice but to rule in favor of the right to own slaves in the territory under the 5th Amendment. So slavery would exist in the territory *after* the territorial decision, too!

What this meant was that a territory could vote to uphold slavery, but it could never vote to expel it. The conclusion is that in operation, if not in theory, popular sovereignty came out exactly the same as the extreme Southern position that "slavery follows the flag." Was there any difference between saying that slavery exists in the territories by constitutional right and Calhoun's doctrine that "slavery follows the flag?" Gerber thinks that there is absolutely no difference whatsoever!

And thus, slavery would have to be legal in every American territory, South, North, West, anywhere. Indeed, in any future territories also! Can anyone really evaluate this seemingly innocuous provision of the Compromise of 1850 as anything but a clear Southern triumph?

If we could put the Compromise of 1850 provisions on a balance sheet they might look about equal, because each side had an equal number of provisions. But in fact they were not equal, because some provisions were more significant than others. The Fugitive Slave Act was more important than the D.C. Slave Trade. The Texas border matter was inconsequential. The admission of California should not be there at all. And because silence about slavery – which all agreed meant Popular Sovereignty – worked out in practice as "slavery follows the flag," Southern interests prevailed.

SLAVERY IN THE TERRITORIES 1787 - 1856

Who "won" the Compromise of 1850? In Gerber's view the Compromise was a major Southern victory over the North. Moreover, it was only the first of many. Bottom line: the Compromise of 1850 counts as Southern Victory #1.

Southern Victory #2: Election of 1852

Southern Victory #2 – came in the election of 1852. The Democratic candidate, **Franklin Pierce** of New Hampshire, defeated the Whig Candidate, General **Winfield Scott**. Scott had been a war hero of the Mexican War. In the campaign the slavery extension issue split the Whigs into Northern and Southern wings. It fragmented the party. The Whigs lost the strength to run another candidate for President after 1852. Scott was the last of them.

The Democrats won in 1852 by a landslide. The Democratic platform strongly endorsed the Compromise of 1850 as the final resolution to the issue of slavery in the territories. Vote for Pierce, the Democrats said, and put away the extension issue forever. Forever would not last long.

The issue of federal internal improvements raised immediately the issue of slavery extension. In the 1850s internal improvements meant a transcontinental railroad. Decisions about railroad building split the sections wide apart once again – and again the South won! Both Northern and Southern states had tried to woo the new Western states into their political camp. Whichever section won the economic connection with the west would acquire a political ally with enough strength to swing the balance of political power in their favor. One offer which both used was the offer of a transcontinental railroad.

Such a railroad would provide a crucial economic and political link between the west and whichever section – North or South – possessed the eastern terminus. Southerners naturally wanted a southern route, from New Orleans, Louisiana, to San Diego, California. From New Orleans eastward the entire South would be connected to the west. Northerners wanted a railroad route from St. Louis, Missouri, to San Francisco, California. From St. Louis eastward, through Chicago to New York, the entire north would be connected to the west.

In 1853 Congress authorized surveys of four routes. The surveys were directed by President Pierce's Secretary of War, **Jefferson Davis** of Mississippi. Davis well understood that a southern transcontinental railroad would be the way to bring slavery into the massive new areas just acquired from Mexico. Even though Davis was a states' rights man, in principle opposed to federal internal improvements, lo and behold he advocated the construction of a railroad by the United States government, under the direction of the war department, via the Southern route. To be sure, the Southern route was shorter than the others. It had fewer mountains to overcome. There was much less danger from Indian attacks. And the southern road would thus be less expensive and easier to build.

The survey indicated that the southern route would have to pass through still another piece of Mexican territory. Davis convinced President Pierce and Congress to purchase the land needed for $10 million. The result was the **Gadsden Purchase of 1853**. Just a little chunk of land lying west of Texas and east of California!

Southern Victory #3: Gadsden Purchase 1853

Certainly the **Gadsden Purchase** was a stunning Southern victory, Southern Victory #3. Potentially it meant the extension of slavery to the West. The economic and political link between South and West would have cemented the long term future of the cotton economy by tying it to the growth of the Western states. The stage was now set for Congress to authorize the building of the railroad from New Orleans to San Diego.

Meanwhile, the "Little Giant," Senator **Stephen A. Douglas** of Illinois, had been trying to get his central route (St. Louis to San Francisco) accepted by Congress. In order to get federal funding, a railroad had to run through areas already organized under federal jurisdiction. Thus the Nebraska territory (including the current states of Nebraska and Kansas) lying between Missouri and Utah, would have to be opened for settlement. It was the last piece of Louisiana Purchase land not yet organized. It was being used primarily for Indian reservations.

Southern Victory #4: Kansas-Nebraska Act 1854

Senator Douglas in 1854 introduced his **Kansas-Nebraska Bill**. Its passage would mark Southern victory #4. This one was extraordinarily significant! The Kansas-Nebraska Bill was not the first attempt to open the Nebraska territory. Southerners, so fearful of new free states being created from this territory, had defeated every previous attempt. What could Douglas offer this time, to get Southerners to change their minds and vote for the Bill? There was lots of bait. In its final form, the Kansas-Nebraska Act set up two new territories, Kansas and Nebraska.

SLAVERY IN THE TERRITORIES 1787 - 1856

Most important, the Bill specifically repealed the Missouri Compromise Line of 36°30', making it inoperative and void! This meant that those two territories were no longer automatically free territories, as they had been under the 1820 Compromise. Instead, Douglas specifically moved to his favorite tactic – popular sovereignty – for deciding the issue of slavery extension. Recall that in practice, popular sovereignty meant that "slavery follows the flag"! The central railroad route, while not formally authorized in this bill, was understood to be approved next.

The Kansas-Nebraska proposal now offered the South a momentous choice. They could take advantage of this golden opportunity to force slavery into Northern territories, something they had been demanding for years and years. In return they would have to approve the central railroad route that Douglas so devoutly wanted. To do this they would vote for passage of the Bill. Or they could defeat Douglas's route and keep the Southern railroad route Jefferson Davis had recommended. In taking that action they would also pass up the chance to extend slavery into northern territories. They could do this by defeating the Bill.

Southern honor and Southern principles were at stake, for Douglas's bill enacted in practice the doctrine that "slavery follows the flag." The South chose to overrule its clear long-term economic and political interest. The Southern delegates in Congress hesitated for hardly a moment. They backed the Kansas-Nebraska Bill enthusiastically.

Northerners on the other hand, were shocked and alarmed by this proposal to extend slavery into the North and to break a 35 year old compromise in the bargain. People could not have been more surprised by a bill to repeal trial by jury! It is significant, further, that Douglas adopted Southern arguments to justify the Kansas- Nebraska Bill. He even declared that the Missouri Compromise was unconstitutional – and ought to be repealed – because Congress lacked power to prohibit slavery in the territories. In some quarters Douglas was severely criticized for being "soft on slavery."

The **Kansas–Nebraska Act** was whipped through Congress by the powerful Democratic Party organization, of course with Southern support. Over terrific opposition it passed, because of party discipline, in May, 1854. The Act had several results. First, there occurred the violence and anarchy of the actual physical attempt to settle Kansas. There was a genuine civil war in that new territory. **"Bleeding Kansas"** was a dramatic story by itself, but perhaps outside our current scope. Kansas became a free state in 1861.

SLAVERY IN THE TERRITORIES 1787 - 1856

Second, the Act clearly marked a major step in the acceptance of the constitutional right to slavery in the territories. That made it a clear Southern victory. The doctrine of "expand or expire" was applied to Northern, formerly free territories. This time, moreover, some prominent Northerners were admitting that the South's view was correct. Can anyone imagine that the forcing of slavery north of 36°30,' with the backing of powerful Democratic Party leaders such as Douglas, was anything but a massive Southern victory?

Third, the Act crystallized Northern political opposition to slavery extension. As a direct result of the Act, the **Republican Party** was formed in July, 1854, under the oaks at Jackson, Michigan. These new Republicans were anti-extension men from every political and economic background. Many of them had been bitter political enemies previously. Were some even Banana Republicans?

They adopted the viewpoint, put forward by New York Governor **William Henry Seward,** that the territories must remain free. Such men as Seward and **Salmon P. Chase** of Ohio, Massachusetts Senator **Charles Sumner**, and editor **Horace Greeley** of the New York <u>Tribune</u>, based their argument against slavery extension upon the 5th Amendment, just as Southerners did. Seward emphasized the word "liberty" in the Amendment. Persons could not be deprived of life, *liberty*, or property without due process of law. Slavery deprived people of their liberty, a position also held by Abraham Lincoln. Lincoln, too, was one of those new-fangled Republicans. Whereas Southerners emphasized the word "property," Republicans underlined the word *liberty* within the 5th Amendment as being the operable word.

Perhaps the most significant statement about the Kansas–Nebraska Act came from the lips of Senator Charles Sumner of Massachusetts, another founder of the new Republican Party. These Republicans were not the Jeffersonian Republicans of the early republic. They were the party of Lincoln and Chase and Seward and Greeley and Sumner – and Warren Harding, Richard Nixon, and George W Bush. That lineup presents another strong case that Darwin was badly mistaken!

About the Kansas–Nebraska Bill Senator Sumner said: "It is at once the worst and best bill on which Congress has ever acted. The worst, inasmuch as it is a present victory for slavery. The best, for it annuls all past compromises with slavery and makes all future compromises impossible. Thus it puts slavery and freedom face to face and bids them grapple. Who can doubt the results?" There would be many doubters, indeed.

SLAVERY IN THE TERRITORIES 1787 - 1856

The emergence of the Republican Party meant a hardening of Northern views against the series of Southern political and legal victories to extend slavery to the territories. That phenomenon escalated and polarized the struggle, of course. A similar phenomenon occurred in the South as well. Just as the advocates of free territories grew more resolute, Southern moderates fell increasingly under the sway of pro-extension **"fire-eaters,"** as Southern hard-liners came to be called. Such men as **Alexander Stephens** of Georgia, the 90 pound future Vice President of the Confederacy and, of course, Jefferson Davis of Mississippi, who would become the President of the ill-fated Confederate States of America. Along with many others in every Southern state they took over the tempo of this struggle. Given the Southern psychology which we have already described, "fire-eaters" began to perceive all Northerners as abolitionists and antislavery fanatics.

Southern Victory #5: Election of 1856

One more victory occurred with the election of 1856. That year witnessed the election of a pro-slavery Northern President, **James Buchanan** of Pennsylvania. Buchanan had served in both houses of Congress, intermittently since 1821. He had served as Secretary of State under James K. Polk; we remember the **Oregon Treaty** of 1846. Buchanan's pro-Southern views became clear in 1854, when he was America's Ambassador to Great Britain.

Buchanan had signed the notorious **Ostend Manifesto**. That document urged the United States to seize the island of Cuba, 90 miles from the American mainland, if Spain would not sell it to the United States. The Manifesto could only be interpreted by both South and North as a grab for a new outlet for slavery extension. Buchanan became the presidential candidate of the Democratic Party, ever more Southern-dominated.

Buchanan's primary opponent in 1856 was the Republican **John Charles Fremont**, the "Pathfinder" as he was frequently called, because of the genuine Western adventures in his background. Fremont had fought in the Mexican War and gained a creditable army record. Fremont also had a dashing image as a Western explorer hero. Above all, Fremont was thoroughly opposed to the extension of slavery to the territories; everyone knew it. Although the Republican Party was only two years old, because of the demise of the Whigs, it now offered the only alternative for Northerners who opposed slavery extension.

Buchanan won, of course. It was a strong victory, but his victory was not overwhelming. Buchanan carried the whole South and the border states of

Missouri and Kentucky. He also won Indiana, Illinois, California, New Jersey and Pennsylvania. He garnered a total of 176 electoral votes. His popular total was 1.8 million plus. As a wholly sectional Northern candidate, Fremont won 114 electoral votes and roughly 1.5 million popular votes.

Republicans were elated with the results of their first race. It promised a bright future – which in fact turned out to be an accurate prediction. Democrats, however, could look forward to at least four more years of pro-slavery policy in Washington.

The history of those next years takes us directly to the Civil War.

CHAPTER TEN: SLAVERY, THE TERRITORIES AND EMANCIPATION 1857-1865

Slavery in the Territories

Chapter Ten continues the crucial issues of the extension of slavery to the territories begun in Chapter Nine. It also contains an analysis of the determination by President Lincoln to emancipate the slaves during the Civil War. The two subjects – slavery extension and emancipation – were inseparable then and hence are examined in a single chapter.

No issue in American history has ever proven more volatile and explosive as the struggle to extend or to prevent the extension of slavery to the territories of the American West. A parade of Southern successes over slavery extension had already taken place. Those included the Compromise of 1850, the election of 1852, the Gadsden Purchase of 1853, the Kansas-Nebraska Act of 1854, and the election of 1856.

Southern Victory #6: *Dred Scott v. Sanford*

The next Southern victory, one most ominous to the fate of the Union, arrived two days after President James Buchanan's inauguration. This was the Supreme Court ruling in the case of **Dred Scott v. Sanford.** March 6, 1857. Buchanan, it should be noted, had prior knowledge of what the Court ruling would contain, because he had discussed the *Dred Scott* decision with Chief Justice Taney beforehand. You can decide what that means about separation of powers.

The facts of the case may be easily recalled. Scott was a slave owned by Dr. John Emerson, a U. S. army surgeon. In 1834 Emerson took Scott to the free state of Illinois, and later, when Emerson was assigned to Fort Snelling, to the free territory of Wisconsin, part of the Louisiana Purchase north of the 36°30' line. Eventually Emerson returned with Scott to his native Missouri, a slave state. When Emerson died, Scott sued Mrs. Emerson for his freedom.

SLAVERY, TERRITORIES, EMANCIPATION 1857-1865

Scott claimed that his residence on free soil, both in a free state and a free territory, made him a free man. The case was brought in a trial court in Missouri, since Scott claimed to be a Missouri resident. Oddly enough, in the lower Court, Scott won - and won his freedom. That decision was immediately reversed on appeal to the Missouri Supreme Court. Scott was not free. In order to get the case to the United States Supreme Court, the title to Scott was sold to Mrs. Emerson's brother, John A. Sanford of New York. As you may know citizens of different states can sue in federal court. Scott's case ultimately found its way to the Supreme Court.

Chief Justice Taney wrote the majority opinion in this critical case. Taney upheld the Missouri Supreme Court and rejected Scott's suit for freedom. He rested his decision on three grounds: First, declared Taney, because Scott was a black person he could not be a citizen of the United States. Only American citizens could sue in federal court. Scott could not bring this suit. Obviously, he could not win it. While blacks might be citizens of states somewhere, they could not be U.S. citizens, said the Chief Justice, not even free blacks. Taney asserted that the Framers of the Constitution intended the Constitution to be a "white man's document." Indeed, the Maryland slave-owner added, black persons had no rights which any white man was bound to respect.

Second. As a resident of Missouri, Taney continued, Scott could not rely on the laws of Illinois, a free state, to be valid in a Missouri Court. Illinois law did not apply in Missouri. If Scott had sued in Illinois, perhaps the law might have had some effect. But he did not, and so it did not. Scott remained a slave.

Third, and the portion of the ruling that most concerns us: as a resident of the territory north of 36°30', Scott had not been emancipated. This was because **Congress could not prohibit slavery in the territories**. To ban slavery would violate the 5th Amendment guarantee to safeguard property. Congress could not deprive a person of property without due process of law. This section of Taney's argument upheld the Southern position that "slavery follows the flag." It was precisely what Southerners had been hoping and praying for! What did it mean that the 5th Amendment prevented Congress from prohibiting slavery in the territories?

The *Dred Scott* ruling meant that the Missouri Compromise of 1820 was always illegal. We may recall that the 36°30' line had been repealed by the Kansas-Nebraska Act of 1854. Now the Court was saying that it had never been valid in the first place. It had always been unconstitutional. The decision had the impact of permitting - the legal term is sanctioning - slavery in any American territory. Oregon was now open to slavery. So were Kansas and Nebraska, New Mexico and Utah. Slavery would also be legal in any territory the United States in its ebulliant expression of **Manifest Destiny** might choose to acquire. The Court had spoken. Slavery was to be protected everywhere the American flag went. The Southern argument was now the law of the land.

Two Justices dissented from the majority opinion. Their views are of note, because of the opportunity to compare ideas, but the dissent was, of course, not the law. They were Justices **Benjamin Curtis** and **John McLean** (not the Bruce Willis character from "Die Hard"). Curtis had been appointed as a Whig by President Fillmore in 1851. McLean, a Democrat, had been appointed by President Andrew Jackson in 1829.

Curtis and McLean argued that Scott could indeed sue in federal court. Because there was no clause in the U.S. Constitution defining who was an American citizen, then under the law if one were a state citizen he or she would automatically be a U.S. citizen as well. The first U.S. Citizenship clause, incidentally, was placed directly into the Constitution in the 14th Amendment of 1868, during Reconstruction, although one had previously been enacted by statute in the Civil Rights Act of 1866.

At any rate, Curtis and McLean observed that there were free blacks in any number of states prior to 1787 and that the Framers meant to include them in all constitutional guarantees. There were actually some 108,300 free blacks in the United States by 1815 – about 11% of the total African-American population. The Constitution, the dissenters said, was not just a white man's document.

Next, Curtis and McLean argued that Scott's residence in Illinois had indeed made him free. There was an Illinois law which freed any slave who lived there for a year and a day and who was not a runaway or just passing through. That law was valid in Missouri, under the "full faith and credit" clause of the Constitution. Article IV, Sec 1: "Full faith and credit shall be given in each state to the public Acts, Records, and Judicial Proceedings of every other state." That provision exists so that you are legally married in every state, not just the one where you subjected yourself to that imprudent condition. Or if you bought an automobile in one state, you still owned it even if you moved elsewhere. Declared Curtis and McLean, Scott should have been freed by Illinois law.

Finally, and again most important, Curtis and McLean argued that of course Congress had power to prohibit slavery in the territories. The power to make rules for the territories went back to Thomas Jefferson and the Louisiana Purchase. They showed no fewer than 14 times since 1789 when Congress had legislated about slavery in the territories. In some instances Congress had approved slavery. In some they had banned slavery. But to assert now that Congress lacked the power to rule on that issue deliberately ignored historical reality. There were too many precedents in favor of the power to legislate on slavery. The dissenters concluded that since Congress had prohibited slavery north of 36°30', it was banned. Having lived in that territory, Scott was a free man!

The Republican Party in general, and Abraham Lincoln in particular, took still another approach to the *Dred Scott* decision. Lincoln held that if Scott could not bring his case to the Supreme Court, then the Court could not hear it, beyond that simple statement that Scott could not sue. Then all of the rulings after that statement were just plain hearsay, personal opinion, and not binding in law. If Scott could not sue the Court could not hear the case. If the Court could not hear the case, it could not rule on the territories. Taney's opinion, Lincoln said, was only **obiter dictum**, a Latin phrase which means incidental opinion or literally "said by the way."

Despite the dissenting judicial opinion and the Republican political objections, the ruling stood. Slavery was legal in every territory! The law was the law, and *obiter dictum* was just advertising. The South had won its greatest victory so far. The sixth in a row!

Aside from the law, the case had major political implications. If the decision were to be put into effect, then the whole reason for the very existence of the Republican Party would be destroyed. The Republicans were the Free Territories Party – and by the ruling in *Dred Scott* there were no such things as free territories. The Republicans, demanding an end to the expansion of slavery in the territories, would be wiped out by a single judicial decision which simply negated the very concept of free territories.

Taney's decision also thoroughly embarrassed Northern Democrats. If implemented, the decision would destroy the Democratic Party idea of popular sovereignty, so openly advocated by Senator Douglas, just as it would abolish the Wilmot Proviso position, the Republican position of free territories. If Congress was barred from prohibiting slavery, because of the 5th Amendment, then so were the residents of the territories themselves. Any law passed by a territorial legislature that prohibited slavery would also violate the Amendment and be overruled by the Court.

The Lincoln-Douglas Debates: August 21 – October 15, 1858

Northern Democrats tried valiantly to reconcile popular sovereignty with the *Dred Scott* ruling. The most important of these attempts occurred in

SLAVERY, TERRITORIES, EMANCIPATION 1857-1865

1858, during the debates between Abraham Lincoln and Stephen A. Douglas, the Lincoln – Douglas debates. Both men were running for Douglas's Senate seat in Illinois in the off-year elections of 1858. Seven debates were held, live and outdoors, up and down the state of Illinois.

During the second debate, at Freeport, Lincoln asked Douglas this tough question: "Can the people of a U.S. territory, in any lawful way, against the wishes of any citizen, exclude slavery from its limits, prior to the formation of a State Constitution?" In other words Lincoln was asking: how can you still argue for popular sovereignty when the Court had already destroyed that doctrine by the *Dred Scott* decision?

This question really put the advocate of popular sovereignty in a tight place. If he admitted that the *Dred Scott* ruling was the law, then he would be admitting that popular sovereignty was a farce. That would ruin Douglas as the leader of Northern Democrats. However, if he rejected the Court's ruling Southern Democrats would disown him for failing to endorse the decision. Without Southern support Douglas would lose any chance for the Presidency in 1860.

Douglas was clever. To some extent he made good sense. At least he found a way to reconcile this pro-Southern ruling with his own face-saving necessity. Douglas stated: "slavery cannot exist a day or an hour anywhere, unless it is supported by local police regulations." He meant that if there was no territorial statute or law to protect slaveholders, then their antislavery neighbors would find some way to make their lives so uncomfortable that slavery would end.

Douglas didn't exactly imply that unless the local cops intervened, slaveholders would have trouble with their kneecaps or that their horses would go lame or that their kids would be ostracized or their wells would have dead skunks in them. Or did he? But public consensus and local pressures would work against slaveholders, if there were no enforceable law protecting slavery. In short: no police protection, no slavery.

Douglas's **Freeport Doctrine**, as this theory was named, had predictable results. (1) Douglas won reelection to the Senate; he deserved it. (2) His statement held northern Democrats in the party. It prevented a mass exodus to the Republicans. A number of abolitionist-minded Democrats did switch their allegiance, but the bulk of northern antislavery Democrats were satisfied with his remark and Douglas remained their leader. (3) The South, ever increasingly under the sway of people like **Jefferson Davis** and **Barnwell Rhett** and **William Lowndes Yancey** and other "fire-eaters," could not brook even the slightest deviation from the official *Dred Scott* line. Despite Douglas's efforts to keep his party united,

SLAVERY, TERRITORIES, EMANCIPATION 1857-1865

Southerners branded him a Judas, who had betrayed his party, the South, and the Nation.

On the other side of the debates, Abraham Lincoln made his position clear as early as June 16, 1858, prior to the debates. In one of his most famous speeches Lincoln declared that "*A house divided against itself cannot stand.*" Lincoln said, "*I believe that this government cannot endure permanently half slave and half free. I do not expect the Union to be dissolved. I do not expect the house to fall,*" he continued. "*But I do expect it will cease to be divided. It will become all one thing or all the other. Either the opponents of slavery will arrest the further spread of it; or its advocates will push it forward till it become alike lawful in all the states, old as well as new, north as well as south.*"

Lincoln had taken a hard-line against the extension of slavery, to be sure. The divided house – the United States – would have to become all free. He did not spell out how this would happen, but Lincoln drew the line clearly and firmly against any more Southern advances. It was time for the North to stand up to the challenge.

Beyond *Dred Scott*

Lincoln's stand, the Republican hard-line stand against slavery, was echoed by Governor **William Henry Seward** of New York. In October 1858 Seward declaimed, "*It is an irrepressible conflict between opposing and enduring forces and it means that the United States must and will, sooner or later, become entirely a slaveholding nation or entirely a free-labor nation.*"

We can see in these statements of Lincoln and Seward just what the Republicans were afraid of. They were fearful that the South would not rest content with the *Dred Scott* principle, just as they had not rested content with the Missouri Compromise, or the Compromise of 1850, or the Kansas – Nebraska position. Now that the South had control of the government, why stop?

It remained for Horace Greeley, the eccentric editor of the New York <u>Tribune</u>, to sum up the Republican fears in brilliant fashion:

> "*Why can't you let slavery alone?*" *was imperiously or querulously demanded of the north, throughout the long struggle...by men who should have seen, but would not, that slavery never left the north alone, nor thought of doing so....*"Buy Louisiana for us*" said the slaveholders.* "*With pleasure.*" "*Now Florida.*" "*Certainly.*" "*Now for*

SLAVERY, TERRITORIES, EMANCIPATION 1857-1865

*Texas." "You have it." "Next, a third more of Mexico!" "Yours it is...."
"Now break the Missouri Compact and let slavery wrestle with free
labor in the vast region consecrated by that compact to freedom."
"Very good-what next?" ...And all this time while slavery was using
the Union as her catspaw, men were asking why people living in the
free states could not let slavery alone, mind their business, and
expend their surplus philanthropy on the poor at their own doors,
rather than on the happy and contented slaves."*

Lincoln, Seward, Greeley, and the Republicans had cause to be alarmed
that the South was going to press its attack further, to force slavery down
northern throats. For example: Jefferson Davis publicly demanded that
Congress enact a **national slave code**, a national law to protect
slaveholders from local antislavery community pressure, and impose it on
all the territories. Support for a national slave code would be inserted into
the Democratic Party platform (at Charleston) in 1860.

Republicans were also afraid that the African slave trade might be
reopened. Prime field hands were expensive. A new influx of slaves from
Africa could lower the price by increasing the supply. There were loud
demands to repeal the African Slave Trade Act of 1808, the federal law
that outlawed that trade. The Governor of South Carolina demanded it. A
businessmen's convention in Mississippi demanded it. The most
prominent magazine in the South, **De Bow's Review** (New Orleans)
demanded it. And Senator William Lowndes Yancey of Alabama argued
quite forcefully: *"If it is right to buy slaves in Virginia and carry them to
New Orleans, why is it not right to buy slaves in Cuba, Brazil, or Africa
and carry them there?"*

Yancey was right, of course! His argument thoroughly disproved the facile
viewpoint of so many that slavery was dying in 1860 and would have died
out if the South had just been left alone. That idea is just pure
crapazoidial nonsense! Make no mistake. Yancey and the South were
demanding enough slaves to populate the Northern and Western
territories, regardless of soil or climate conditions. This was not about
economics. It was about Southern culture and the Southern way of life.
Slavery was necessary to keep the South a white man's country!

Of course Republicans were alarmed over the next Southern demand and
the next and the next. Their concern caused them to dig their heels in
against slavery extension. Abraham Lincoln took just such a hard line in
his debates with Douglas in 1858.

It must now be plain that after a parade of legal victories, the South had
achieved total success in the law. The South had won the legal argument

155

SLAVERY, TERRITORIES, EMANCIPATION 1857-1865

regarding slavery extension in the territories. All the North had left was the power of moral argumentation. It would take the deaths of 625,000 young men and one President to alter the constitutional law of slavery.

The story of the demise of slavery may be briefly told.

Emancipation

The issue of emancipation of America's four million slaves is so clouded by misconceptions, false information and half-truths that it is difficult to deal with it without getting hung up in current ideas about race relations and 21st century mental attitudes. Some people think Abraham Lincoln was a noble and idealistic emancipator. Some think him just another racist politician. Some are altogether indifferent. What matters is that everyone understands emancipation as it existed within the context of the Civil War. This is very much a problem of historical circumstances, of historical cosmology. To remove the emancipation struggle out of its historical context, to view it with 21st century eyes, means that our interpretation of the emancipation issue is a joke we play on the 19th century. Instead, we must appreciate the emancipation controversy in its historical moment.

Factors Operating Against Emancipation

1 – Racist Attitudes of 19th Century America

Once the Civil War broke out, several factors limited any rapid movement for emancipation. The first is plain old racism, the racist attitudes of 19th century America. Most Americans, North as well as South, shared a 19th century view of black inferiority. To most northerners of 19th century America, African Americans were hardly the equal of any white man. Many Northerners saw black folk as "Sambos." The term "Sambo" represented the stereotypical image of the shuffling, illiterate, subservient black. Whatever his views about slavery, it is fair to say that Abraham Lincoln himself had no concept of black equality – certainly not as we understand equality today. Given northern racial attitudes it is almost amazing that anything could be done to free the slaves.

2 – Theory of War as Insurrection

The second limiting factor was the idea of the civil war as a giant insurrection. The Union notion of rebellion also operated against

156

emancipation. In a war between two independent nations the conqueror had no obligation to respect the rights or the property of the defeated power. For the Union this military struggle was not a war between nations. Millions of individuals had rebelled against their legitimate government, but there was no such species as the Confederate States of America. One can imagine that that view was precisely what Lord North thought about his colonial rebels in 1776.

To prevent even the hint of legitimacy of the Davis government in Richmond, and to prevent British recognition and assistance to the South, the U.S. portrayed itself as fighting an internal rebellion, an uprising against the rightful government. If the Confederacy gained recognition abroad, the U.S. might well lose half the nation. It is hard to imagine how an independent Confederate States of America would ever emancipate its slaves.

It might well be noted that a great many Americans opposed force to compel reunion. Without the South the United States would be essentially a free nation, with free institutions. In that climate of freedom the Union slave states – Missouri, Kentucky, Maryland, and Delaware – would eventually move to emancipation.

The insurrection theory limited the drive for emancipation. Under the Constitution Southerners who had not been convicted of some crime against the United States were still entitled to their rights, including property rights, just as if they had been loyal Northerners. If the government could not strip a Connecticut citizen of his or her property rights without due process, then it could not arbitrarily take a Southern slaveholder's property, either. Or a Northern slaveholder's! Whatever action might be taken against slavery would have to occur by constitutional means only. Some sort of trial and conviction would most likely have to occur. Or some other idea concocted.

3 – Risk of Secession of Missouri and Kentucky

The third factor operating against emancipation may have been the most powerful. Emancipation risked the secession of Missouri and Kentucky. If Lincoln moved toward emancipation too fast, Missouri and Kentucky, huge Union slave states with enormous resources, would secede and join the Confederacy. Leaders of Missouri and Kentucky warned Lincoln that if he abolished slavery, those states would immediately join the Davis government

The Confederate government actually included unofficial representatives from Missouri and Kentucky in both houses of Congress. Those representatives actually voted in that Congress, even though the two states were still in the Union.

If Missouri and Kentucky did secede, or perhaps if even one of the two joined the Confederacy, the Union could kiss the war goodbye. From a military viewpoint those two States contained too many men and horses to take the risk of losing hundreds of thousands of soldiers to retake them. The point remains that if Missouri and Kentucky joined the Confederacy the Union would lose the war. Someone will have to explain how a Confederate victory would help one slave.

That is why, when General **John C. Fremont** and General **David Hunter** issued orders liberating the slaves in their military areas, which were located in Missouri and Kentucky, Lincoln promptly overruled them. He could not risk the secession of Missouri and/or Kentucky. To Lincoln, the hasty actions of these abolitionist commanders, however idealistic, would have caused the Border States to secede. Of course Lincoln took all kinds of heat from antislavery people, who used this incident to show that Lincoln was a hypocrite, a racist who did not care about antislavery whatsoever! You can understand the larger issue here.

5th Amendment Protects Slavery

Fourth: the 5th Amendment to the Constitution was also a limiting factor. Slaveholders held that their property was protected by their state constitutions. Northerners generally believed that internal state institutions were their own business, beyond the reach of the national government. Moreover, the Supreme Court had already ruled that slavery was protected by the Constitution. No statutory legislation passed by Congress to ban slavery could survive against the 5th Amendment guarantees of due process and just compensation.

Antislavery legislation might make 21st century civil rights advocates feel better, but any congressional antislavery laws would have been declared unconstitutional. If the American government simply wiped out property rights by majority will, why couldn't it also wipe out other constitutional rights – to free speech or jury trial?

The logic of 5th Amendment supremacy must be followed further. If Congress could not emancipate the slaves by legislating against it, does anybody think that a president could eliminate property in slaves and override the Amendment by executive order alone? If Congress cannot pass a law depriving a slaveholder of property, can any mere presidential order take that property? Does the word "dictatorship" come to mind?

SLAVERY, TERRITORIES, EMANCIPATION 1857-1865

From a constitutional viewpoint there were only several options open. The states themselves could free their slaves. This was clearly a doubtful option but a possible one. Alternatively, emancipation could be accomplished by constitutional amendment. Two-thirds of Congress and three quarters of the states would have to ratify that amendment. Even if somehow the amendment cleared congressional muster, where were those three quarters of the states going to come from? At least four Confederate states would have to vote for it. That could not happen before the Civil War, and it would not happen during it. After all, the Southern states were still in the Union.

Factors Operating For Emancipation

While powerful pressures limited efforts to emancipate the slaves, there were also strong counter pressures working for emancipation.

1 – Lincoln's Antislavery Ideology

First: President Lincoln's strong antislavery views. Lincoln had always hated slavery. He said very simply: *"if slavery is not wrong, nothing is wrong!"* Lincoln was hamstrung on this issue at the outset of the war. He proclaimed himself President of all Americans, not just antislavery Americans. *"I am naturally antislavery,"* Lincoln said, *"and yet I have never understood that the Presidency conferred on me an unrestricted right to act officially upon my judgment and feeling."* This reference to the heeding the aggregate wishes of the American public may be contrasted with recent presidential attitudes.

He explained over and over that his primary purpose was save the Union. In his famous letter to **Horace Greeley** in August 1862 he said, "*My paramount object...is to save the Union, and is not either to save or destroy slavery. If I could save the Union without freeing any slaves, I would do it. And if I could save it by freeing all the slaves, I would do it. And if I could save it by freeing some and leaving others alone, I would also do that.*"

Considering the 19th century context, Lincoln was no hypocrite. One did not have to believe in racial equality to be against slavery. Millions of Americans, however bigoted, held slavery immoral. One could believe that no one should own another human being without also believing that everyone should have equal access to restaurants or have integrated schools. Lincoln was typical of Americans in this respect.

SLAVERY, TERRITORIES, EMANCIPATION 1857-1865

Some pundits proposed colonizing slaves (some also added free blacks as well) in Africa or Haiti. Even Lincoln, as late as 1863, counseled African-Americans that bare freedom would not put an end to discrimination. He recognized how hard it would be to persuade whites that blacks were first class citizens. Colonization would at least give blacks a homeland of their own.

Frederick Douglass, the prominent black abolitionist, talked Lincoln out of that position. America was the rightful home of African Americans. The U.S. could not solve its racial problem by simply deporting it. America must deal with the issues of emancipation and equality squarely and live up to its ideals. Douglass's arguments persuaded the President. The point is that, whatever his motives, antislavery views were antislavery views. Abraham Lincoln was flat out antislavery. When he could find opportunity to act against that hated institution, he would not hesitate

2 – U.S. Must Prevent British Recognition of the Confederacy

Second. The need to prevent Britain (and France) from recognizing the new Confederacy as a sovereign nation among the nations of the world also worked in favor of Emancipation. Without some moral cause, the C.S.A. had the advantage in foreign circles. Much like the United States in 1776 the South was fighting for its independence. Without some moral cause the U.S. was in the position of Lord North in 1776. America, like England sought only to crush a rebellion. Ah, but the Union fighting for emancipation would throw the weight of world opinion against the Confederacy.

That is why Lincoln appointed strong antislavery men as ambassadors to foreign capitals. **Charles Francis Adams**, the son and grandson of presidents, served America in London. **Carl Schurz**, a German immigrant, a hero of the Revolution of 1848, Lincoln sent to Madrid, Spain. He posted New Yorker **John Bigelow**, co-owner and editor of the Evening Post, to France. And Lincoln appointed **Cassius Marcellus Clay** of Kentucky to Moscow. Lincoln knew that those men would lend an antislavery cast to American policy, even though it was not officially the government position. They in turn helped persuade him that he must move against slavery or risk foreign aid to the Confederacy.

Customarily, we do not think of the Northern motivation for war as antislavery. However, there is one sense in which this was certainly an antislavery war. **Once the war became protracted, it became an antislavery contest. Never was there a moment's thought of bringing the defeated south back into the Union with the institution of slavery intact.** Surely not after all the carnage and sacrifice of war. That would only leave the basic argument unresolved. It might lead to a future war all over again. The Civil War doomed slavery. At some point Northerners understood that the Union would have to be restored without slavery. Somehow! Some way! Emancipation became a means of preserving the Union.

3 – Abolitionist Pressure on Lincoln

The third factor working toward emancipation was pressure from abolitionists. Antislavery pressure on Lincoln was enormous. One should not underestimate this pressure, especially with a presidential election looming in 1864. Abolitionists, such as **Wendell Phillips** continually beat Lincoln's door down with demands that he take a firm stand against slavery as did **William Lloyd Garrison** and black militant **Martin Delaney** and of course **Frederick Douglass**. These abolitionists were a strong force, however hard to measure their precise influence.

4 – Need for Additional Troops

The fourth factor favoring emancipation was the clear need for additional troops. Abolition became connected to the war effort. Northern governors told Lincoln that great numbers of antislavery white men would not enlist in the army and fight just to win the war but preserve slavery in the South. General **Ulysses S. Grant** pointed out the need for men, especially for those who were waiting for the government to alter its position on slavery before joining up. Grant cited the large number of African American men willing to serve in the Union army, but who would not do so if the government refused to act against slavery. Nearly one quarter of a million African American soldiers ultimately served in the Union army.

Thus there were great pressures against emancipation – and great pressures for emancipation! For Lincoln the real question was not whether but rather how to emancipate the slaves, without losing Missouri and Kentucky – and thus losing the war – and without tearing up the Constitution entirely.

Steps Toward Emancipation

Lincoln's first proposal called for **gradual compensated emancipation** in the Border States. He recommended that Congress pledge financial aid to any state which adopted gradual emancipation. Under this plan freedmen might be settled outside the United States, but only if they wished.

SLAVERY, TERRITORIES, EMANCIPATION 1857-1865

Lincoln had in mind that his plan would destroy any hope of the Confederates that the Border States would join them. Moreover, the financial outlay would cost far less than war itself. Congress never seriously considered the President's proposal. Lincoln, furthermore, could not persuade Border State leaders in Missouri or Kentucky to initiate any emancipatory steps. Proslavery majorities in those states would have nothing to do with any form of emancipation, gradual or otherwise.

Congress, however, did enact several emancipation-related measures. On April 14, 1862, Congress abolished slavery in the District of Columbia, an action within their power, since D.C. was not a state or territory. Congress provided $300 to slave owners as compensation for the freedom of each slave, and appropriated $100,000 for freedmen who wanted to emigrate. Lincoln actually thought the success of the D.C. abolition would encourage the Border States to follow suit. But they still refused.

More significantly, in June 1862, Congress passed legislation abolishing slavery in the territories. **In the territories!** Without any compensation whatsoever. What about Chief Justice Taney's *Dred Scott* ruling? Republicans, who had never accepted the decision, now openly and frontally repudiated it, and the Supreme Court along with it. This congressional action has received scant historical attention from historians, but as a constitutional issue it held portent for the doctrine of judicial review and of separation of powers. As a political matter, however, abolition of slavery in the territories satisfied a long-standing Republican commitment. Republicans now kept their campaign promises and enacted their ideology. **The struggle for free territories was won**.

The first serious effort to destroy slavery in the Southern states was the **Confiscation Act of July 1862**. In part, this law provided that all slaves of rebels or those who aided the rebellion would be deemed "captives of war" or alternatively "contraband" if they were captured or escaped to the Union. Whether "captives of war" or 'contraband" they would be forever free, and never made slaves again.

The Confiscation Act also provided for enrolling contraband freedmen into the Union army. This war measure, however, was not enforced with any vigor by the Lincoln Administration. The reason is that Lincoln was moving toward a larger notion of emancipation by a means that we have just noted was constitutionally dangerous, even dictatorial. Lincoln intended emancipation by executive order!

SLAVERY, TERRITORIES, EMANCIPATION 1857-1865

The Emancipation Proclamation

On Sept 22, 1862, Lincoln issued his **Preliminary Emancipation Proclamation.** The formal **Emancipation Proclamation** was issued as the year 1863 began. It is imperative that we understand this document as a war measure issued by the Commander-in-Chief. Lincoln proclaimed that in all areas still in rebellion on January 1, 1863, slavery would be abolished immediately and completely. Emancipation would take place in areas still in Confederate hands – but not in Union hands. Emancipation would occur only where Union armies had not yet conquered by the beginning of 1863. That is all the Proclamation encompassed. It did not apply to slaves in areas already captured by the Union army, such as Louisiana. It did not apply in the four Union slave states.

Indeed, the Proclamation did not free anybody instantly. It had no effect until the conquering Union armies moved through a Southern state. Wherever the Union armies appeared, however, the Proclamation functioned perfectly. Slaves flocked to Union army lines, essentially emancipating themselves.

Some abolition-minded people thought then, and some people still think today that the Emancipation Proclamation was a sell out. But was it? We can examine how politically perfectly crafted this limited executive order really was! Relying on his authority as Commander – in – Chief of the armed forces in time of actual rebellion, Lincoln was able to circumvent the constitutional prohibition against federal interference with the internal institutions of any state. Moreover, by freeing only slaves in the rebellious areas, he would not interfere with the rights of private property in the Union slave states; Missouri and Kentucky would not secede over this form of emancipation. Radical abolitionists might consider the Proclamation a half-measure, but the larger issues were in play.

Further, by issuing a proclamation, rather than letting military successes dictate policy, he appealed to the growing antislavery feelings of foreign nations. Given the limited options Lincoln had to work with, the Emancipation Proclamation must be counted a brilliant political maneuver. As Commander-in-Chief Lincoln claimed that he could use whatever legitimate weapons of war he had available. Eliminating slavery was a weapon of war. It was better then relying on states to enact abolition, because it obtained the strongest possible impact abroad. The Proclamation acted to offset Confederate pressure on Britain and France to recognize the Davis regime.

SLAVERY, TERRITORIES, EMANCIPATION 1857-1865

Of course it was better than the silence of inaction. Lincoln would have considered inaction immoral. At the same time the Proclamation encouraged antislavery advocates and promoted enlistments in the army. In Lincoln's mind his limited action was better than total emancipation, because any President who attempted to wipe out the property rights of loyal union men, who were also slaveholders, would drive the Union slave states over to the Confederacy in an instant.

In evaluating the Emancipation Proclamation, we observe that this antislavery action was no flaming manifesto of liberty. It was no Declaration of Independence. It was no Gettysburg Address. That it was not still bothers people who simply do not appreciate the limitations within which Lincoln had to work. In Gerber's rendition the Proclamation stands as the ultimate tribute to Lincoln's sense of innovation and flexibility. We must understand it in its historical moment or we do not understand it at all.

Was the Emancipation Proclamation constitutional? Judged by peacetime standards in the 21st century, probably it was not. As historian Allen Guelzo has noted, even Lincoln thought the Proclamation would be declared unconstitutional if it ever found its way to the Supreme Court. Given the influence of Chief Justice Taney Lincoln probably was right in that prediction.

Opponents of emancipation, North and South, condemned it as a gross usurpation of the power of the President. If Lincoln's suppression of civil liberties and dissent was tyrannical, then logically the Emancipation Proclamation was tyrannical as well. But was emancipation the right thing to do? Was the Purchase of Louisiana the right thing to do? However regrettable, it occasionally befalls the American constitutional system that virtue can be achieved only beyond the bounds of conventional constitutional orthodoxy. Emancipation was one of those cases.

Lincoln understood that he had transgressed constitutional boundaries. "*I felt that measures otherwise unconstitutional might become lawful by becoming indispensable to the preservation of the Constitution by the preservation of the Union.*" Thomas Jefferson might have smiled at such a sentence. He might not have smiled about the idea of emancipation.

As early as December of 1863, as Lincoln developed his plans for setting up new loyal governments for Louisiana and Arkansas, Confederate states securely in Union hands, he included emancipation as a condition of permitting civil government to be reestablished in those states. Lincoln made it a condition of Reconstruction that restored states must abolish slavery in their state constitutions.

SLAVERY, TERRITORIES, EMANCIPATION 1857-1865

It is important to note that the Union slave states – Missouri, Kentucky, Delaware, and Maryland – interpreted Lincoln's Reconstruction conditions as the ultimate demise of slavery. Those states, finally, began their own emancipation processes early in 1865. But they had lost the opportunity for compensation, as originally offered by the President. Thus the Union slave states, too, would finally abolish slavery. The handwriting on the wall spelled "Emancipation" at long last.

The Thirteenth Amendment

To make emancipation uniform throughout the nation, and to eliminate all doubts about its constitutionality, the only available mechanism was a constitutional amendment. The Framers has made it difficult to amend the Constitution. There had been no written alterations since the Jefferson Administration some fifty years before. It was most difficult to get two-thirds of each house of Congress to approve. It was virtually impossible to get three-quarters of the states to ratify.

Lincoln pushed for a constitutional amendment anyhow. There simply was no other way. Finally on January 31, 1865, the 13th Amendment – the antislavery Amendment – passed Congress. The 13th was the first constitutional amendment to change the substance of the Constitution, rather than its rules or procedures.

Was ratification of the 13th amendment legal? It was certainly questionable. There were 36 states. 27 were needed to ratify. The Union contained only 25 states, if you do not count the states of the Confederacy. Two Union slave states, Kentucky and Delaware, rejected the Amendment. That meant that four of the seceded states must be counted for ratification. Lincoln's provisional governments were counted in the ratification process.

On Dec 18, 1865, the official declaration of ratification was announced and the 13th Amendment went into effect. Congress was wild with enthusiasm! Eventually eight Confederate states were counted as having ratified the Amendment. Those Southern ratifications were made by provisional governments set up under President **Andrew Johnson's** reconstruction program. There is the utmost irony in that those were the same governments which Congress refused to recognize as valid for readmission to the Union. Nonetheless, Congress was willing to let them stand as competent to ratify the Constitution.

SLAVERY, TERRITORIES, EMANCIPATION 1857-1865

Abraham Lincoln did not live to see emancipation accomplished. **John Wilkes Booth** shot and killed the President several days after Lee's surrender to Grant at Appomattox in April 1865. In the 21st century, at a time in our history when some African Americans and other advocates of absolute racial justice complain that emancipation was a barren gift, because it did not also eliminate racism and economic disadvantages, it may be useful to recall that those who struggled for emancipation did not see it that way. For former slaves emancipation was the greatest gift of all.

CHAPTER ELEVEN:
THE DILEMMA OF AMERICAN HISTORY –
THE PROBLEM OF INTERPRETIVE CONSISTENCY

It is valuable to make some rough historical comparison between the circumstances surrounding the American Revolution and the circumstances surrounding the American Civil War. Customarily, those two large events are examined and interpreted without any particular reference to the other. Comparative history is an unusual species even among American historians. Opening the comparative lens, however, catches a wider picture. However, to consider the circumstances behind the American Revolution compared to the circumstances behind the Civil War immediately leads to a serious dilemma, a problem of interpretive consistency. What we think about one event must influence what we think about the other. They are joined at the historical hip. We shall name this problem *"The Dilemma of American History: the Problem of Interpretive Consistency."*

Historians strive to make order out of the events of the past, so that history means something to us. In examining the relationship between the American Revolution and the American Civil War, we also can strive for order – and meaning.

Was Confederate Independence Justified?

Should the **Confederate States of America** have become an independent nation? The answer to that question must influence what we also think about the American Revolution. In one sense, it is quite appropriate to think that the South should have become its own nation. That is how the United States itself was born. And Israel, and now, perhaps, Palestine. The number of examples may be multiplied. What is the foundation of this proposition?

The **right of self-determination** is a precious idea. Should not the people of every society determine who rules them? That is what government by consent means, after all. Government without consent is tyranny. Every society has a right to assert its own integrity, its right to self-determination.

THE DILEMMA OF AMERICAN HISTORY

If it was right for the United States to determine that America should be an independent country, apart and separate from the British Empire, then logically, why should not the Confederacy also have that same right of self-determination? That was what **Robert E. Lee** and his fellow southerners believed in 1861. That was what **Thomas Jefferson** believed in 1776.

The downside of Confederate self-determination, of course, is that the horrid system of slavery would become permanent and perpetual in an independent Confederacy. The Confederacy was born to protect the institution of slavery and the culture and power structure which supported slavery. Slavery formed the basis of a separate Southern nationhood. Slavery existed in the new America of 1776, too. But in the cosmology of latter 18th century, slavery was not the paramount issue it had become by 1861. There was certainly a difference about the issue of slavery between 1776 and 1861. It is, therefore, difficult to give moral countenance to any nation – self-determination or no self determination – born because of slavery.

The historian must decide whether the right of self-determination was more important than the moral issue of slavery. On one hand, we may decide that it was morally wrong to invoke government by consent if that self-determination was based on the institution of slavery. On the other hand, if societies are born out of a unity of values, then ought we to judge what those values are? Who are we to decide what is good for other societies? If we are allowed to make such judgments, we are in the position of saying that only good societies should be allowed to exist. And of course good soceities are the ones we agree with! That is simply an unacceptable conclusion.

Should the Union Have Been Preserved in the Civil War?

The opposing point of view is that the Union should have been preserved in 1861. The Southern rebellion should have been crushed. Doesn't every nation have a right to protect its integrity against the chaos of every faction that wants to go its own way? Is every little splinter group with a website and a printing press, that wishes to call itself independent, have justification to destroy an established society? When do such groups speak for a society?

If we clearly understand the dangers of anarchy and the destruction of civil society, then even the fancy formulations about Southern secession and state sovereignty – which really amount to declarations of self-determination – cannot justify the fragmentation of the American community. That was certainly **President Abraham Lincoln's** position.

Ah, but who would support the preservation of the Union in 1861 if it meant putting down the rebellion and restoring the South with all of its institutions intact, including slavery? The positive side of the alternative of preserving the Union is emancipation. There was a clear and definite bond between preserving the Union and emancipation! That was also Abraham Lincoln's position.

Unity or national integrity was made a worthy cause precisely because slavery was abolished. There was not enough impetus to suppress the rebels based on unity alone. Emancipation superseded even Southern self-determination. If only territorial integrity matter, the Soviet Union should also have been preserved. And the former Yugoslavia. And the Ottoman Empire. Bare union in America, without any moral edge, such as the eradication of slavery, does not trump Southern self-determination.

Comparing the American Revolution and the Civil War

Indeed, If there was no reason for union, except that each nation has authority or power of preserving its national integrity against division and fragmentation, then the British Empire was also covered by that same reasoning. How, then do we justify American independence in 1776? There is a serious intellectual dilemma here, is there not?

It is intellectually insufficient to declare that 1776 was 1776 and 1861 was 1861. To argue that that was then and this is now is a weak justification. What about interpretive consistency? Are we not driven to conclude that if the Union should be preserved in 1861, then the British Empire should also be preserved in 1776? Conversely, if the American revolutionaries were justified in 1776, were not the Confederate revolutionaries justified in 1861? If Thomas Jefferson was right, why wasn't Jefferson Davis? If Lincoln was right, why not George III? Here we identify the problem of interpretive consistency in a rather succinct nutshell. There are no easy answers to this dilemma. Reexamination of the problem of interpretive consistency is certainly in order.

Similarities and Differences

What were the similarities and differences between the Southern States of 1861 and the American Colonies of 1776 that can get us out of our dilemma? Or perhaps prevent us from resolving it?

THE DILEMMA OF AMERICAN HISTORY

Recall that John Adams captured the idea of the American Revolution as a consciousness that Americans were not British any longer. The Revolution, said Adams, was in "the hearts and minds of his countrymen." That shock of recognition, that awareness of separation, made America a separate political community. Whatever the cause, there was a distinction between the American Revolution as a shift in consciousness and the War for Independence as an action to implement that Revolution.

America was a separate nation psychologically and emotionally before the War for Independence brought about formal nationhood. Had the Redcoats prevailed, there still would have been an American Revolution, albeit a failed revolution. American revolutionary leaders, the Radicals of 1775 and 1776, even though not an outright majority of colonists, had convinced themselves of British tyranny. Tyranny, or at least the perception of tyranny, was the principle which caused Americans to crystallize in their brains and guts that they were not British, but rather a separate community, a separate nation.

In identical manner Southern leaders in the 1850s came to a moment when in their minds compromise on slavery became impossible. That is when they became revolutionaries, the Radicals of Southern secession. In the hearts and minds of Southern leaders the Confederate revolution occurred prior to their War for Independence against the United States. Southern nationalism in 1861 was not different from American nationalism in 1776. War or no war, Southerners believed themselves a separate people.

Just as in 1776, the tyranny of the United States – or the perception of tyranny – by 1861 was the principle which caused Confederates to crystallize in their brains and guts that they were not American, but rather a separate community, a separate nation. The perception was the reality. The perceptions of tyranny in 1776 and 1861 were indeed parallel cases.

The threat from the "Black Republicans," the [incorrect] view that all Northerners were abolitionists and Abraham Lincoln was the abolitionist chieftain, was the shock that crystallized Southern thinking. In that sense Lincoln stood in the same relation to Southern revolutionaries that Lord North had occupied in the views of American revolutionaries.

The Dilemma of American History

170

THE DILEMMA OF AMERICAN HISTORY

Thus we are confronted once again by this colossal dilemma. Most Americans certainly understand, sympathize and support the American revolution in 1776. By those very standards are we not just as bound to understand, sympathize and support the Confederate cause in 1861? Southerners certainly thought they were repeating the experience of 1776 when they revolted in 1861. They had history on their side.

Was not the principle of self-determination, the idea that people should decide who their rulers are and the rules they live under, the same in both cases? An honest appraisal suggests that the situations were rather parallel.

If we turn the problem around, does it change anything? If we believe that a nation must have a right to prevent the disintegration of its national integrity by quelling the aspirations of factions which seek to fragment that nation, we can surely understand, sympathize and support the preservation of the Union in 1861.

Applying once again the same standard of objectivity, we can appreciate the Union, but not the Confederate cause in 1861. We want the Confederate rebellion to fail. Lincoln was right. Jefferson Davis was wrong. However, by that very same standard, are we not just as bound to appreciate the British cause in 1776? Did not the Empire have the same right to preserve its national integrity in 1776 as the Union did in 1861? Was not George III quite as justified in suppressing revolt and the disintegration of England's domain as Abe Lincoln was? And by the same methods? If Lincoln was right, so was Lord North!

We can have it either way that suits us. But not both ways. For the sake of interpretive consistency – for the sake of historical objectivity – we can favor either independence in 1776 and the Confederacy in 1861. Or else we can favor Union in 1861 and Empire in 1776. One or the other. Yet everyone knows that neither of those alternatives is particularly satisfying. Everyone finds both of those propositions unacceptable. What we all really want is to find a way to favor the Union in 1861 and American independence in 1776. We most of us want further is to find some consistent principle that allows us to favor the preservation of the American empire in 1861 and also favor breaking up the British Empire in 1776. We want some point of interpretive consistency to support American independence but not Southern independence. This is one tough dilemma.

There is one easy out, of course. One can simply proclaim that: "This is my country. I'm an American! No issue of interpretive consistency is as important as my emotional attachment to my historical roots." Patriotism

THE DILEMMA OF AMERICAN HISTORY

– nationalism – however attractive an option, remains insufficient justification for historians. Is there nothing more powerful than emotional loyalty to create some intellectual harmony in favoring Independence in 1776 and Union in 1861?

Resolving the Dilemma

There is one singular consideration. Both independence and union are united by the drive to **preserve free institutions.** The validity of the American Revolution rests in large measure upon the enactment of the free institutions of republican government. Similarly, the validity of the Union cause in 1861 also rests largely on the preservation of free institutions. The methods were flatly contrary and contradictory. However, the objectives in both cases were related to the enhancement of a society that would strengthen and protect individual liberties.

The American Revolution was fought to enhance the free institutions that Americans had learned during 150 years of experience of autonomy and salutory neglect. Freedoms could not be unlearned. Moreover, the decision to choose a republican, rather than a monarchical form of governance, became the operating principle in 1776. That is what Jefferson's Declaration of Independence was all about. America would emerge as a society without kings, without a hereditary aristocracy, without an established state religion, without a standing army. In America individual rights were sacred and protected. Consent of the governed -- self-determination – was the operating principle in 1776.

Similarly, the Civil War was fought to preserve free institutions from attack by a feudal society in the South. Northerners surely believed that Southern victories, represented by the extension of slavery to the territories, threatened free institutions as nothing else possibly could.

Abolitionists such as **Wendell Phillips** and **William Lloyd Garrison**, believed in personal liberty more than in any other principle. That is why they, who had hated the Union and the Constitution, because it protected slavery, changed their minds and supported the reunion. That is why Abraham Lincoln converted the war from merely putting down a revolt of unhappy rebels into an antislavery war. This is not to suggest that Lincoln viewed the war as an abolition war from the outset. He clearly did not. It does mean that at some point in time, when it became clear that the war would be a protracted affair, it also became unthinkable and untenable to consider reintegration of the Confederate states into the Union with slavery intact. The safety and security of free institutions required eradication of slavery as an institution.

THE DILEMMA OF AMERICAN HISTORY

Somehow, in some manner, slavery would have to be destroyed, lest another secession occur down the road, with another half-million dead required to maintain the United States as a free nation. This view of the Civil War as an antislavery war led to freedom for four million slaves. Whatever the issues of race relations unleashed by emancipation, the end of slavery was inevitable. For the United States to preserve its national integrity, Union included emancipation.

Alexander Hamilton's idea that protection of individual rights was the responsibility of the national government energized the spirit behind the idea of Union. That is what Union meant, what the United States meant – the right of every person to equal citizenship, equal rights and equal opportunities.

To preserve the Union without emancipation would be the equivalent of preserving the British Empire in 1776. To maintain national integrity meant free institutions in 1861, just as independence did in 1776. It may be repeated that while the means were contradictory, the objectives were consistent. That is the greater synthesis.

Examining very briefly several significant consequences of the Civil War provides evidence that eludicates this viewpoint

Consequences of Civil War:

1 - The U.S. Preserves Free Institutions

The first and most significant consequence of the Civil War was, as just observed, the preservation and enhancement of free institutions. That preservation took place on several levels and took several forms. The massive emotional upsurge of national spirit in the Northern states in favor of Union translated both consciously or unconsciously into a mass desire to free the slaves. Even if antislavery ideals were not the direct or original motives for war, it is nonetheless the case that the war transformed itself into an antislavery crusade. One of the primary effects of Civil War was to exterminate forever in America one of the most tragic and savage institutions ever to deface the dignity of humanity.

2 – Emancipation Plus Civil Equality

A second consequence of the Civil War was the movement beyond bare abolition to a concept of civil equality for freedmen. Slaves freed as the Union armies moved throughout the South would have to be guaranteed something more than merely dissolving the fetters of ownership by which masters claimed their slaves as chattel property. That basic augmentation was the conferral of collection of rights aggregated under the name of **civil equality.**

Civil equality translated as a set of legal rights to the same protection before the law as enjoyed by whites. The right to the prerogatives of American and state citizenship, the right to own and to dispose of real and personal property, the right to sue and be sued, and the right to be subject to the same criminal penalties as whites, all fell under the definition of civil equality.

Some advocates of civil equality thought that the extension of the right to vote to black males, once granted United States citizenship, also met the definition. Others considered voting rights political rights. Civil equality would be conferred in the various Reconstruction programs following Appomattox, as we shall note in the ensuing two chapters of this volume.

Were those guarantees sufficient to protect the freed people from their white neighbors? We must be careful about this issue. We must not impose 21st century cosmology upon the makers of Reconstruction. Our current notions of equality are different from those of the 1860s and 1870s. Civil equality was indeed enacted during Reconstruction. If those rights appear minimal by today's standards, they were not minimal to the 19th century. In an era of small government and with a work ethic that stressed earning one's way up the economic and social ladder without any support or handouts from Uncle Sam, enactment of measures of civil equality were major feats, indeed.

Those guarantees were embedded in the **Civil Rights Act of 1866,** in the **14th Amendment**, in the **15th Amendment.** These receive attention in Chapter Twelve. Beyond civil equality the right to equal public accommodations would be extended to the former slaves in the **Civil Rights Act of 1875.** Civil equality never included land reform. No forty acres; no mules. There was no public school integration, no affirmative action, no fair housing policies, nor any of the other current notions of equality which we today associate with equality. Civil equality, so critical as a floor of basic rights, became a critical consequence of the Civil War.

3 – Location of Sovereignty in Nation – Not States!

A third consequence of the war that has not been challenged was the question of the location of sovereignty in the American constitutional system. The Civil War established forever the sovereignty of the United States against the occasional challenges of state sovereignty. State sovereignty surfaces from time to time when regional minorities cannot capture a majority of votes in Congress or otherwise lack national support. They fall back on some imaginary moment at the outset of the American republic when they claim state sovereignty and national sovereignty were somehow equal. It is a ruse that denies majority will.

The Constitution had originally determined that sovereignty resided in the people, through the national government, and not the states. That was the purpose of the Framers in replacing the Articles of Confederation with the Constitution in the first place. The South challenged that transfer of power and embedded it in the Constitution of the Confederate States of America. It took until 1865 – and 625,000 dead young men – to enforce the Framers' original principle. Today, perhaps more than any time since the Civil War and Reconstruction, the national government protects individual rights better than states or localities. Americans owe that to Hamilton and Madison and Lincoln.

What a tragic waste of lives just to reenact and reinforce the concept that each individual is best protected and most happy, when he or she possesses the fullness of rights and when those rights are extended to everyone in the society. That was the idea spoken so well by James Madison when he wrote the Bill of Rights: that the rights of each of us are best protected when we rely on the whole community, through the national government, to enforce those rights. That is what the Civil War and indeed, Reconstruction, demonstrated at last!

If we can be comfortable accepting that analysis, it is possible to emerge from our intellectual dilemma. The idea of free institutions, of individual rights, extended to all, equally protected by the nation, permits an escape from that problem of interpretive consistency.

CHAPTER TWELVE:
RECONSTRUCTION – RIGHTS FOR ORDER

As the guns of the Civil War fell silent after Appomttox, the nation awaited Reconstruction. Could the anger and hatred which prevailed in the exhausted nation be supplanted by emotional healing and a cleansing revival of the spirit? The opportunities to bring change were now at hand.

For the victorious North, after all, the purpose of fighting the Civil War was precisely the chance to remake the South once the shooting ended. The purpose of the war had always been Reconstruction. Ah, but what sort of Reconstruction? Many in the Union states believed in a lenient and rapid Reconstruction in 1865. Advocates of a quick, lenient peace have contended that the South would have changed its own governance system, its own values, its own institutions, if only the South had been left alone. Most Northerners, however, thought that to abandon the South to its own devices would amount to fighting the war for nothing. As Northern editor **Edwin L. Godkin** put it:

> *What Mr. Davis and his fellows ask us to do is to treat everybody who chooses to get up a rebellion, and gives some plausible reason for it, as an honest fellow, only a little mistaken. What would he have said to this plea if put forward on behalf of John Brown? Was he not honest?*

Could Abraham Lincoln have unifed the resolve of a people who had risked so much for the opportunity to translate their views into action? Lincoln largely agreed with those objectives. Historical evidence indicates that the President was leaning toward the Radical Republicans at the time of his murder. What his second term in office might have achieved remains loudly silent.

Surely, if the Civil War had been what so many historians think it was -- an **irrepressible conflict** between hostile cultures and divergent systems of belief and behavior -- then it would have been largely impossible to expect the South to accept the spirit of a Union victory. If the South had won its independence, would Northerners thereupon have admitted that states had a legal right to secede? Or that slavery was right? If the great differences between the sections could not be reconciled before the war, there is little reason to suppose that the war would make reconciliation easier. If anything, the war embittered both sides. Each strengthened its belief that its cause had been right and righteous.

Reconstruction by Phases

Reconstruction falls into four distinct phases or periods. Chapter 12 covers Phase 1. The others are covered in Chapter 13.

(1) Presidential Reconstruction. The first phase is a period of Presidential Reconstruction, beginning during the war under Abraham Lincoln and then continuing under President Andrew Johnson. In this phase Southern states were permitted to organize themselves into civilian governments. Those governments were run by pro - Southern white Southerners and led by people who had received pardons from the Chief Executive. Acting under President Lincoln's **Ten Percent** plan, and then the continuation of that plan by Andrew Johnson, each of the eleven former Confederate states had reorganized itself by the end of 1865. Presidential Reconstruction lasted for two additional years until supplanted by renewed military control in March, 1867. State constitutions drawn up during Presidential Reconstruction limited the freedom of former slaves and enacted white supremist governments.

Congressional reactions to Presidential Reconstruction also took place in this phase. **The Freedmen's Bureau**, the **Civil Rights Act of 1866**, the passage of the **14th Amendment**, and the introduction of military rule all took place in this presidential phase of Reconstruction.

(2) Military Reconstruction. The second phase, military rule, began on March 2, 1867, with the passage of the **First Reconstruction Act** of that date. That law divided the South into five military districts, each governed by a major general who had practically absolute power. The military presence was not strong, since demobilization was rapid and effective, but the army, nevertheless, was obeyed by the South.

The role of the army -- in addition to maintaining law and order -- was to supervise the organization of a second set of civilian governments controlled by pro - Union loyalists. Military rule in each state lasted until Congress satisfied itself that the state had fulfilled all the conditions laid down for it. Then the state was formally readmitted to the Union, symbolized by the seating of Representatives and Senators in Congress. At that instant military rule ceased.

(3) Congressional Reconstruction. This phase is sometimes called Radical Reconstruction or Black Reconstruction. It was a phase of Congressional supervision of the new set of civilian governments which were established under military aegis and which replaced the military itself. In contrast to the first set of civil governments under Presidential Reconstruction, these were dominated by Southern Unionists, branded Scalawags by their pro - Confederate brethren; by Northern settlers in the South, labeled Carpetbaggers by their former foes; and by male freedmen, called by their former masters names which may not be reprinted here.

During this phase a second series of state constitutions were written. This time those documents incorporated all of the guarantees Congress thought necessary to protect the rights of the former slaves and to insure Southern loyalty to the Union. These included the ratification of the previously passed 14th Amendment, and in many cases the 15th Amendment as well, civil rights protections, and free public schools. These governments rebuilt the South and were primarily responsible for resolving at the state level the problems identified as major postwar issues.

(4) "Redeemer" Reconstruction. This last phase of Reconstruction was the period of the return to power of the Democratic Party in the Southern states, dominated by whites and largely pro - Southern in attitudes. In this phase federal restraints on the South were removed and Reconstruction officially ended. It is difficult to place dates on this phase, because some states were "redeemed" as early as 1870 and 1871, while others remained under Republican rule until 1877. Most states fell in between. All states were "redeemed" by 1877 when the last federal troops were removed from Louisiana, South Carolina and Florida.

The Problems of Reconstruction

Obviously, Reconstruction of the South involved complicated and enormous tasks, which, even under the best of circumstances amounted to rebuilding an entire society -- in values, in spirit, in governance, and, of course, in brick and iron. Even if the South had not been resistant to change (which it clearly was), and even if the North had been unified in its goals and methods (which it clearly was not), Reconstruction would have been most complex and tortuous. The problems to be solved may be partially listed here, but even to state them briefly suggests the degree of difficulty in overcoming them.

RECONSTRUCTION – RIGHTS FOR ORDER

Most immediately there must be reestablished a sense of order in the South. Order meant the suppression of the lawless bands who roamed the countryside, forerunners of the **Ku Klux Klan**. In a larger sense order meant the resumption of an acceptance to an obedience to law and the restoration of the routine of peace by a people whose lives had been disrupted by wartime mobilization and the trauma of war itself.

It was necessary to reestablish the South economically, to end fiscal chaos, to resume the reliability of trade, and to reopen links with Northern markets. Cotton had to be planted; cattle fattened. A new labor system must be invented, since slavery was a relic of the past, a victim of the war. Wages must be paid or some substitute found. Railroads must be built and shipping restored. Roads and public buildings must be erected out of bombed out devastation. This is to say nothing of the private construction required to rebuild homes, businesses, and the fertility of the land.

A new social system must also be formulated and the relationship between whites and blacks worked out. The question of race relations was unquestionably the thorniest of all. Civil government must be renewed. Schools and churches, and, indeed, all institutions in the South had to be reestablished. A new sense of direction for the South in values must be implanted and take root. There must be a restoration of the spirit of a people who had, even for a brief moment in history, considered themselves a separate nation. In constitutional terms, furthermore, the relationship of the Southern states to the Union must be determined. The South must undergo Reconstruction.

Each of these was a monumental problem. Together they were staggering. Amid the emotions engendered in any discussion of Reconstruction those realities of 1865 are frequently forgotten.

A Word About the Freedmen's Bureau

Even before the war ended the Lincoln Administration (and then Congress after the President's murder) began to cope with the chaos in the South that resulted from the destruction of Southern institutions. Most particularly Union leaders sought both to combat the vigilante terror of white gangs who intimidated the unsettled freedpeople and to provide for the physical and economic welfare of those former slaves.

In March of 1865 Congress established the **Bureau of Refugees, Freedmen and Abandoned Lands,** the Freedmen's Bureau. That agency, located in the War Department to save the taxpayers the expense of another civilian bureaucracy, was placed under the leadership of

RECONSTRUCTION – RIGHTS FOR ORDER

General Oliver Otis Howard (for whom Howard University in Washington D.C. is named). The Bureau was unique in 19th century American history in that it resembled an embryonic welfare state. The Bureau was a service - dispensing benevolent government agency, not unlike the federal relief agencies of the New Deal era of the 1930s. The Bureau provided food, shelter, clothing, schools, hospitals and legal aid. it did whatever it could to help the freed people and protect them. The most significant achievement of the Bureau was the establishment of schools for freed folks. As many as one quarter million students, children and adults alike, learned to read and write in schools staffed frequently by Northern white teachers. The literacy rate for African Americans skyrocketed. The teachers did not have to pass Praxis II.

The agency also had jurisdiction over abandoned lands. In many cases the Freedmen's Bureau settled freedmen on lands which white owners had abandoned, especially in the Sea Islands of South Carolina. That action was later overturned. However, the Bureau was also inefficient, slow, and subject to local Southern political influences – perhaps the eternal way of the military. Nonetheless, it did a world of good in the critical period of 1865 - 1866 to restore order to an uprooted society.

Current Interpretations of Reconstruction Require Revision

Reconstruction remains something of a mystery to students of history. Today the conventional thesis among historians holds that Reconstruction failed, because the Republican Party, which had won the Civil War, provided insufficient guarantees for the freed people. Congressional Republicans may have claimed to believe in justice for a people oppressed for centuries. They may have believed in liberty and equality. They had the votes in Congress to enact their ideological beliefs. Yet they nonetheless abandoned the newly freed former slaves to the tender mercies of their Southern white neighbors. Why? How could a "sell out" of such major proportions occur?

One variety of this argument contends that Congressional Republicans limited their programs to mild and relatively uncontroversial enactments related to civil and legal equality: the **Civil Rights Act of 1866**, the **14th and 15th Amendments** to the Constitution, and analogous state-based programs. The Republican Congress armed the freedmen with civil rights and the vote but then declined to take on the tougher issues. They enacted no public school integration. They enacted no land reform for freedmen – no forty acres with or without a mule. They punished no Southern traitors. Worse, along with their Republican President, Ulysses S.

RECONSTRUCTION – RIGHTS FOR ORDER

Grant, they refused to protect black Southerners from intimidation, violence, even outright murder perpetrated by white Southerners.

An alternative (but congruent) thesis contends that the American public became distracted from Reconstruction efforts because of new issues. The rise of corporate power after the Civil War, a huge economic depression that coincided with the latter years of Reconstruction, westward expansion, and corruption in government all combined to sidetrack Congressional Republicans from their commitment to the freed people. As Reconstruction continued Republicans weakened in their commitment to the freed people. They either lost their determination to pursue social or economic programs for the freed people or they never had that motivation in the first place. Thus a Reconstruction program, well initiated, just fizzled out because of newer problems that required energy and funding.

A third position holds that many Republicans had limited objectives for the freed people in the first place. All people should have equal civil rights and the franchise. By 1870 those goals had already been achieved. For many moderate Republicans, and even some Radical Republicans, who later became **Liberal Republicans**, the ratification of the 15th Amendment armed the African Americans with full power to protect themselves. Anything more would fall into the category of social equality – something the freed people must earn for themselves. Reconstruction measures, according to this view, granted the blacks the weapons to function successfully in Southern society. It was time to let them do it.

Taking these three versions together critics of Reconstruction have sought to discover the origin of continuing 21st century racial inequities in the limitations of Reconstruction. The Reconstruction program, historians claim, was deliberately confined to the mild concept of equality before the law. Even the written guarantees of citizenship, property rights, due process, equal protection, and the right to vote were limited gifts, conferred by a Congress more concerned with peace than justice, with reconciliation more than genuine racial equality and democratic equity.

Whichever version one adopts Reconstruction failed because the Union did not commit itself to the long-term, hard-nosed measures to alter the life of the South. Land reform, military occupation, and certainly the practical enforcement of equality for the freed persons would have worked if instituted over the long run. The North lacked stamina, or will power, or humanitarian sentiments, or became distracted by the lure of enterprise – or simply did not care enough about blacks – to install the guarantees necessary to cause genuine equality to work in the South.

RECONSTRUCTION – RIGHTS FOR ORDER

Reconstruction should not have ended until all of those results were permanently incorporated into Southern attitudes and institutions.

Present-Mindedness

However enticing these perspectives, they present two serious historical problems. First: there is a certain **present-mindedness** at work lurking in these approaches. All of us are bound to view the world through the eyes of our current cosmology. We have been influenced by the Civil Rights revolution and we live in a time when legal, political and civil equality has largely been achieved. Given our current mental equipment, is it any wonder that historians concentrate their attention in Reconstruction on the plight of African Americans?

Current historians have projected their current values back onto Reconstruction. They demand that the Republicans who claimed to share a modern ideology about racial equality be held accountable for not permanently implanting that racial equality in the fallen South and making it stick. They focus on what was left undone. It is somehow the fault of 19th century Republicans for not enacting what 21st century Americans see so clearly. For this historian such present-mindedness causes a missed focus. We need instead to examine Reconstruction from the inside out, as the participants viewed it. We may not "play tricks on the dead."

The Inherent Dilemma of Reconstruction

Second: This same present-minded focus prevents appreciation of what we may regard as the **inherent dilemma of Reconstruction**. Radical Republicanism, or what we may define as pre-war abolitionism, carried into the post-war period. But Radicalism was only one (and the minority one at that) of two primary strains of Northern thinking. Most Northerners would have said that they fought the Civil War as a Union War—a war to put down rebellion and restore a single nation.

But what did Union—actually reunion—actually mean? Today we feel deeply the tragic death of a single American soldier killed in Iraq. Just one. How about 23,000 in one day, as at Antietam? Or 625,000 deaths in the bloodiest war in the entire nineteenth century? As noted (in Chapter Eleven), no Northerner could imagine fighting for the Union only to bring the South back into the fold with the institution of slavery still intact. No one could picture restoring the South the way it was before all that carnage.

182

RECONSTRUCTION – RIGHTS FOR ORDER

Somehow, some way, there would have to be emancipation. Somehow, there would have to be uniform institutions established in a reunited America. You did not have to be an abolitionist to demand the end of slavery as a war aim. You did it to remove the seeds of discord between North and South. There must be one nation, not two, inside the same constitutional system. The South could not be allowed to rebel again ten years down the road. Slavery had to go. This was not particularly ideological. It was a practical, even a conservative, objective for the future security and peace of the nation. Lincoln held this view. Thus one thing Union meant was emancipation.

Then what? Could the United States government simply free four million people from shackles and turn them loose without protection? Moreover, how protect white Unionists in the south? How change the culture of nine million southern whites who a few weeks before would shoot you on sight and who thought themselves a sovereign nation? Thus a second thing Union meant was that additional measures to support the freedmen must be enacted. What measures and how would they work?

That question brings us to the inherent **dilemma of Reconstruction**. Reconstruction was an all-out war carried out in peacetime. One Northern objective of the war was to achieve loyalty to the Union from the defeated Southerners, the reestablishment of allegiance to the United States. Not by some oath to support the Constitution that Southern whites took under duress, but rather by a signficant cultural shift, a sense of being Americans once again, not sullen Confederates. Reconstruction must end division and hatred and terrorism against local enemies. It must bring about a genuine peace.

To accomplish this objective the conditions of Reconstruction must be mild and generous. Former Confederates, indeed all white Southerners, must have their rights and property (excluding slaves) restored. They must elect their own leaders unimpaired. There could be no humiliation of the vanquished. No retaliation. No punishment. No vengeance. No overhaul of society. What was needed was the sort of humane – some say lenient – idea of Reconstruction that had been initiated by Abraham Lincoln before his murder.

To achieve reconciliation the thing that must never happen is for the government to make equals of former slaves. Southerners might accept, however, grudgingly, the reality of emancipation. But racial equality in any form would be guaranteed to produce anger, alienation and resentment. It would delay and perhaps even defeat any restoration of positive feeling toward the Union. Even the most minimal guarantees for freed people – the right to own property, a horse, a rifle, the legal capacity to make a contract or to learn to read and write, to sue in court – would provoke white resistance exactly to the extent that any of those were attempted. To gain white allegiance the government must leave the future of the freed people to the white South.

This is not theoretical. We know that even the mildest requirements leading toward equality proposed first by President Lincoln and then by **President Andrew Johnson**, met with the stiffest Southern backs. We remind ourselves about the **Black Codes** enacted in 1865 by white pro-Southern civil governments that attempted to reduce the freed people to conditions as close to slavery as possible. We know of the daily violence perpetrated against freed people who had the temerity to exercise their freedoms. If baby steps toward equality evoked such reactions, how much more severely would white Southerners resist more substantial strides, such as the Civil Rights Act of 1866, or the 14th Amendment, or omigod, the right to vote! And worse yet, the right to sleep in the same hotel and ride in the same railroad car as whites! Go to the same schools! Confiscate white property and distribute it to blacks! For the white South, the greater the escalation of support for the African Americans, the greater the resistance. The depth of racist white supremacy must be understood – then and now.

However, since the other Northern objective of Reconstruction, as noted, was to insure the results of the war by providing rights to the freedmen, how would that happen? Too many young Northern lives were sacrificed in this uncivil war only to lose the victory as a condition of pacification. Again, as with emancipation, equal rights were not grounded in abolitionist ideology of justice and egalitarianism. They were based on the pragmatic need to preserve the victory on the battlefield and honor the "hallowed dead," as Abraham Lincoln referred to them.

How could the government prevent whites from reducing their former slaves to a status of all-but-slavery? How prevent them from intimidating, killing and maiming blacks and white Unionists? How prevent a potential race war in the South? How maintain civil order? There were two alternatives: one was a permanent military occupation of the South by the United States Army. A permanent army of occupation to rule the Southern states. Such an idea was of course absolutely unthinkable in the 19th century.

Rights For Order

RECONSTRUCTION – RIGHTS FOR ORDER

The other method was for the freed people to protect themselves by possessing equal rights. Thus, all Republicans could insist on equality before the law, the same American citizenship, the same due process of law, the same equal protection of the laws, the same criminal penalties for blacks as for whites. Those rights might be enforced for a time by the army, if need be, until they became accepted by Southern state governments. This is how the U.S. managed Germany and Japan, the defeated powers in World War II.

Moving from moderate Republican toward Radical, the **right to vote** would become the key requirement **to preserve civil order.** For some Republicans **equal public accommodations** was a necessary component of promoting civil order. For the more Radical Republicans the great gift of learning in **integrated schools** was deemed necessary for the purposes of order! And for some extreme Radical Republicans nothing less than land for the freedmen, carved from the fields of the vanquished, would suffice. Order coupled with justice! Guarantees of equal rights, fully enforced, was the mid-road alternative to abandoning the freed people to their former white masters on one hand or installing a permanent military force in the South on the other.

The dilemma is this: sectional harmony and racial equality were incompatible outcomes. The restoration of white allegiance and the requirement of civil order by granting rights to blacks lay in direct conflict with one another. To enact racial equality would defeat the goal of regaining the loyalty of Southern whites to the Union. To fail to enact racial equality would be to win the war and lose the victory in the peace process. Present-minded historians have blamed Radical Republicans for failing to achieve a task that was inherently doomed.

To untangle this web we may begin by reexamining major aspects of Reconstruction.

Reconstruction: Northern War Aims Versus Southern Culture

Reconstruction may be viewed as a struggle between Northern war aims and Southern culture. For the victorious Union, after all, the purpose of fighting the Civil War was precisely the chance to remake the South once the killing ended. The purpose of the war had always been Reconstruction. At the minimum the South would have to scrap its doctrine of secession and pledge acceptance to national supremacy and national loyalty. It must also guarantee equality before the law to the black population that Southerners regarded merely as chattel property.

RECONSTRUCTION – RIGHTS FOR ORDER

In addition, a great many Northerners – with differing motives – thirsted to make the South over in the Northern image. To some that meant the establishment of free institutions and Yankee values, including the virtues of private enterprise and free labor. To others it meant that the South must rip out white supremacy and the aristocracy of class, and replace them with the ideals of democratic equality, including the doctrine of racial equality.

For the vanquished South, conversely, simple military defeat could never be equated with acquiescence to Northern principles. Southern mores and behavior, molded by generations of slavery and aristocracy strongly resisted change. The South had fought long and well to preserve intact its vision of society. That purview included a total commitment to white supremacy. Mere physical force would hardly convince white Southerners that they had been wrong!

Somebody, North or South, would have to back down sooner or later. In a major sense Reconstruction tested the commitment of both antagonists to their particular ideologies and interests. Reconstruction continued the Civil War from the battlefield into other forums. Reconstruction was a conflict between Northern war aims and Southern culture. To repeat, Reconstruction was an all out war carried over into peacetime.

The Constitution itself was not much help in providing guidelines for Reconstruction. The constitutional system had been powerless to prevent the Civil War and the mass slaughter of the flower of the nation's young manhood. The conflicting interest groups had come to a moment when they could not be accommodated within the same constitutional framework. The system was really broken and must be fixed. It could not and would not be repaired without major revisions in the Constitution itself.

Where does that leave students of American history? As individuals we can indulge in wise-sounding statements which start "if only this" or "if only that." As historians, however, we must leave the "if only" speculation to philosophers and prophets, and to contemporary idealists. And of course to political scientists!

Southern Attitudes Regarding "Lenient" Reconstruction

One way to re-examine this issue is to consider once again Southern attitudes in responding to the relatively lenient presidential authority to establish new civil governments in the Confederate states. Both Abraham Lincoln and then Andrew Johnson required each former Confederate state

186

RECONSTRUCTION – RIGHTS FOR ORDER

to abolish slavery. They must also repeal and discard their ordinances of secession. All public officers must swear to be forever loyal to the U.S. from that moment forward. With those few conditions fulfilled, Southern states were permitted to restructure their civil governments. President Lincoln had reconstructed three states prior to his death under these conditions: Louisiana, Arkansas and thr occupied part of Virginia. various proclamations by President Johnson throughout the spring and summer of 1865 permitted the remaining eight states to restore civil governments. Moreover, Johnson's **Proclamation of Amnesty** of May 29, 1865, despite some exceptions, essentially restored white Southerners to their rights as American citizens. Southern states did what they were required to do. All eleven states had fully functioning civil governments by the end of 1865.

But with what mind did Southerners promptly and speedily accomplish these actions, proceed to reorganize their governments, and hold elections? Did ready acquiescence to presidential conditions prove that the South was prepared to accept the result of the war? If Southerners resisted Lincoln's and Johnson's **Ten Percent Plans,** or performed the very minimum they could get away with – or accepted the conditions in order to forestall more severe or drastic requirements – how would they receive any more substantial pro-freedmen measures enacted by the Republican Congress?

Some Northerners certainly thought the South had accepted with good grace and a positive attitude the changes required by the Lincoln/Johnson plans. **General Ulysses S. Grant**, surely no friend of the South, made an inspection tour of the Southern states shortly after the fighting ceased. He reported to President Johnson that the South appeared to him ready to accept the conclusions that the war had wrought and on that basis ought quickly to be readmitted to full status in the Union. Grant's report had a large influence upon Johnson's policy.

Not everyone agreed. General **Carl Schurz** had also been touring the South after the war. Schurz, it may be recalled, was the German revolutionary of 1848, an antislavery advocate who had risen to become Lincoln's Ambassador to Spain. He would become Senator from Missouri, founder of the Liberal Republican Movement of 1872, and President Hayes's Secretary of the Interior. Following his political career he became a prominent newspaper editor in New York City. Today Carl Schurz Park is home to Gracie Mansion, the residence of New York's mayors. He had, like Grant, been commissioned by Johnson to observe and comment.

Schurz claimed that the South was anything but ready for readmission, precisely because Southerners had not changed their attitudes one whit.

RECONSTRUCTION - RIGHTS FOR ORDER

President Johnson chose to ignore his report, but historians cannot. In part, Schurz said:

> *Treason, under existing circumstances, does not appear odious in the South. The people are not impressed with any sense of their criminality. And there is yet among the Southern people an utter absence of national feeling...Now the difficulty lies here: the Southern people have not abandoned their proslavery sentiments. They accept the abolition of slavery because they must...*

Who was right? Grant or Schurz? Just a few years later, even before he became President, Grant admitted to Schurz that he had been wrong and that Schurz had been right. What this may demonstrate, if Schurz was indeed accurate, is that well before the Congress ever took over the reins of Reconstruction the South had determined to refuse to accept, in any spiritual or emotional sense, the defeat of the Southern way of life or even the freedom of the slaves.

That is, Southern objections to Reconstruction were not just reactions against Congressional Reconstruction or military rule. Rather, the South only acquiesced in Presidential Reconstruction because that was the easiest way out! Better to accept a few mild requirements than refuse them and risk more stringent and severe ones. Southern states adopted the President's requirements. But Southerners were not persuaded.

Every former Confederate state elected to Congress under the Lincoln and Johnson white-only governments the same men who had served previously in government. Those naturally happened to be former Confederate officers and soldiers including the Vice President of the Confederacy, **Alexander Stevens** of Georgia, elected to Congress from his native state. Among those who presented themselves to be seated by Congress were four Confederate generals, five Confederate colonels, six Confederate cabinet officers, and 58 Confederate Congressmen. Was there also a partridge in a pear tree?

The same thing happened in state and local elections under those Presidential Reconstruction governments. Southerners quite naturally elected to office the talented, experienced people who had served their needs so well before. These people still represented the interests of the Southern whites, although, we might remind ourselves, those elections occurred after the loyalty oaths to the Union had been sworn.

In response Congess simply refused to seat the newly elected Representatives and Senators. The Republican leadership instructed the Secretary of the House of Representatives, **Edward McPherson**, not to

RECONSTRUCTION – RIGHTS FOR ORDER

call their names in the roll call of delegates. They were not seated. Northerners could not tolerate the idea of welcoming Congressmen who, only a few months before, it had been legal to shoot on sight! Can anyone imagine allowing Nazis into the German Reichstag in 1946? While the Constitution permits Congress to determine the qualifications of its own members, Congress had no jurisdiction over state and local officials.

The new Southern state governments also enacted a series of **Black Codes**. These state statutes, passed in every former Confederate state, fixed the place of the freedpeople as close to slavery as they could get within the technical realities of emancipation. The purpose of the Codes was to restore the traditional relationship between the races. They were designed to bring renewed order into the labor force and to compel social relations between the races in the traditional Southern manner.

Under these various Codes African Americans could not own land. They could not testify in court against whites. They could not hold office or possess any political or civil rights except the right to marry and own certain kinds of personal property (but in some states not horses or firearms). There were criminal penalties for contract violation and for vagrancy, defined as not having a job. Freedmen were limited to certain occupations, usually agricultural and domestic in nature. In some states they had to apprentice their children. In some cases they could not go to town without their employer's approval. In short, freed people were reduced to slavery in all but name. Indeed, if the planters of an area agreed not to hire each other's former slaves, then the freedmen had to work for their former master, like it or not, or flee the area, or risk arrest and prosecution for vagrancy.

The Civil Rights Act of 1866

As soon as the 13th Amendment was ratified, the 39th Congress acted. In direct response to the Black Codes, Congress passed the Civil Rights Act of 1866. This statute (currently #1982 of the United States Code) was one of those unstoried, but nonetheless momentous, actions of the 39th Congress. Its primary sponsor was Illinois **Senator Lyman Trumbull**, Chair of the Senate Judiciary Committee and a moderate Republican. Just as the Codes limited the rights of blacks and made second class persons of the freed people, the Civil Rights Act directly overruled those provisions. For the first time in American history the **Act conferred equal American citizenship on all persons born or naturalized in the United States.** The law then granted **full civil capacity** to the newly freed African Americans. Section #1 of the 1866 Act says:

RECONSTRUCTION – RIGHTS FOR ORDER

All persons born in the United States and not subject to any foreign power, excluding Indians not taxed, are hereby declared to be citizens of the United States; and such citizens, of every race and color, without regard to any previous condition of slavery or involuntary servitude...and shall have the same right in every State and Territory of the United States, to make and enforce contracts, to sue, be parties, and give evidence, to inherit, purchase, lease, sell, hold, and convey real and person property....

This short statement stood extraordinarily tall, for it meant that private persons could not discriminate on the basis of race, in the purchase or sale of land, a home, a horse, a rifle, or any other property transaction in which any white person could engage. "Sorry, I don't sell houses to black people," would no longer fly!

The 1866 Act also affected the criminal justice system. There could be no legal racial double standard in the conduct of a trial, or in the rights of accused persons, or in sentencing. All persons were entitled to the...

...full and equal benefit of all laws and proceedings for the security of person and property as is enjoyed by white citizens, and shall be subject to like punishments, pains and penalties, and to none other, any law, statute, ordinance, regulation or custom, to the contrary notwithstanding.

Any denial of equal rights by any person was made a federal offense punishable by fine or imprisonment. The Act could be enforced by the U.S. armed forces. The Act was meant to apply against private individuals as well as against a state or local agency or official.

When the Civil Rights Act was first passed, in early 1866, President Johnson vetoed it on the grounds that welfare and civil rights legislation were routinely state functions. He was correct, in terms of precedent, for the Civil Rights Act was surely unprecedented. A coalition of Republicans, mostly moderate Republicans but also some Radical Republicans, overrode Johnson's veto in April 1866.

Was the Civil Rights Act constitutional? The answer lies in appreciating the meaning of the 13th Amendment, the antislavery amendment. The simple eloquence in Section #1 that *"Neither slavery nor involuntary servitude...shall exist within the United States, or any place subject to their jurisdiction"* nonetheless requires explanation. The debates in the 39th Congress indicate that the language in that clause meant to abolish both the legal foundation of slavery, by eliminating the right to hold property in persons, and also to abolish the discriminatory laws, customs and practices – the **"badges and incidents of slavery"** – which made a person less than totally free. The Amendment did not stop at bare freedom, even if one dares call emergence from chattel slavery "bare." Both the legal conditions of slavery and the conditions imposed by social custom which allowed a person to be treated like a slave would be eliminated by the 13th Amendment.

Congress therefore, justified the Civil Rights Act under Section #2 of the Thirteenth Amendment, which announced that *"Congress shall have the power to enforce this article by appropriate legislation."* Oddly, the new Act was not legally challenged for a century, until 1968.

The Fourteenth Amendment

Congress did not stop with the Civil Rights Act. Two months later, in June 1866, **the 39th Congress proceded to enact the most significant alteration in the U.S. Constitution since the Bill of Rights – the 14th Amendment**. Today that Amendment provides constitutional support for integrated schools, for women's rights (including abortion), for applying freedom of speech, religion and the other liberties of the Bill of Rights to the States, and for generally prohibiting state and local governments from enacting discriminatory practices of every variety. Together with the 13th and 15th Amendments, the 14th has been regarded as a second American Revolution or at least a second Constitution.

Should not the Reconstruction amendments, therefore – especially the crucial 14th – have Framers, too, just as the original Constitution does? The Republican leaders of Reconstruction rarely get plaudits for their efforts, given current negative interpretations of Reconstruction. Following a suggestion from historian **Garrett Epps**, perhaps they should be elevated to status of a second set of Framers. If we applaud the Framers of 1787 for erecting our constitutional system, even though many were slaveholders, should we not also applaud the Framers of Reconstruction for having destroyed slavery, and for erecting the national government as the guarantor of civil equality for former slaves?

This group of new Framers might consist, at a minimum, of several moderate Republicans: the aforementioned Senator **Lyman Trumbull** of Illinois, plus the primary sponsor of the 14th Amendment, **John A. Bingham** of Ohio. Additional others might include the Chairman of the Joint Congressional Committee on Reconstruction, Senator **William Pitt Fessenden** of Maine and the Chairman of the House Judiciary Committee, **John F. Wilson** of Iowa. Radical Republicans must also be included: Representatives **Thaddeus Stevens** of Pennsylvania and **James A.**

RECONSTRUCTION – RIGHTS FOR ORDER

Garfield of Ohio, plus Senators **Charles Sumner** of Massachusetts and **Jacob Howard** of Michigan.

The 14th Amendment repeated the language of the Civil Rights Act of 1866 that made U.S. citizens of the former slaves, thus conferring on them the guarantees in the Bill of Rights. The Amendment, moreover, enshrined into the constitutional law the provision that banned states from denying to any person "due process of law" and "equal protection of the laws" – guarantees against discriminatory state action which have held states accountable to this very day.

By the 14th Amendment and for the first time in American history, the United States government pledged itself to intervene between the actions of a state and the effects of state actions, if those actions discriminated against any person. The United States would intercede to protect citizens and non-citizens alike against state sanctioned discrimination. That colossal achievement remains, without question, a revolutionary constitutional concept. Or was it indeed what James Madison and Alexander Hamilton had in mind at the outset of the American republic? The 14th Amendment advanced significantly, and continues to advance, the cause of equal justice under law!

But that was not all. Another provision of the 14th Amendment was to penalize state discrimination against black male voters by the denial of representation in Congress by the discriminating state. The original Constitution had provided that slaves be counted as three/fifths of a person in determining the number of representatives of a state in Congress. This had given the Southern states 23 "extra" representatives before the war, which they would not have received if blacks had not been counted at all. With emancipation, freed people would be counted as five/fifths of a person, a whole person, in the population count, thus giving the South an additional 12 seats in Congress (or 35, if blacks were not counted at all).

The Republicans who proposed the Amendment in Congress on April 30, 1866, believed that the South should be given these additional representatives **as long as the blacks had the right to participate in government equally with whites and were made citizens with full civil rights.** Of course, given the Black Codes, the South received the full 35 votes essentially for nothing. The 14th Amendment countered this condition by denying representatives in Congress to any Southern states which denied civil rights to any citizen, in proportion to the denial. Had that provision been enforced, the South would have lost all 35 seats. It was never enforced. Congress had moved swiftly to gain civil rights for the former bondsmen.

RECONSTRUCTION – RIGHTS FOR ORDER

Why did Congress, having two months earlier passed the Civil Rights Act, enact the 14th Amendment and send it to the states for ratification? The conventional historical wisdom claims that Congress was shaky over the constitutionality of the Civil Rights Act of 1866, particularly as it applied to private discrimination. They need not have been, but one could never tell about the Supreme Court in such matters. Some historians claim that the Republicans were concerned lest a future Congress simply repeal the Civil Rights Act altogether. Consequently, Congress promulgated the 14th Amendment in June 1866. The purpose of the new Amendment, the standard interpretation suggests, was to fulfill the same basic purposes as the Act, but to do so in an ironclad manner, not subject to repeal, legislative revision, or judicial declaration of unconstitutionality. That interpretation cannot be sustained by historical evidence.

The 14th Amendment, to be sure, omitted any reference to the issues of private discrimination covered in the 1866 Civil Rights Act. But that omission was not intended to narrow the scope of protection for the freed people. **In 1870 Congress readopted the entire Civil Rights Act of 1866, incorporating the complete text into the Enforcement Act of 1870.** Thus, subsequent to the passage and ratification of the 14th Amendment, Congress reenacted the same language it used to ban private discrimination that it had originally formulated in the rights granted in 1866. Whatever Congress intended the 14th Amendment to mean, it was surely not to retreat from the ban on private racial discrimination in property transactions. If Congress passed the Amendment to supersede the Civil Rights Act or guarantee that it would not be declared unconstitutional or repealed, why would they re-pass the Act? So what was the real reason for the 14th Amendment?

An alternative interpretation is suggested. The 39th Congress sought to enact its war objective of protecting the freedmen. The Republicans devoutly intended to provide for the freed people the full array of civil rights that constitutional law would allow. Thus, some means must be found to overturn the pro-white civil governments erected under the presidential ten percent plans. Those governments suppressed the former slaves through the Black Codes and through intimidation and violence. Congress understood Southern recalcitrance. Republicans were determined to install a new set of state governments composed of persons loyal to the Union who would protect the wartime victory.

The Republican leaders recognized the connection between the capacity of the former bondsmen to protect themselves before the law and the capacity to rebuild the South on Northern principles. Without a floor of civil equality the restored Union would not be safe. Blacks must be secure against public and private discrimination. The alternative to genuine civil equality would be some semi-permanent military occupation of the South by Union troops.

Thus, Congress made ratification of the 14th Amendment the single and sole test of loyalty. Any state which ratified the Amendment would be readmitted to the Union without any further conditions. Their Congressmen and Senators would be seated. There would be no further reconstruction measures taken. Congress would consider ratification evidence that the state would honor the provisions of the Amendment. Conversely, rejection of the Amendment would lead to a military response. Refusal to ratify the Amendment would be all the evidence Congress would need to replace the civil governments with military rule by the U.S. Army. All civilian government would end. Troops would rule Southern towns and cities. Martial law would prevail.

Southerners understood the choice. Grant blacks civil equality by ratifying the Amendment or live under military rule! **They rejected the Amendment vehemently and instantly.** As the Florida Legislature put it: *...We will be taxed without representation; we will quietly endure the government of the bayonet; we will see and submit to the threatened fire and sword of destruction, but we will not bring, as a peace offering, the conclusive evidence of our own self-created degradation."* The conferral of racial equality before the law struck the hardest blow at the Southern idea of white supremacy.

For a wary Congress, that rejection, repeated throughout the South, furnished the most articulate evidence of Southern resistance to deep cultural change. Ten Southern states, every Southern state except Tennessee, refused to ratify. Indeed, Tennessee's ratification was compelled, because Radical Republican Governor **William G. Brownlow,** called "Parson" Brownlow, threatened to shoot legislators if they voted against ratification. Tennessee was instantly restored. The other ten states remained in constitutional limbo. It would take until July 28, 1868, before the 14th Amendment was ratified.

The ratification issue did create a constitutional oddity, a constitutional Catch 22! To become fully restored as states, Southern states must ratify the Amendment. But, of course, only full-fledged states could vote on any Amendment in the first place. Southern states, who always claimed to be out of the Union, did not hesitate to vote negatively.

Southerners received what they knew was coming. As Congressman James G. Blaine put it: *The Southern whites knowingly and willfully brought it upon themselves. The Reconstruction Act would never have*

RECONSTRUCTION – RIGHTS FOR ORDER

been demanded had the Southern States *accepted the Fourteenth Amendment in good faith."* As a direct response to the failure of the Southern states to ratify the 14th Amendment, military rule was instituted in the South. Since ratification had been made the test of loyalty, and since the South had failed that test by deliberately rejecting the Amendment, then this defiance must be met with sufficient force to insure loyalty. Congress instituted military government in the South in **The First Reconstruction Act on March 2, 1867.**

The date of the First Reconstruction Act is significant. Radical Republicans had won an overwhelming victory at the polls in the Congressional elections of fall, 1866. Too frequently it is assumed that it was this incoming Congress, which initiated military rule. But the Act was passed on March 2, 1867 by the outgoing 39th Congress. That Congress had been elected along with Abraham Lincoln in November, 1864. They had taken office officially in December 1865 (although Lincoln called them into special session in March) and left office on March 4, 1867. The new 40th Congress did not take their seats until the first week of December 1867. Thus, military rule had been enacted by the outgoing, "lame duck" Congress.

This means that military rule for the South had the support not only of Radical Republicans but also of the moderates and even some conservative Republicans. That party united in the belief that Southerners had not accepted the results of the war. Indeed, the Civil Rights Act, the 14th Amendment, and military government represented a far more general attitude in the North than simply the wishes of the Radical wing of the Republican Party. Indeed, the Reconstruction Act was largely written by conservative Senator **John Sherman of Ohio,** brother of General William T. Sherman.

Once again what is obvious must find articulation. Southerners prefered military rule to civil equality. Rather than accept equal rights before the law for freed people and free blacks, the white South chose to eliminate altogether the precious gift of self-government and be ruled by hated Union generals! For the white South to supersede civil government with military government was preferable to allowing blacks the basic equal rights of citizenship, due process and equal protection. The Southern states had determined to refuse to accept in any spiritual or emotional sense their defeat, or the substantive freedom of their former slaves, or the other changes which constitute Northern war aims. Schurz had made an astute observation.

CHAPTER THIRTEEN: RECONSTRUCTION
COMPLETING THE AMERICAN UNION

Military Rule – Phase Two of Reconstruction

With the enactment of the **First Reconstruction Act** on March 2, 1867, the momentum for Reconstruction shifted to Congress. The Radicals in the new 40th Congress would now set the conditions for reconstructing the Southern states. Congress justified its actions on the basis of its constitutional responsibility to provide for each state a "republican form of government." Congress chose to interpret the so-called **"guarantee clause"** [Article 4, Sec. 4] to mean equal rights for all citizens. Meantime, President **Andrew Johnson**, as expected, vetoed the Act as a tyrannical usurpation of the rights of the states. He was promptly overridden, 135 to 48 in the House, 38 to 10 in the Senate. The size of those majorities, the results of the elections of 1866, suggests that the people of the Union meant to insure their war aims.

Under the First Reconstruction Act the ten states not yet "readmitted" were divided into five military districts under five federal commanders, all Union Major Generals. Military governments supplanted the civilian governments previously established under presidential authority. The military commanders exercised plenary power. Their first role was to take over the governing functions of the state governments, all the legislative, executive and judicial functions, as a prelude to establishment of new loyal civilian governments.

The next task of the military commanders was to oversee the formation of new state constitutions to replace those of the Lincoln and Johnson governments. New lists of voters, deemed eligible under Section Two of the 14th Amendment, would be drawn up, even though that Amendment was not yet formally ratified. The military would supervise elections to those constitutional conventions. Black males were authorized to vote in the election of delegates to those conventions.

In addition the Reconstruction Act required the new constitutions to enact the right of male blacks to vote and hold office. They must also disqualify former Confederate leaders from voting and holding office. Otherwise the constitutional conventions could structure their state governments as they wished. The new documents would have to be ratified by a majority of eligible voters, not merely ten percent of the eligible voters needed by the earlier presidential civil governments.

Once the state constitutions were ratified, then civilian state governments could be drawn up. Elections would occur. Once in office, those new governments must ratify the 14th Amendment. That action completed, the state would be entitled to readmission, with its representatives seated in Congress. At that point military rule would end.

"The problem before us," wrote Editor **Edwin L. Godkin**, "is to pacify the South, and to secure the freedmen against legalized degradation and oppression." Representing the opinions of millions of Northerners, Godkin insisted that the path to pacification and security lay in "the retention of the South under the present military regime until the whites have got rid of whatever delusions as to the possibility of defeating the Congressional policy Mr. Johnson may have inspired them with." In the meantime, asserted Godkin, "military rule is doing no harm. It is the best and most civilizing rule to which the South has ever been subjected..."

By itself the Reconstruction Act, while moving the South from Presidential to Military Reconstruction, did not work. Deliberate Southern resistance, in the form of passive aggressive behavior, compelled Congress to retreat to an even more stringent measure. The new 40th Congress passed the **Second Reconstruction Act** to make the first law operative. The Second Act gave military commanders the power to take initiative in launching voter registration drives, in getting delegates elected to constitutional conventions, and in adopting new state constitutions. That Congress should act so quickly indicates another point: that Radical Republicans disliked the idea of military government on principle as much as anyone else. They were installing military regimes, not for the purpose of punishment, but for supervision of the restoration of loyal civilian authorities.

The Second Reconstruction Act passed Congress on March 23, 1867. It was vetoed by President Johnson the same day. That very day his veto was overridden, 114 to 25 in the House, and 40 to 7 in the Senate. The Radical Republicans were in the saddle. They had been placed there not by any political trickery but by the overwhelming sentiment of the great mass of Northerners. The American people were unwilling to brook Southern defiance overlong. They refused to lose the peace.

The second law did not work any better than the First. Neither did a third supplemental act, even tighter than the second. Three laws had passed without getting the new governments started. The reason is not complicated. Congress required a majority of registered voters in each state to approve their new constitutions. To register Southerners had to swear that they had not supported the rebellion. Southerners blithely took the oath and registered to vote. When it came time to cast that vote, however, they stayed home and did not vote. It was hence impossible to get a majority of registered voters to begin the Reconstruction process. Perhaps the fault lay in the oath of allegiance. Loyalty oaths have little or no effect, as Southern actions demonstrated. This set of oaths was certainly among the most perjured in history.

Finally, Congress wised up! **The Fourth Reconstruction Act** passed on March 11, 1868, because of the "ten day" rule, without the President's signature. That law changed the number needed to elect delegates to the constitutional conventions and then to approve the new constitutions to a *majority of votes cast, not the majority of voters registered.* That change worked, and finally Radical Reconstruction could get under way. It had taken three years since the close of hostilities before the Radicals could win themselves the power position from which to enact their war aims. Most of what Congress could do had already been instituted, albeit in milder form than many Radicals might have wished. Beginning in March, 1868, Republican civil governments in the Southern states took over the direction of those states from the military.

Military rule was not oppressive to Southerners. In the first place the grand total of Union troops in the ten former Confederate states numbered just over 20,000 men. The army had been almost totally demobilized after the war. There were normally no more than perhaps 500 soldiers in any one garrison. As a force powerful enough to compel obedience, the army was simply too weak. And yet the South totally acquiesced in military administration. There was no serious physical resistance to the troops. This is not that Northern soldiers were liked, but only that there were no uprisings. This indicates that the military authorities were essentially fair and not punitive to Southerners. If they had been unfair, there would have been resistance. If soldiers had molested Southern women, or if there had truly been the brand of injustice sometimes meted out by military rulers, there would have been outright rebellion.

If anything, the reverse was the norm. In cases heard in military courts for violation of election laws -- such as voting when one was disenfranchised -- only roughly 20 percent of defendants were found guilty. Only some 750 former Confederate officeholders, both civil and military, were ever prohibited from holding office. What is even more significant is that, despite Southern anger over what they considered military tyranny, the Southern states took no active steps to overturn military rule by establishing the constitutional conventions called for by the Reconstruction Acts. Southerners, who defended states' rights and local control, who passionately hated federal interference, preferred to remain under military administration rather than to admit even the barest civil equality to the freedmen. White supremacy was more vital to them than even their principles of government!

Congressional Reconstruction – Phase Three

Beginning in March 1868, Republican civil governments in the Southern states took over the direction of those states from the military. If Reconstruction was, indeed, a struggle between Northern war aims and Southern culture, enactment of Northern war aims appeared to be ascendant.

In recalling the exhausting list of problems facing the victors with the end of the war, it is critical to note that it was these Republican civilian governments, composed of Northern men who settled in the South, Southern Unionists and freedmen, which now had to come to grips with the daily working out of these issues. These Radical governments enacted the state laws, and enforced them, that established legal and political equality for the freed people. These governments rebuilt the public roads and began the process of rebuilding railroads. They established the credit of the states.

These Southern Republican governments also erected for the first time in the South a system of **free public schools**. They were segregated schools, to be sure, but they were nonetheless based on the principles of compulsory public education so common in the North and so alien to the South. The new governments also restored the routine of business life and the daily reliability of public service. They did all this despite the relative lack of experience in government about which so many people complained. Of course they had help from the federal government, and sometimes took direct orders. Some did their jobs better than others, considering the complexity of the problems and the passivity of the white majority population. Overall, the record for a society emerging from the shattering ravages of a brutal war is a highly positive one.

How Radical Was Congressional Reconstruction?

It is clear with hindsight that the Radical Republicans sought only one major war aim: their objective was to give to African Americans legal and civil equality, equality before the law -- and enforce it! This was the entire essence and extent of their program. All other war aims were subsidiary to civil equality enforced. The Republicans accomplished this by enforcing the 14th Amendment and then by enacting and enforcing the 15th Amendment as well. **The 15th Amendment**, of course, gave black males the ballot, a measure which worked with remarkable success. Toward the end of the Reconstruction period, Congress also enacted the Civil Rights Act of 1875, to be discussed later in this chapter.

The whole crux of Reconstruction was to provide civil equality as the price of reunion. Radical Republicans more than moderate Republicans were inclined to use force to insure those guarantees. Radicals were perhaps a bit more suspicious of white Southern protestations of loyalty than their moderate Republican colleagues. They would have preferred that white Southerners accept the new condition of the blacks in their midst in their hearts and minds. But at least whites would have to change their behavior toward blacks. Thus the term "Radical" ends at civil equality enforced!

Nonetheless, the label "Radical" still sounds severe to the modern ear. Perhaps the doctrine that people who had been slaves in one year should have the same rights before the law and hold office and vote the next year really was a radical political position. For the latter 19th century such a view seemed to many, if not most, to be flatly outrageous. Southerners regarded it in that manner. So did many Northerners. Today some Americans take civil equality for granted and even belittle it as a minor achievement at best. 19th century Americans did not take that view. Civil equality was a stunning achievement. The Radicals accomplished it.

Every measure built into the Reconstruction process was designed to connect with the implementation of that concept of civil equality. Hence Radical Reconstruction did not mean vindictive punishment of the South for the sins of secession, rebellion and Civil War. Neither were any economic policies instituted on behalf of the freed people, although several were proposed. There were a number of schemes for land reform, including the redistribution of plantation land to the freedmen. The best known was the famous "40 acres and a mule" -- and that never had a mule in it! Those plans were too advanced for the context of the 19th century and could not pass even the most Radical Congress.

Neither were any rebels punished as war criminals. There was only one execution, that of **Henry Wirz**, the Commandant of **Andersonville Prison**. Wirz was hanged for war crimes against Yankee prisoners of war, but, interestingly, not for treason. No Southern property was confiscated after the war, unless one considers slaves property. A few Confederate leaders went to jail. President Jefferson Davis remained in prison the longest, a term of two years. The others were released after a few months. Nobody was tortured or deported. Some men lost their right to hold office. Some 150,000 lost their vote for a time. If we contrast this Reconstruction with the treatment of German War criminals after World War II, we can see how mild and limited Radical Reconstruction was in truth.

"Redeemer" Reconstruction – Phase Four

The name "Redeemer," a Southern appellation, suggested a longing for a return to traditional mores embodied in the concept of home rule. With the return to power in the South of white, Democratic Party, "Redeemer" governments, Reconstruction entered its final phase.

Perhaps the best evidence of the limited scope of even the Radical program is to observe just how easy it was that those Republican state governments were replaced by white Democratic governments during the final phase of Reconstruction, "Redeemer" Reconstruction. Radical Reconstruction did not last from 1868 to 1877, as so many think. The shift from Radical Republican to Democratic "Redeemer" governments occurred as quickly as white Southerners decided to make it happen. In Virginia and North Carolina Democratic white conservative "Redeemer" governments came into power in 1870! Georgia 1871. Texas, Arkansas, and Alabama 1874. Mississippi 1876. Those seven states also sent white Democrats to Congress. In three states only: South Carolina, Florida and Louisiana, were there any Radical governments to overturn or any troops to pull out in 1877.

The Emergence of "Redeemer Reconstruction"

Those simple dates reveal much. They require us to ask: how did the "Redeemer" governments overthrow the Radical regimes in the several Southern states? How did they get into power? There is, obviously, one way only. They were voted into power. But if they were voted in, where did the votes come from? Surely not from the newly enfranchised freedmen! Blacks voted for the people who had freed them and given them civil equality, the party of Abraham Lincoln, the Republican Party. The votes had to come from white Southern Democrats. But weren't all the whites, according to Southern mythology, disqualified from voting under the 14th Amendment? And even if they could vote, can it possibly be the case that the Republicans calmly stood by and allowed themselves to be voted out of power? Weren't the Radicals motivated by a thirst for political power in the South so that could keep themselves and their Party in office? Would Radicals who had struggled so hard to attain the ability to enact their war aims simply accept a democratic decision to elect Democrats? The answer is definitely yes!

RECONSTRUCTION – COMPLETING REUNION

Again the fact is that only approximately 150,000 men, out of some 630,000 whites who volunteered for the Confederate armed forces were ever disfranchised. The right to vote was not withheld from those who were drafted into the Confederate army, because those men could claim, however deceptively, that they served the rebel cause against their will. Thus, out of an army of over two million men, and all those others who aided them, only a handful lost their vote. What appears to have occurred is that many thousands more simply did not register to vote under the Radical governments, or else they registered to vote but refused to vote. Out of apathy or out of protest, or whatever motive, whites simply stayed away from the polls.

The point is that when they did bother to vote, they won! Neither the military nor the Radical Republican regimes tried to stop them. By the time Reconstruction officially ended in 1877 all but three of the eleven states of the Confederacy had voted Republicans out, Democrats in! If the Radicals in those states had been interested primarily in political power for the **Grand Old Party**, they never would have let that happen. Neither would the Republican Administration in Washington. Moreover, in April 1872, Congress itself passed an Amnesty Act, by which even the disenfranchised were pardoned and received their full rights once again.

Let the case be put thus: **IF** the Radicals had been motivated primarily by political considerations -- **if** their aim was political control over the Southern states -- why did they permit the "Redeemer" governments to come into power? And why re-enfranchise the last cohort of men who they knew perfectly well would vote Democratic? So much for political motives! Much like the Federalists who had launched the new American Republic and then surrendered political power to Thomas Jefferson in the election of 1800, the Republicans of Reconstruction also yielded power peacefully.

How about economic motivation? This idea, so compelling, also lacks historical evidence. It is often argued that the North wished to exploit the South economically. Certainly the Republicans were the party of economic development during the years that coincided with Reconstruction. However, businessmen themselves were divided about what economic policies to follow. Some wished to maintain the South as a sort of economic colony, providing raw materials for Northern industry. Others wished to integrate the South into the mainstream of the national economy so that America could better compete with European business interests.

Radical leaders in Congress were badly divided. No single economic interest could gain a majority in that legislature. Massachusetts Senator **Charles Sumner**, perhaps the Senate's leading Radical, favored low tariffs, while Representative **Thaddeus Stevens** of Pennsylvania, who wrote the 40-acre proposal for freedmen, advocated protective tariffs. As a result no major laws were proposed to help the South recover economically or to favor the emerging interests of large corporations in the South. The utter absence of economic legislation suggests once again that economic interests were not the primary Radical focus.

The most likely explanation is that the Radicals had already enacted their primary war objective: of civil equality enforced. They surrendered power because they believed that they must accede to the will of the majority. The democratic process was more important than staying in office. Men capable of believing that the 14th and 15th Amendments were the alternative to permanent military occupation in the South surely could also believe that once those Amendments were in place they would be upheld even by those who disliked them, especially if blacks had the legal and political means to protect themselves.

Ideological Considerations: Rights-for-Order Reiterated

If the Radicals were not primarily moved by political power or by economic interests, then we are left to consider ideological concerns as their major motivator for Reconstruction. Ideology accounts for the drive for *civil equality enforced.* Ah, but what ideology? Radicals believed primarily in the old Yankee virtues of good character, personal and public integrity, culture, and morality. It was their constant desire to improve the ethical level of human relationships.

The environment for implementing these values depended directly on stability and order in society. The prime directive of every government is to preserve order. The Radicals sought to impose a moral order in the South, a uniform social order which would resemble that of the North. Order, in turn, required the extension of free institutions. Free institutions included a system of laws, judicial fairness, an independent press, educational institutions, citizen political participation, and a set of individual rights protected by government. Free institutions provided those adaptive mechanisms by which new circumstances and new power realities could be channeled to the public. Free institutions defused divisions in society and prepared people to accept new realities. They preserved social order.

The great threat to order was its opposite, disorder. Disorder included the agitation, violence, and anarchy of degraded and depressed classes in American society. In the case of the South, civil and legal inequalities spelled smoldering unrest, constant conflict and disorder. Under those circumstances society could not genuinely exist. The remedy for disorder lay in civil equality. Society must be democratized, so that no minority, no class, no interest, no region would remain alienated. James Madison would have applauded that reasoning. The reasons for violence and discord must be removed before they burst into flames. Civil equality became the key to restored social harmony and the implantation of Northern values.

Let it be clear that civil equality for the freedmen was necessary not so much because it was humane or because it fulfilled the demands of justice, but rather because the exercise of individual rights, guaranteed by the United States, permitted African - Americans to protect themselves against white society. Equal rights were required precisely because inequality bred disorder. Disorder flatly contradicted Northern values. This was exactly the "rights-for-order" mentality shared by moderate and Radical Republicans alike.

Thus Radicals proposed and supported measures for the freed people as a way of striking a blow for civilized society. They supported civil equality as a means of reforming order in Southern society toward Northern ideas and values. Rights for blacks would be an enormous stride forward, no matter how difficult to implant.

The Impeachment of President Andrew Johnson

The impeachment and trial of President Andrew Johnson, March through June, 1868, represents a significant event in the development of Reconstruction. Historians have perspired over the apparent paradox of the Johnson impeachment just at a time when the Radicals had such a commanding power in both houses of Congress and at a time when Johnson had less than a year to go of his term of office. It seems somewhat strange that President Johnson was impeached when Radical Reconstruction had already passed over his veto, when he seemed less threatening than ever. Maybe the real question is not why he was impeached -- for there might have been good reason in the minds of the Radicals who supported and operated that process -- but rather why in mid - 1868? It was an issue of historical timing.

It may be recalled that the outgoing 39th Congress, on March 2, 1867, enacted the **Tenure of Office Act**. That law prevented the President from removing from office civil officers he had appointed, without the advice and consent of the U.S. Senate. The law reversed the customary practice which had grown up since the Washington Administration of allowing the President to remove officials at his own discretion without congressional consent. The Tenure of Office Act, of course, served as the pretext for the impeachment of Johnson. Johnson's attempt to fire Secretary of War

RECONSTRUCTION – COMPLETING REUNION

Edwin M. Stanton, a Radical Republican, was a conscious, deliberate violation of the Tenure of Office law -- or so Congress decided.

That law, however, said nothing about the removal of military officers, nor could it. Those officers came under the direct jurisdiction of the President as Commander-in-Chief. Andrew Johnson had in fact removed various military commanders in the five military districts, and elsewhere, who had been zealous in their efforts to carry out the mandate of the Reconstruction Acts. He removed General **Philip Sheridan** from the Louisiana-Texas District, because Sheridan had fired certain pro-Southern civil officers from their jobs in the Johnson governments. Johnson also got rid of General **Daniel Sickles** (who had lost a leg at the Battle of Gettysburg) in South Carolina, because Sickles had eliminated debtors' prisons and established schools in his region, actions Johnson regarded as usurping strictly state functions. He dumped General **John Pope** for removing from the voter lists the names of ex - Confederates known to have served in the Confederate army, but who had taken the loyalty oath, swearing that they had never aided the rebel cause. General **Edward O.C. Ord** was removed for similar offenses. General **Rufus Saxton**, second in command of the Freedmen's Bureau, was fired for settling blacks on lands confiscated from former slaveholders. The remaining district commander, General **John Schofield**, was a moderate, acceptable to the South; he retained his position.

Johnson finally replaced Edwin Stanton as Secretary of War, once the impeachment trial was over, and once Stanton came out from behind his barricaded office in the War Department, and resigned. The point is that Johnson was quite within his authority in making those removals, whatever that meant in terms of the implementation of policy. Despite huge Radical majorities in Congress, Johnson was hardly hog-tied. Congress could pass any law, but the President must still enforce it. The Radicals obviously believed that Johnson's obstructionist tactics threatened the entire Radical program they had worked so diligently, and at such cost, to get into place. With Johnson out of power they were free to implement the war aims they had enacted without impediment from the executive branch.

What remedy exists to discharge a President during his term of office when he is hopelessly at odds or out of touch with the American public? There really is none at all. Impeachment stands as the lone constitutional remedy by which to remove the President. In the American system the people speak at election time. Between elections only impeachment (a form of indictment) by the House of Representatives and conviction in a formal trial before the U.S. Senate -- with the Chief Justice presiding -- can legally remove a sitting President. To impeach and convict there must be clear criminal activity, what the Constitution calls "high crimes and misdemeanors." Not political error, not personal ineptness, not policy incompetence, not disagreement with the majority party and not even disreputable personal behavior. The Framers of the Constitution wished to maintain separate powers, to prevent legislative supremacy, but still provide a means for removing a President for genuine crimes in office.

In the absence of any political remedy, Congress attempted to use the only means at hand. The evidence for Andrew Johnson's "high crimes and misdemeanors" was flimsy at best and trumped up at worst. That became apparent at his trial before the Senate. The Tenure of Office issue, for example, turned on the issue of who had appointed Stanton. Had Johnson appointed Stanton, he would have technically been in violation of the Act by firing him. Whether that would constitute a high crime or misdemeanor within the meaning of the Constitution is certainly doubtful. But Stanton had been appointed by Lincoln, not Johnson, as the President made quite clear, and it was simply unknown whether the Act meant to include appointees of a previous President.

In any event the Senate Radicals failed by one vote short of the two-thirds needed to convict the president. Seven Republican Senators voted along with the Democratic Senators for his acquittal. They included Senators **Fessenden, Fowler, Grimes, Henderson, Ross, Trumbull and Van Winkle.** Each of those men was either compelled to resign or was defeated in the ensuing elections; their vote spelled the end of their political careers, a certain indication of the Radical mood of the nation.

On the other hand the trial served its purpose. Johnson never again obstructed the actions of Congress in the several months he had remaining before Ulysses S. Grant became President. The Tenure of Office Act, by the way, was not formally repealed until 1887, in the Administration of Grover Cleveland, but it was never applied and lay unenforced and unexecuted after Johnson left office.

Reconstruction Policies of President Grant

Ulysses S. Grant took office as President on March 4, 1869. As the nation's ultimate war hero during the Civil War, he had accepted Robert E. Lee's surrender at Appomattox, Virginia, on April 9, 1865. He remained commanding general following the war and then served briefly as Andrew Johnson's Secretary of War prior to running for the Presidency as a Republican. Moderate Republicans praised him for his constant comment, "Let us have peace." Radical Republicans knew, moreover, that Grant had always advocated for the rights of the African Americans, within the limits of his military position. They expected him to take an active stance in securing the gains of Reconstruction.

RECONSTRUCTION – COMPLETING REUNION

Grant's Reconstruction policy catered directly to the national temper of America. First and foremost it fulfilled the Radical aims for civil equality. With the passage of the **15th Amendment**, ratified in 1870, Congressional Reconstruction reached its peak. It is difficult to underestimate the significance of the enfranchisement of black males. No element in the entire panoply of enactments designed to protect the freedmen and hence assure an orderly Southern society, could match the right to vote. The bestowal of that precious act of participation in the political process signaled the highest achievement of the Republican program.

White Southerners hated the idea of black voters. Only five years earlier these new voters had been chattel property, owned as a horse might be owned and treated as horse might be treated. Now they were not only the civil and legal equal of the former masters but they could actually cast ballots and hold office as equals. Nothing infuriated white Southerners as the sight of freedmen voting. It had to be stopped at whatever cost!

Congress understood that issue quite well. So did the President. In the year beginning with May 30, 1870, Congress enacted three laws designed to enforce both the 14th and 15th Amendments. **The First Enforcement Act** (not to be confused with the First Reconstruction Act) prohibited voting discrimination in local elections on the basis of race. It also provided criminal penalties for intimidating voters or for depriving a man of his job in order to control his vote. The **Second Enforcement Act** followed the Democratic victories in the off-year (Congressional) elections of 1870. It provided for supervisors of elections to oversee voter registration and to certify voting returns to insure honesty. This law, incidentally, was used not only in the South, but against **Tammany Hall** Democrats in New York City.

The **Third Enforcement Act,** popularly known as the **Ku Klux Klan Act**, made it a federal crime to conspire to overthrow the government by force and to prevent anyone from enjoying the equal protection of the laws. This statute banned hooded night-riders and allowed the President to call out the army to enforce the law. President Grant was even authorized to suspend the *writ of habeas corpus*. This third law in very short order broke the power of the KKK in the South. [The current Klan is not a continuation of the old Klan; the "new" Klan was formed in Atlanta in 1915.] In any event, these enforcement provisions went about as far as any Radical wished to go. The enforcement provisions certainly disturbed people who disliked the abuse of civil liberties inherent in the use of military force. Is it possible the white South regarded those laws as the equivalent of the Coercive Acts of 1774?

Because of presidential strict execution of the Enforcement Acts the turbulence in the South began to subside. As long as the Grant

RECONSTRUCTION – COMPLETING REUNION

Administration continued to prosecute criminals who perpetrated violence against black voters or otherwise intimidated them, Republican regimes flourished in the South. Once that force was withdrawn, as it would happen after Grant's reelection in 1872, renewed violence remerged and white "Redeemers" took over the Southern states.

Moreover, as national attention turned to problems of the economy, the West, and foreign affairs, Grant was required to turn away from Reconstruction. Northern public opinion would not have sanctioned further actions in the South while newer and major issues seemed to threaten the nation. The Republicans stood to lose the power to act on any of those by sticking strictly to the enforcement of further Radical Reconstruction. They might well have lost the Presidency and their majority in Congress in 1872. The Grant Republicans recognized this circumstance by passing, in April, 1872, the aforementioned Amnesty Act. This law re-enfranchised those whites still proscribed from voting or holding office in the South.

Then, with the onset of the **Depression of 1873**, a serious economic downtrend unlike anything in previous American history, more immediate matters became primary. Not more vital, perhaps, but more imminent, more pressing, more "now." Should we condemn Grant for being "wimpy" on the Northern commitment to Reconstruction after 1872? He was clearly following the popular will in this matter. All that remained was for Southern governments to be returned to the hands of the majority of voters in those states. As previously noted, that happened in the mid-1870s in eight states and in the final three in 1877. It is critical to note, moreover, that the softer policy, if that is the proper term for it, beginning with the Amnesty Act of 1872, did help ameliorate hostilities between North and South.

The Liberal Republican Movement of 1872

Another significant force which assisted in reconciling the sections was the Liberal Republican Movement of 1872. A substantial number of Republican leaders disagreed with the Reconstruction policies of the Grant Administration. Actually, many of these Liberals had started out the Reconstruction period as Radicals, even before that position took prominence in the halls of Congress. As Republicans they shared the Radical concern with the rights of the freed people. They continued that commitment as Liberal Republicans.

Their number included **Carl Schurz**, now Senator from Missouri, author of the report declaring that the South had not accepted the results of the war. Nation magazine editor **Edwin L. Godkin**, who had so devoutly

RECONSTRUCTION – COMPLETING REUNION

favored military rule in the South on behalf of the freed people was now a Liberal Republican. So were Illinois Senator **Lyman Trumbull** author of the Civil Rights Act of 1866, and abolitionist Congressman **George Julian** of Indiana. Even Senator **Charles Sumner** of Massachusetts, could be counted among numerous other Republican luminaries who joined the Liberal Republican ranks [Sumner fell out with Grant over foreign policy]. What caused their defection to this new political organization?

By 1872 Liberals believed that with the postwar amendments in place, and with civil equality enforced, the government had done all it could do or ought to do in the South. Now, they said, it was time to let the Southern people who had to live together get used to the changed conditions. They believed that the Grant Administration continued the passions of the war, without any cause, because the Southern states were in safe hands. The former bondsmen had been given all the power they needed to protect themselves. The South did not need any more Reconstruction. Now that civil equality had been enacted, it was time to pay attention to sectional harmony.

In tandem with their criticism of Grant's Southern policy Liberal Republicans also condemned his support for a protective tariff. High tariffs had become a Grant trademark. Liberal Republicans believed that high tariffs fostered monopolies, led to the exploitation of workers and to an overemphasis on materialism in American life. They believed in 1872 that the laws of supply and demand should be left to work without government interference. They were genuine advocates of governmental *laissez faire,* that government should keep its hands off the free capitalist market. That is the origin of the term "Liberal," quite a distinct difference from 21st terminology.

Liberal Republicans further distrusted the centralization of power in the hands of the executive branch. They thought Ulysses Grant was edging close to becoming a dictator. They disliked his system of appointment by patronage and preferred a **civil service system** for government employees. Some feared Grant would seek a third term as President if he won a second term. Some even disliked Grant personally for what they claimed was a lack of sophistication and cultivated tastes. What could they expect from a man who once said that Venice would be a lovely city if they only drained it!

The Liberal Republicans held a national political convention as a third party in Cincinnati, Ohio, May 1-4, 1872. After a tremendous struggle they nominated New York Tribune editor, **Horace Greeley** of New York, as the Liberal Republican presidential candidate. Greeley had defeated Lincoln's Ambassador to Great Britain, **Charles Francis Adams** and several other hopefuls in a bruising six-ballot convention fight. The feisty editor had been one of the founders of the Republican Party in 1854. His credentials as a Republican loyalist were clear. He had, however, at considerable personal cost, become a symbol of forgiveness toward the defeated South. For example, he had signed the bail bond to get Jefferson Davis out of jail, an act which cost his newspaper thousands of readers. Greeley also represented a strident nationalism. Americans remembered his dictum to go west, young man, and grow up with the country.

The Liberal Republican strategy was to ally with the Democrats, but only on Liberal Republican terms. They would unite to put a swift end to Reconstruction, and then move ahead with the issues of tariffs, finance, monopoly, civil service reform, corruption in office, and decentralization of power. In short, the Liberals wished to get on with the issues of the 19th century. **Creating a Fusion ticket, the Democrats actually went so far as to nominate Greeley!!!** How strange was that? It would be as screwy as the Republicans of 2008 nominating Hillary Clinton for President. Passing strange, indeed!

It didn't work, either. Grant won reelection in 1872 by a huge majority. Grant Republican campaigners condemned Greeley and the Liberals as having sold out the freed people to the white South. That was unfair political campaign propaganda. The Liberal Republicans had pressured the Administration to pass the Amnesty Act and to correct some of the worst abuses of the tariff system. But the Liberals did not back off one inch from their support of the rights of African Americans. The Liberals were primarily interested in social order and wished to restore tranquil conditions, orderly institutions, and to put an end to sectional hostilities. They remained "rights - for - order" Republicans.

The Liberal Republican Party was the first and to this very day the only third political party with sufficient political clout to persuade one of the two major parties to nominate its candidate for President. That had never happened before and it has not happened since. They lost, but they had a definite modifying effect on sectional bitterness, a positive impact in promoting national harmony.

Colfax and *Cruikshank*

On Easter Sunday, April 13, 1873, in a little Louisiana township in rural Colfax Parish [county], an armed mob of some 165 local whites, including numerous Confederate veterans, murdered approximately 100 black freedmen. Fearing an attack, the former slaves had holed up in the Colfax courthouse. The whites set the building on fire. They opened fire on the blacks as they tried to escape the flames, despite a white flag waved by those attempting to save their lives. Perhaps sixty who managed to evade the first barrage were rounded up and mercilessly executed in pairs by the crazed marauders. The conclusion of this properly named **Colfax Massacre**, as will be noted, would severely inhibit the federal government in its protection for the freed people.

After a long manhunt in the swamps, conducted by a small contingent of Union soldiers, a number of the assassins were caught and tried in federal court in New Orleans. The accused murderers claimed that they were defending their homes against a gang of blacks who had threatened to rape their women and kill their children. This was the customary appeal to white supremacy so frequently enticing to juries and to the white community.

Despite eyewitness intimidation and a mistrial, several defendants were found guilty of violating the Enforcement Act of 1870. They appealed their convictions. Ultimately the case was reviewed by the U.S. Supreme Court in *U.S. v. Cruickshank, et.al.* (1876). Bill Cruikshank was one of the defendants; Jim Hadnot and Bill Irwin were the remaining others. The Supreme Court held in their favor. Their convictions were reversed. They were released from prison and returned home to Colfax as heroes.

The Court in *Cruikshank* ruled that Congress lacked power to create ordinary crimes – "common law" crimes such as murder or arson – the crimes for which the defendants had been convicted. The Enforcement Act could not be used to try cases of murder. Only states, not the United States, had jurisdiction to try individuals for criminal acts. The Enforcement law, according to the Court, permitted trials for civil rights violations, but the Justice Department must prove that the motivation for the murders was to prevent the blacks from voting! The original federal prosecutor, **James Beckwith**, and Attorney General **George Williams**, according to the Court, had failed to prove those claims conclusively.

Moreover, said Justice **Joseph P. Bradley**, writing for the Supreme Court, the government could not rely on the enabling clause of the 14th Amendment as grounds for trying the defendants. "No state," declares Section #1 of the Amendment, could deprive a person of "life, liberty or property" without legal due process. But Cruikshank and his cohorts were not the State of Louisiana, but rather private citizens and thus not subject to the jurisdiction of the Amendment.

The effect of *Cruikshank* was to turn cases of white crimes against blacks over to local courts, where no self-respecting white man would ever convict another white man for killing or maiming any black person. The ruling prevented the U.S. government from intervening to punish white defendants, except for civil rights violations, actually hate crimes virtually impossible to prove. Historian **Charles Lane** calls the decision in

RECONSTRUCTION – COMPLETING REUNION

Cruikshank "the day freedom died." Certainly, the Court's attitude required a retreat in the national government's defense of civil rights and liberties.

The Civil Rights Act of 1875

The spree of violence and mayhem against African Americans, of which the Colfax Massacre was only the most prominent of many occurrences, did not deter the Republicans in their determination to enact rights-for-order. One additional measure must be examined, because it has been either overlooked as unimportant or otherwise rejected as meaningless by historians. After several years of proposals and postponements on March 1, 1875 Congress enacted a new civil rights statute, the **Civil Rights Act of 1875.**

The new Act fulfilled the commitment of even the most advanced Radical Republicans for granting and enforcing civil equality. The statute banned racial discrimination in public accommodations. The Act imposed stiff penalties on private persons who denied the right of any citizen to *"full and equal enjoyment of...inns, public conveyances,...theatres, and other places of public amusement."* Penalties were also placed on the denial of equal rights to serve on juries. By this law blacks could sleep in the same hotel as whites, ride the same bus as whites, attend public events without segregation, and even serve with whites on the same jury.

As originally proposed by Massachusetts Senator Charles Sumner (who died in 1873 prior to passage) and sponsored by Massachusetts Congressman **Benjamin Butler** the Act even required public school districts to establish "mixed" (integrated) schools. That provision was struck out in committee at the very last minute, perhaps because it frightened Northern Congressmen as well as Southern, or perhaps because they were fearful that President Grant would veto the law if that provision remained in it. Or perhaps that idea was just too far ahead of its time.

Why did Congress enact the Civil Rights Act of 1875? The motivation and the timing of this statute remain intriguing. As a statement of Radical attitudes the new law was controversial to the max! Yet Republicans passed it during the time when the white Democratic "Redeemer" regimes of the Southern states were returning peacefully to power, when Radical Republican influence in the South was clearly waning. Why would Congress enact this socially provocative and politically risky law at all? Why enact it just when the social and political elements in America seemed conducive to a conclusion to the Reconstruction process?

Was the Civil Rights of 1875 some last - ditch effort to win the support of African Americans voters in both North and South? Was it one final attempt to punish the South by enacting Yankee values, as many Southerners have claimed? Was it a legislative tip of the hat to the late Senator Sumner, as some Northern historians have suggested? Or did the Republicans of the outgoing 43rd Congress remain steadfast to the ideological principles that had guided them throughout Reconstruction?

Ideals sometimes rise above politics. No Northern member of Congress would risk his seat and his political career over some far-out interpretation of private rights unless he totally believed in it. As with the case of the Civil Rights Act of 1866, and the 14th and 15th Amendments, Congressional Republicans in 1875 genuinely believed in the principles of **civil equality enforced**.

But they did risk their seats and their political careers. Many paid the price for their commitment to civil order. For having campaigned on behalf of the Civil Rights Bill some 100 Republicans, North and South, lost their House and Senate seats in the 1874 off-year elections. Even Congressman Butler was defeated for reelection. This Republican defeat was one of the most lopsided shifts in power of any congressional election in American history. It was not as if they had no idea they would lose control of Congress if they insisted on pursuing such a bold and progressive political position. The Republican Party would be ruined, they were warned. Nonetheless they dug their heels in. As then Congressman **James Garfield** of Ohio put it, "If ruin comes, I welcome ruin."

Thus they prevailed. As lame ducks of the 43rd Congress, the defeated and the reelected alike, the Republicans returned to the short session of Congress and on March 1, 1875, they passed the Civil Rights Act – albeit with the school clause stricken out!

In constitutional terms, Congress grounded the new law upon the enabling provisions of the 14th Amendment. Had that justification been acceptable to the Supreme Court, the Act would have moved the nation far in the direction of banning private discrimination in accommodations open to the public. [Restaurants were not included in the Act unless they were located inside an inn.] Since inns, theaters, and carriers of one kind or another were privately owned, the Civil Rights Act of 1875 went even beyond the ban on private discrimination located in the Civil Rights Act of 1866. To have made these rights stick would have added a dimension to the content of private rights which would take America until the civil rights legislation of the 1960s to accomplish!

Once again, the U.S. Supreme Court would have none of it! In 1883, in the *Civil Rights Cases* the Supreme Court held unconstitutional the Civil Rights of 1875. That law was, the Court declared, an unconstitutional exercise by Congress of the enforcement provision of the 14th

RECONSTRUCTION – COMPLETING REUNION

Amendment. The guarantees of the 14ᵗʰ Amendment operated only against state – sanctioned actions, but not against private discriminatory actions. Inns, hotels, theaters, public conveyances, while open to the public, were essentially private in nature. Hence, discrimination against blacks would be the action of private persons against other private persons. Those rights could not be enforced under the 14ᵗʰ Amendment.

Could they have been enforced under the enabling clause of the 13ᵗʰ Amendment? Justice **Joseph Bradley**, who wrote the Court's opinion in this case and who had earlier written the *Cruikshank* decision, acknowledged that the 13ᵗʰ Amendment had clothed Congress "with power to pass all laws necessary and proper for abolishing all badges and incidents of slavery in the United States." However, Bradley held, acts of private discrimination at hotels, theaters, railroads, etc., did not constitute badges and incidents of slavery. They were not themselves barred by the 13ᵗʰ Amendment. "It would be running the slavery argument into the ground," Bradley stated, "to make it apply to every act of discrimination which a person may see fit to make...."

The *Civil Rights Cases* thus invalidated the Civil Rights Act of 1875. Equal public accommodations would not be made enforceable until the passage of the **Civil Rights Act of 1964**, an Act based not on the 14ᵗʰ Amendment, but rather on an interpretation of the Interstate Commerce clause of the Constitution.

The *Civil Rights Cases* also held clear implications for the Civil Rights Act of 1866. It is probable that if that statute had come up to the Court for adjudication, it might well have been struck down as unconstitutional, too, at least to the extent that it encompassed private acts of discrimination.

Remarkably, the Civil Rights Act of 1866 remained unchallenged until 1968. In the unusual case of ***Jones v. Alfred Mayer Company*** (1968) the Supreme Court under Chief Justice **Earl Warren** upheld as constitutional the validity of the ban against private discrimination in the 1866 Act. The capacity to dispose of property and make contracts and other actions protected in 1866 were basic to citizens, the Warren Court ruled. Their denial would amount to badges of slavery and hence could be eliminated under the 13ᵗʰ Amendment. For the Court of 1968, the rights protected in that law did not amount to "running the slavery issue into the ground."

The Election of 1876

This most controversial election represents the winding down of Reconstruction in its most obvious and clearest form. It competes with the election of 1800 as the most complex, controversial and contentious of any presidential contest in American history.

The Republicans had nominated the respectable Governor of Ohio, the man who had written the regular (pro-Grant) Republican platform in 1872, **Rutherford B. Hayes**. The Democrats put up the Governor of New York, a wealthy corporation lawyer, **Samuel J. Tilden**. Both parties were trying to shake the image that they were led by men lacking character and high moral stature. Both Hayes and Tilden were considered men of unblemished innards. They were gentlemen down to their boxer shorts.

The early results of the election showed that the Democrats had won. In an election in which 81 percent of eligible voters actually cast ballots, Tilden received 51 percent of the popular vote [4,288,546 popular votes] while Hayes 48 percent [4,034,131]. Tilden had received 184 electoral votes. He needed 185 to win. Hayes had 165. However, there were 20 electoral votes in question: one in Oregon, seven in South Carolina, six in Louisiana, and six in Florida. It is significant that these three Southern states were the last to hold on to their Radical Republican regimes, and where federal troops remained.

The Republican leaders, particularly the Chairman of the Republican National Committee, Senator **Zachariah Chandler** of Michigan, well understood that Hayes could win if he could capture those 20 votes. Chandler proceeded to wire the Republican leaders in the four doubtful states, telling them to "hold their states."

In Oregon the Republicans actually had won. One of the Republican presidential electors also happened to be a federal officeholder, and so he was disqualified as an elector. The Governor of Oregon, a good Democrat, recognized the critical nature of the situation. He appointed a Democrat as the new elector, although by rights he should have appointed a Republican, since Hayes carried the popular vote of Oregon. The Republicans objected. They sent in their own set of electoral votes. There were thus two sets of returns. The Democratic set showed two votes for Hayes, one for Tilden. The Republican showed three votes for Hayes. If the Democratic set was counted, Tilden would win.

In the three Southern states the Democrats were afraid that the Republicans would tamper with the **Returning Boards**, the public agencies which certified the results of the election – today's Election Commissions. They therefore sent delegates to those states "to insure honesty." What else! Later, Senator **John Sherman** of Ohio would find good political jobs for all the Republican members of the Returning Boards in those three states.

RECONSTRUCTION – COMPLETING REUNION

In South Carolina there were more ballots cast than voters registered! Even the casual observer will appreciate the high percentage of voter participation of South Carolinians in the 1876 election. The Republican Returning Board awarded the state offices to the Democrats, but they gave the presidential electoral votes to Hayes. The Democrats, noses bent out of shape over this, sent in their own set of returns anyhow. Thus in the Palmetto State there were two different sets of returns with two different presidential winners.

In Louisiana, scene of the Colfax Massacre, the Democrats appeared to have a majority of from 6,000 to 9,000 votes. In this state the Republican-appointed Returning Board disqualified approximately 13,000 Democrats and 2,000 Republicans. Hayes swept the state. Again the Democrats sent in their own set of returns.

In Florida Tilden enjoyed his best chance for victory. The Republican Returning Board disqualified enough Democratic votes to permit Hayes to win. The Board even awarded the state offices to the Republicans. The State Supreme Court, dominated by Democrats, authorized a recount of the votes and appointed a new Returning Board, this one run by Democrats. Lo and behold, Tilden won the recount election and the electoral votes. Once again two sets of returns were submitted, one set from each Returning Board. This was Florida, after all.

Much of the so-called Republican fraud was not really fraud at all, but rather the invoking of disfranchisement procedures long unused. The Reconstruction laws of the states required Southerners to swear, as a prerequisite to voter registration, that they had not voluntarily taken part in the rebellion. Many former Confederates had registered falsely, swearing that they had never aided the rebellion when, of course, they had. Those men should have been disqualified from voting, but the disfranchisement provisions had never been enforced. In 1876, however, with a real chance for a Democratic victory, large numbers of Democrats voted who never should have been eligible to vote. Most of the disqualifications were quite proper by law.

Eventually, two sets of electoral votes arrived in Congress from those four states. Each set gave the victory to the candidate of the Party that submitted them. Which set counts? The Constitution is unclear on this point. It says that the electoral votes go to the President of the Senate, and in the presence of both houses of Congress "the votes shall then be counted." The Constitution does not actually say who counts the ballots. The President of the Senate, presumably the Vice President of the United States, opens them. But who counts them? In 1876, to compound matters, Grant's Vice President, **Henry Wilson** of Massachusetts, had died in office in 1875 and there was no sitting Vice President. The Republican *president pro tempore* would fill in.

Further complications arose because the Democrats had swept the House of Representatives in the 1876 election, while the Republicans had held on their majority in the Senate. Of course the Republicans argued that the President of the Senate should count the votes, since that was the traditional practice. Since the Republicans controlled the Senate, its president would be a Republican. He would count the Republican votes and Hayes would win.

The Democrats argued that the same procedure should be followed as had been used in the previous three elections, since that was the traditional practice. If any state's votes were disputed by one House of Congress or the other, that state's votes would not be counted at all. In 1876 the (Democratic) House of Representatives would formally protest the votes of the four disputed states. None of the 20 votes would count. Neither candidate would have a majority of the Electoral College. The election would go into the House of Representatives where the Democrats would elect Tilden.

No settlement of this issue could be made. Late in January, with the President to be inaugurated on March 4, 1877, there still was no President-elect. Finally, Congress bestirred itself. They decided to establish an **Election Commission** with the final power to decide which electoral votes to count. The Commission's decision would be final unless both Houses of Congress objected (unlikely!). The Commission would be composed of five Representatives – three Democrats, two Republicans; five Senators – three Republicans, two Democrats; and five Justices of the Supreme Court – two Republicans, two Democrats, and the members would pick the fifth Justice.

The expected fifteenth person was Justice **David Davis** of Illinois, a theoretical Independent. The Democrats agreed to this Commission because they believed Davis would be honest enough to discover fraud in one electoral vote. Tilden only needed one of the 20 outstanding. On the same day that the bill establishing the Commission passed Congress, the legislature of Illinois elected Davis to the United State Senate from that state.

Historians are divided about Davis's election to the Senate. Some claim that since the Republicans controlled the Illinois legislature, they maneuvered to get Davis off the bench, since the remaining members of the Supreme Court were all Republicans and one of them would have to be chosen. They told Davis (falsely) they would support him for President in 1880. That certainly would have been good strategy. Other historians declare that Tilden's Democratic managers actually manipulated that election for Davis in the hope that he would feel disposed toward Tilden while still serving on the Electoral Commission. In any case Davis decided that his election disqualified him from serving on the Commission altogether. Finally, Justice **Joseph P. Bradley**, a Republican, was chosen the fifteenth member.

The Commission's greatest problem was whether to go behind the electoral count and study possible mishandling or fraud. While that method would be fairest, it would take months to do it properly. March 4 would pass without a President being elected. That would precipitate a constitutional crisis, since no law could be enforced nor Congress called into session. Anarchy, perhaps renewed Civil War, might result. Already Rifle Clubs were forming in some states, ready to compel acceptance of their man.

The Commission's alternative was simply to decide which votes were the official votes and to decide whether those votes were procedurally in order. For the sake of abiding by constitutional process, and to head off violence, the Commission selected the latter choice. The Commission voted 8 to 7 that each of the 20 electoral vote should be awarded to Hayes. Each Commission member had voted for the candidate of his party. None of the fifteen could rise above partisanship in this most crucial process. The House of Representatives objected. The Senate did not. The ruling stood.

The reading of the electoral votes by the *president pro tempore* of the Senate was thus scheduled to resume. The Democrats, however, having amassed a substantial quarter million popular vote plurality for Tilden, and furious that they had been outflanked and cheated of victory, threatened to filibuster the reading of the electoral returns past March 4th. A crisis was at hand. **Somehow**, an agreement was reached! Rutherford B. Hayes was duly elected on March 2, 1877. He was inaugurated officially and on schedule two days later.

The Compromise of 1877

The content of that **"somehow"** is significant. It is sometimes referred to as **The Compromise of 1877**. Sometimes in is labeled the **Wormley House Conference**, because of the hotel in Washington where the bargain was constructed. How that agreement came about is still unclear, despite thorough historical study, the best of which has been written by historian **Keith Polakoff**. The results may be summarized.

RECONSTRUCTION – COMPLETING REUNION

Democrats, even Southern Democrats, were of different types. Northern Democrats, generally *laissez - faire* in their attitudes even before the War, were opposed to high tariffs and certainly opposed to government intervention after the War. They had had enough of Grantism and scandal and Reconstruction. They were joined by the Liberal Republicans of 1872 who fused with those Democrats who wished an end of Reconstruction and an end of government privileges generally. This was the rising group of *laissez faire* liberals, who believed in private initiative, economic laws, and governmental non-intervention. They supported that "Archbishop of *Laissez - Faire*," Governor Samuel J. Tilden.

Another strong group of Democrats, primarily Southerners, did wish federal aid, however, for internal improvements projects, for aid to businesses such as railroads, and ironically for high tariffs. In the *antebellum* period these people (or their fathers) had been Southern Whigs. Of course they had united with Southern Democrats. Just as Republicans were of different economic and social views, but joined together to block slavery extension and fight the Civil War, so did various Democrats unite to protect the South, whatever their internal economic differences. If Tilden were elected, there would probably be a general curtailment of government assistance to business.

If Hayes were elected, however, Republican programs, better - managed and cleaner than under Grant, would likely continue. Old Southern Whig types, now certainly Democrats, were willing to bargain with the Republicans to elect Hayes President! It would be in their interests, even if not in the political interests of their Party. The liaison between the Hayes forces and the Whig/Southern Democrats was a lobby of major proportions. It was led by **Thomas Scott**, President of the Pennsylvania Railroad and the Texas/Pacific Railroad. A compromise was cooked up between Hayes's managers -- Hayes himself knew nothing about it -- and Southern Democrats.

The "terms" of the Compromise of 1877 may be cited briefly. Republicans agreed to support a huge federal subsidy to build the **Texas/Pacific Railroad** and other federal internal improvements projects such as Mississippi River levies. In return the Whig-type Democrats agreed to stop any filibuster engineered by their Democratic colleagues. They also agreed to elect a Republican, **James Garfield** of Ohio, as Speaker of the House of Representatives, even though the House was Democratic. This was because the Speaker appointed all of the House committees; Garfield would be sure to support the right people for positions helpful to move forward the appropriate economic policies.

The two groups also agreed to build a new Republican Party in the South based on conservative white votes, rather than black and pro - Union white votes. This amounted to a major revolution in party arrangements in the South and certainly vastly altered Republican attitudes about the South. Further, Hayes would appoint Tennessee Senator **David M. Key**, a Democrat, as Postmaster General. In those days the Postmaster General had great powers of appointment because he distributed a great number of jobs to the faithful. Key would appoint many loyal Democrats to Post Office positions in every local post office in America.

Finally, any remaining United States troops in Southern states would be pulled out. Home rule for the South would be final. Reconstruction would finally be over. In return, Southerners would promise to safeguard the rights of the blacks as granted during Reconstruction. **Only the "Home Rule for Black Rights" provision of the Compromise was made public.** All the other provisions, naturally enough, were secret.

How did this agreement work out? The threatened filibuster was blocked, and Hayes was elected on March 2, 1877, as noted. Hayes was personally angry and ashamed when he discovered what had been done to secure his election, but he felt he must in good conscience honor the terms of the deal. He did appoint Senator Key Postmaster General. In turn Key worked with Hayes to build a new Republican Party in the South by appointing to office white Republicans not offensive to the South in addition to numerous Democrats. The Republicans, it must be observed, were notably unsuccessful in building a white-based party in the South. Only in the 1990s did a lily-white Republican Party begin to take the Southern "red states." away from the Democratic "solid South." The Democrats swept to giant victories in the South in 1878 and again in 1880. The Republicans lost whatever hold they had on the South during Reconstruction.

In addition, Hayes came out publicly for the Texas/Pacific and supported aid to that railroad. Most significant, he did withdraw the federal troops remaining in the South. In short, Hayes carried out as best he could his part of the bargain. But other parts of the agreement fell through. Garfield was not elected Speaker of the House. Northern Democrats balked at the idea of a minority party Speaker in the predominately Democratic House. Aid to the Texas/Pacific also failed; there was already a **Southern Pacific Railroad** in the same area in which the Scott lobby wanted its rail line to run, and the Southern Pacific had been built without federal subsidies. Hayes could not afford to push too hard for this. The failure of the Republicans in the South was also momentous, for Blacks were left unprotected. Although they did not actually lose their rights until the 1890s and after, they lost their political protectors in Washington.

RECONSTRUCTION – COMPLETING REUNION

Of what significance was this bargain? Most immediate, of course, was the resumption of constitutional government without violence with the election of Hayes. The Compromise of 1877 also reflected the degree to which the Reconstruction issues had faded from the postwar national consciousness. Northerners to a very substantial extent either accepted Southern views about blacks or simply turned to solutions to problems they saw as more immediate. Furthermore, conservatives of both Northern and Southern stripes recognized their common interest and began to work together politically to put forward their economic and fiscal policies. This conservative union still votes together in Congress -- its roots may be found in the arrangements of 1877.

President Hayes never quite got over the stigma of his election. He never gained any particular popularity with the American people, even though he was hardly an ineffective Chief Executive. People called him "Rutherfraud B. Hayes" or "Old 8 to 7," referring to the Electoral Commission's vote. Hayes did not seek a second term in office. He was not re-nominated by his Party.

Evaluating Reconstruction

Reconstruction has been presented in these chapters as a postwar form of "irrepressible conflict," the same Civil War carried over into peacetime. In a sense the victorious Union had to win this battle all over again. Only this time they must utilize peacetime methods within the boundaries of the Constitution. That was the mountain the authors of Reconstruction must climb.

Between 1865 and 1875 congressional Republicans had enacted massive protections to guarantee to the former slaves their freedom, their full citizenship and their constitutional rights before the law. In one decade a population of four million, for so long regarded as chattel property, had risen to civil equality, the voting equals and in some respects the social equals of their former owners.

Despite the best efforts of the Republicans white supremacy could not be rooted out of Southern hearts and minds. Southern states, acting with unparalleled deception, would substantially weaken the precious protections of the postwar amendments and the civil rights acts. The 19th century Supreme Court weakened those guarantees still further. The Northern public ultimately turned away from support of Reconstruction. The promise of genuine equality for African Americans was compromised in 1877 in something of the same manner as the slavery issue had been compromised in 1787.

RECONSTRUCTION – COMPLETING REUNION

Contrary to conventional popular belief, however, the freedmen did not immediately lose their hard won rights under "Redeemer" regimes. The official organs of government largely implemented the Reconstruction Amendments and the provisions of the new state constitutions. Many white Southerners generally, if grudgingly, acknowledged black rights, from property ownership to the suffrage, in order to control the freedmen for their own interests. There is considerable evidence that the Democrats converted many black votes from the Republican camp to their own by supporting black candidates who supported Democratic policies.

This is not to suggest that racial harmony existed in the South. Far from it! White supremacy had lost none of its virulence. Unofficial or personal interaction between whites and blacks remained marked by hostilities smoldering under the surface. Violence and intimidation secured white Democratic regimes. However, if attitudes had not changed, there was substantive alteration in behavior. For so many Southern whites, just as for the Republicans, Reconstruction was a reality and there was no going back. At least not yet! The era of **Jim Crow**, replete with full scale segregation, lynching, and the reduction of African Americans to second class citizenship, began in the 1890's. It did not begin when Reconstruction ended in 1877.

It has taken a century to recover most of what the Reconstruction Congresses had originally erected. In the America of the 21st century the goal of constitutional protection against private acts of discrimination remains frustrated. Racism and subtle discrimination surely persists. The farsighted intention of the Reconstruction Congresses to enact safeguards for the principles of racial equality before the law, including prohibitions against private discrimination, offers a cogent model for contemporary America.

A word about President Grant is in order. The hero of Appomattox is frequently considered by historians, in one survey or another, to be one of the worst Chief Executives in American history. Sometimes he finds himself placed into a flat footed tie for last place with that other monument from Ohio, **Warren G. Harding**.

That characterization requires rethinking. Grant had been such a successful general during the Civil War that people expected too much from him as President. The American public anticipated that Grant would be the strong man, the miracle man the nation needed. To a frustrated and rapidly changing nation, Grant would be the superhero who would smooth over all the bloody years of sectional hostility and fratricide. Under Grant everybody would be happy. Everybody would get rich. Grant would be the healer, the force through which Americans would be purged of the years of sin and strife. Americans would "clasp hands across the bloody chasm."

But the process of Reconstruction, from emotional healing to physical rebuilding, from slavery to freedom, was clearly too complex to be settled by the efforts of any one man. People nonetheless expected Grant to bring peace overnight. Of course, if Grant is measured up against those standards, certainly he failed miserably. But then Superman would also have failed miserably. And he didn't come from Ohio!

In one fundamental and profound sense Reconstruction worked. The Reconstruction process reestablished constitutional government in America! Whatever one may think about the policies and programs of the post-Civil War years, Reconstruction did restore the patterns of constitutional government under which America still operates. There can be no dispute about this achievement. A new relationship between the United States and the states had been forged. Reconstruction reconnected America's constitutional dynamics that had been detached by war. The constitutional system would once again function. America became a single nation, perhaps for the first time. The Union was at last complete.

CHAPTER FOURTEEN:
CONSTITUTIONAL DYNAMICS – CONSTITUTIONAL CHANGE

Even after more than two hundred years the American Constitution remains a dynamic force. What is the secret of its longevity? Why has a document written in 1787, the one Americans celebrate as the oldest written national constitution, lasted so long? How did it survive the Jeffersonian Revolution and the Civil War and Reconstruction? If the answer indicates some capacity for change, what species of alteration can historians and students identify? The next pages may strike some as theoretical but this book's readers will convert theory into history. What, then, are the dynamics of constitutional change?

American constitutional dynamics rest upon some darwinian capability for adaptation to changing historical circumstances. How long could the Constitution have lasted if it had been interpreted only according to its literal language? Does the virtue of "original intent" of the Framers interfere with the requirements of adjusting to meet altered realities? What is the secret potion which creates constitutional life through adaptation?

Means by which the Constitutional System Addresses Change:

(1) Constitutional Amendment. There are few written alterations in the Constitution. Those amendments which have been added have tended to reflect or to endorse changes in power which have already taken place. That is because the Framers made the amendment process difficult to accomplish. Amendments cannot be whimsical in nature. Moreover, nobody amends the Constitution as a matter of altruism. Powerful interests are required to cause amendments to meet the congressional approval of two-thirds of each house to pass and three- fourths of the states to formally ratify. The Constitution reflected the power structure of 1787. Similarly, amendments ratify power.

A few examples may serve. The **Bill of Rights** of 1791 reflected the institutionalization of power of the Framers of the Constitution. The Twelfth Amendment of 1803 insured the Jeffersonian Republicans of

CONSTITUTIONAL DYNAMICS

Jefferson's reelection. The three post-Civil War Amendments **(13th, 14th, 15th)** enacted the war aims of the victorious Union. Constitutional amendments most overtly change the constitutional system, but amendment is an uncommon procedure.

(2) Reinterpretation of the written words or phrases of the Constitution by the United States Supreme Court. Over time constitutional (re)interpretation of particular provisions or words in the written Constitution has changed the meaning of those words from their original intent to some meaning appropriate to the reinterpreters. For illustration, the Supreme Court has continually updated the words "free speech." That term now includes a variety of symbolic actions, as well as verbal or written declarations. The right peacefully to picket, an interpretation the Framers would have rejected out of hand, is one instance of freedom of speech. Free speech also includes the right to burn the American flag as a political protest. The Court has revised the ideas to match current realities. Similarly, the power of Congress to regulate interstate commerce has expanded, because the Supreme Court has redefined what interstate commerce means. Today that clause bans racvial discrimination in public accommodations. What failed in 1883 finally succeeded in 1966.

This brand of reinterpretation is not a cynical procedure by the Supreme Court. The new meanings give the provision or words new validity. The Constitution, unamended in written form, has evolved through judicial ruling largely because the rulings have already evolved in common practice.

(3) Invention of the Unwritten Constitution. There is an unwritten Constitution as well as a written one. Without amendment of any sort to the written document, the invention and institutionalization of new institutions, new practices, and new concepts has proven the most central dynamic in continuing the life of the written Constitution. Primarily, the unwritten Constitution consists of powers not written down anywhere, but which have been invented to meet changing requirements. Once in place the system could not function without them. These developments, measured against the original intent of the framers, or customary conventional readings of the Constitution, would likely be interpreted as unconstitutional. **Generally, these innovations supersede the "traditional" constitutional system**.

Inventions occur because conditions demand them. Were the literal Constitution to remain in force, decisions could not be made, opportunities would be missed, power could not assert itself. Without innovations to extend the constitutional system beyond customary borders, it is quite possible that the Constitution would collapse. American life constantly and rapidly changes; a static system with no capacity to change with realities would be doomed. **Realities have historically superseded the Constitution.**

A number of significant instances deserve brief notice:

The unwritten Constitution began at the outset of the new Washington Administration with the creation of the doctrine of **implied powers of Congress.** The need for a **national bank**, as proposed by Treasury Secretary **Alexander Hamilton**, trumped any prior ideology that limited Congress strictly to enumerated powers. The **Purchase of Louisiana** by President Thomas Jefferson in 1803 serves as another classic example of an innovation that superseded the Constitution, because Congress does not anywhere in the written document have power to acquire new territory. Jefferson concluded the Purchase nonetheless, in total violation (as he thought) of the written document. How ironic that had Jefferson not taken such a hard line against Alexander Hamilton's doctrine of implied powers, his Louisiana Purchase would have caused him no constitutional anguish.

Andrew Jackson's veto of the congressional statute to recharter the **Second Bank of the United States** established the signal precedent for the exercise of presidential discretion beyond the original meaning of the Constitution. Prior to Jackson's action, the veto had been thought useful only to declare a law unconstitutional, but never to challenge a policy that Congress had enacted into law. Policy was the legislature's business, the people's busness, after all. The president must execute the law, like it or not. Jackson's policy veto substituted executive discretion for the will of the majority. Jackson had attacked the original separation of powers doctrine. His action, so common to the modern presidency, superseded the Constitution.

Emancipation is perhaps the most significant historical example of realities superseding the Constitution. That one person could own another person as chattel property was a reality that cannot be denied, only abhorred. The **5th Amendment** guaranteed that property rights were safe from the actions of majority will. Congress could no more abolish slavery than it could abolish free speech. Nor could the President take a person's property by executive order. Yet that is precisely what President Abraham Lincoln decreed in his **Emanipation Proclamation**. War measure or not, the Proclamation arrogated to the Chief Executive power that the Constitution expressly denied. Lincoln's actions, however virtuous, superseded the customary Constitution.

CONSTITUTIONAL DYNAMICS

A number of recent examples similarly demonstrate that this constitutional dynamic did not end with Reconstruction. President Woodrow Wilson's establishment of the **War Industries Board** during World War I comes to mind. Wilson set up the War Industries Board on his own authority. No executive agency had ever before been established without congressional approval. However critical to managing the entire American economy in wartime, the Board was Wilson's own creation. Its director, financier **Bernard Baruch**, answered only to Wilson.

President Wilson also took the position that the President must propose legislation for Congress to pass. This action would previously have been regarded as an intrusion into the hallowed halls of Congress, where the legislators converted the interests and needs of the American public into statutes for administrative implementation. Wilson, however, believed that Congressmen could not possess the expertise to legislate on matters of trade regulations, consumer protection, tariff rates and a myriad of subjects requiring specialized talent and experience. The executive branch would have to furnish that expertise. Congress would now react to administration proposals. Can anyone today imagine a budget proposal actually being constructed by Congress? That the President should take this initiative, however, superseded the Framers' doctrine of separation of powers.

President **Franklin Delano Roosevelt's** plan to reorganize the federal judiciary, and particularly to enlarge the size of the Supreme Court, clearly muddied the line between the executive and judicial branches. The plan, which detractors called **"Court Packing"** and supporters called **'Court Unpacking,"** would have permitted the President to appoint a new Supreme Court Justice for every sitting Justice over seventy years of age, who did not retire (up to a total of fifteen Justices). .

There were precedents for altering the size of the Supreme Court. The real motive for the proposal, however, was to change the political composition of the Court, from conservatives who struck down some fifteen **New Deal** legislative initiatives, to liberals who would support the next wave of FDR's efforts to rescue the nation from the jaws of the Great Depression. This dramatic attempt at intervention with the federal Judiciary had only Jefferson's attack on the Federalist judges in 1801-1802 as precedent.

Pushing the outer limits of constitutional authority affected the arena of foreign policy, too. Presidential deployment of American armed forces occasionally remains politically controversial but constitutionally accepted. Need anyone be reminded that Congress has declared war five times in American history [1812, 1846, 1898, 1917, 1941], while presidents from John Adams to George W. Bush have deployed American troops abroad upwards of 200 times.

There is more. When, in 1940, President Roosevelt and British Prime Minister **Winston Churchill** made a deal to trade fifty over-aged unused American destroyers for 99 leases to British bases in the Caribbean, no treaty was ever signed and ratified by the U.S. Senate. Maintaining the need for confidentiality, lest information leak to German submarine commanders, the two leaders signed an **Executive Agreement.** That document had the power of a treaty but without the "advice and consent" process any formal treaty required. While no one would quibble with the need for secrecy in this case, the Executive Agreement did override and supersede the express intentions of the Framers of the Constitution.

Each of the previous actions had addressed a public policy objective. None had been designed for the personal aggrandizement of a President. **Richard Nixon**'s **Watergate** coverup of 1973-1974, however, occurred precisely for the personal political gain of this flawed President. Watergate might well be considered more a series of events in criminal law, rather than in constitutional development. Because the Watergate scandal reflected the height of arrogance of a President mired in the bunker of his own paranoia, it falls under the heading of superseding constitutional bounds. An object lesson, perhaps! A tragic and sickening spectacle that should humble and warn any future President.

President **George W. Bush** has invented "signing statements" as the most recent strategy to avoid presidential responsibility to enforce the legislation passed by Congress. The President first invokes the amorphous shield of "national security," a technique that precludes investigation or even criticism. Then, instead of vetoing a law, he simply declares just what portions of the law he will implement and what he will not implement. In the Bush White House this action has been taken more than 750 times. The sworn oath of the President to "faithfully execute" the law, so precisely delineated in the Constitution, is thus supreseded. Acording to the President, national security demands it!

(4) Political Accommodation and Constitutional Argument. American society is composed of interest groups. There are thousands of them; each of us belongs to many. An interest may be economic (small business, for example) or ideological (abolitionism), or social (the Baptist elders of a local community), or anything else. Obviously it is the objective of each interest first to make itself legitimate, and then to achieve its agenda through pressure or influence of some sort against contrary interests that wish to block that agenda or merely wish it to go away!

The Dynamics of Constitutional Change

It is the nature (some would say "genius") of the American system that it accommodates interests to one another. In America eventually most questions work themselves into policy or political issues to be resolved by policy makers on some level. Or they are determined by the courts. Each interest group attempts to muscle into the power structure. To a remarkable degree the system allows interests groups to flex those muscles, to bang heads with other interests, and, ultimately, to arrive at some momentary accommodation with those others.

Accommodation is a fleeting commodity, for it shifts according to whoever in fact has power and influence. It modifies, similarly, according to the pressure and relative influence of one group in competition for power with another. Again, the resolution of power questions is made in policy, in political decision making. To examine who has political power – in a community, a state, or in the United States – is to study who has the strongest interests and how the accommodation of interests has resolved itself at any given moment.

The logic of this process is that there may be times when the constitutional system (elections, legislation, appointments, the courts, etc.) simply cannot respond sufficiently to some interest group(s). The interest may have become so strong that it cannot be modified by the system or be bound by any transient political accommodation. When the system cannot contain interests within its institutions, it breaks down. In the absence of peaceful forums violence results. Interests must then come into conflict in more primitive, naked, and fundamental quarrels. That was precisely the case within the British Empire in 1776 and again in the American Union in 1861.

The process of accommodating interests also means that the American constitutional system tends to be conservative, or perhaps preservative, of what exists whenever that is possible. It allows change, but gradual change primarily. The system tends to preserve the *status quo*, part of which is the power structure, and part of which is the peace of the society. This viewpoint may not sit well with some, but it accords with historical reality.

CONSTITUTIONAL DYNAMICS

If politics reflects power accommodations, and does so within the system, then constitutional arguments are the highest form of political accommodation. Constitutional argumentation determines whether a policy or an action has constitutional legitimacy or not. Constitutional arguments reflect the highest expression of the attempt to gain or maintain power. We can be certain that once a conflict of interests reaches the stage of constitutional argument that some resolution will be worked out which will be acceptable to the parties to the conflict. Constitutional arguments indicate a peaceful working out of issues of power.

Constitutional agencies, primarily the legislatures and the courts, provide the forums in which interests convert their power objectives into rhetoric. Arguments about power convert to arguments about constitutionality. Those agencies, in turn, buffer and modify power, preventing it from colliding primitively with other power. If those agencies are inflexible, then extra-constitutional arrangements occur. Or anarchy, or some other means of reflecting change will supplant what currently exists. If the forums are flexible, a system of law results. One need think only of the acceptance of the Constitution after over one hundred years of local autonomy and state sovereignty. One need recall the eventual acknowledgement that the institution of slavery must be shattered and the enslaved given freedom and rights.

In America both the quality and quantity of freedoms enjoyed by individuals have grown over the years. In the early 21st century more persons possess more and better liberty than ever in American history. There is a huge irony, however, in that improvement in the condition of liberties and in their dissemination to larger numbers of persons has occurred in direct proportion to the intervention of the United States government into society. At the start of our constitutional system only a few people enjoyed a number of real, but modest, liberties. These were primarily white male property owners. It has taken the entrance of the national government into the relations between state or local government and individuals, or between one individual and another, to enlarge the reality of liberties for (almost) all Americans.

This has happened precisely because the American constitutional system reflected interests which associated themselves with stability and order. Those twin qualities, please recall, are the common source of our rights for ourselves and for others. The democratization and enforcement of individual rights and liberties is the surest way to prevent disorder. Social order and tranquillity depend directly upon inclusion of the disaffected inside the system. It is in the interest of the most powerful to include dissident elements in the rights enjoyed by themselves.

CONSTITUTIONAL DYNAMICS

The U.S. government has been the active agent in the inclusion process. This assertion, that directly connects the national government with the growth of rights, runs counter to the oft-taught maxim which tells Americans that the least government is best and certainly that the government closest to the people governs best. The American historical reality is that it has not.

What will happen in the conservative climate of our own moment one can merely surmise. If the Constitution is to survive the 21st century, the principles examined in the **Revolution and Union** must also continue their own living history.

HISTORICAL READING

For readers who wish a highly select list of significant classic and recent books.

PART ONE: REVOLUTION

Bruce Ackerman, *The Failure of the Founding Fathers: Jefferson, Marshall and the Rise of Presidential Democracy* (2005)

Akhil Reed Amar, *America's Constitution, A Biography* (2005)

Bernard Bailyn, *Ideological Origins of the American Revolution* (1967)

Carol Berkin, *A Brilliant Solution: Inventing the American Constitution* (2002)

Alexander DeConde, *This Affair of Louisiana* (1976)

Susan Dunn, *Jefferson's Second Revolution: The Election of 1800 and the Triumph of Republicanism* (2004)

Stanley Elkins and Eric McKitrick, *The Age of Federalism: The Early American Republic, 1788 – 1800 (1993)*

Joseph Ellis, *American Creation: Triumphs and Tragedies at the Founding of the Republic* (2007)

John Ferling, *Adams vs. Jefferson: The Tumultuous Election of 1800* (2004)

John Ferling, *A Leap in the Dark: The Struggle to Create the American Republic* (2003)

Cecilia Kenyon, "Men of Little Faith: The Antifederalists on the Nature of Republican Government," 12 <u>William and Mary Quarterly,</u> 3 (1955)

Pauline Maier, *From Resistance to Revolution, Colonial Radicals and the Development of American Opposition to Great Britain, 1765 – 1776* (1972)

Matthew Mason, *Slavery and Politics in the Early American Republic* (2006)

Michael I. Meyerson, *Liberty's Blueprints: How Madison and Hamilton Wrote the Federalist Papers, Defined the Constitution, and Made Democracy Safe for the World* (2008)

Jack N. Rakove, *Original Meanings* (1996)

Robert Rutland, *The Ordeal of the Constitution: The Antifederalists and the Ratification Struggle of 1787 – 1788* (1966)

Robert A. Rutland, *The Birth of the Bill of Rights, 1776 – 1791* (1955)

Gordon Wood, *The Radicalism of the American Revolution* (1992)

Gordon Wood, *Revolutionary Characters: What Made the Founders Different* (2006)

PART TWO; UNION

Michael Les Benedict, *A Compromise of Principle: Congressional Republicans and Reconstruction, 1863 – 1869* (1974)

G. Sidney Buchanan, *The Quest For Freedom: A Legal History of the Thirteenth Amendment* (1976)

Richard Carwardine, *Lincoln, A Life of Purpose and Power* (2003)

Garrett Epps, *Democracy Reborn: The Fourteenth Amendment and the Fight for Equal Rights in Post-Civil War America* (2006)

Eric Foner, *Reconstruction, America's Unfinished Revolution 1863-1877* (1988)

William W. Freehling, *The Road to Disunion: Secessionists Triumphant 1854-1861* (2007)

Richard Allan Gerber, *The Liberal Republican Alliance of 1872* (1967)

Richard Allan Gerber, *The System: The American Constitution in Historical Perspective* (2007)

William Gillette, *The Right to Vote: Politics and the Passage of the Fifteenth Amendment* (1965)

Allen C. Guelzo, *Lincoln's Emancipation Proclamation: The End of Slavery in America* (2004)

Michael F. Holt, *The Political Crisis of the 1850s* (1978)

Harold M. Hyman and William M. Wiecek, *Equal Justice Under Law: Constitutional Development, 1835-1875* (1982)

Charles Lane, *The Day Freedom Died: The Colfax Massacre, the Supreme Court, and the Betrayal of Reconstruction* (2008)

Michael Perman, *The Road to Redemption: Southern Politics 1868 – 1878* (1984)

Keith Polakoff, *The Politics of Inertia: The Election of 1876 and the End of Reconstruction* 1973)

Heather Cox Richardson, *The Death of Reconstruction: Race, Labor and Politics in the Post-Civil War North 1865-1901* (2001)

Heather Cox Richardson, *West From Appomattox, The Reconstruction of America after the Civil War* (2007)

Anne Sarah Rubin, *A Shattered Nation: The Rise and Fall of the Confederacy 1861-1868* (2004)

Brooks Simpson, *Let Us Have Peace: Ulysses S. Grant and the Politics of War and Reconstruction 1861-1868* (1991)